Confessions of a Middle-Aged Babe Magnet

One Man's Brave Adventure into Dating Again in the 21st Century

Confessions of a Middle-Aged Babe Magnet

One Man's Brave Adventure into Dating Again in the 21st Century

by

Chad Stone

SOULMATE MEDIA

Published by Soulmate Media
www.soulmatemedia.com

First Printed Edition

ISBN 978-0-9850479-1-7

Cover designed by Ken Wilson Design

Check out the Middle-Aged Babe Magnet blog at

http://middleagedbabemagnet.blogspot.com

To subscribe to Chad Stone's free eNewsletter, send an email to:

babemagnetchad@aol.com

To Finding True Love

Acknowledgments

A book is a labor of love, and this book would not have been possible without the loving help of friends and family. I am grateful for all of the support I received as I walked the path told in this story. I am also eternally grateful for the helpful assistance I received during the writing and editing process.

I won't mention anyone by name, but you know who you are. Thank you. I couldn't have finished this book without you.

Special thanks go to the wonderful woman who provided the happy ending that this book needed. I love you.

The Author's Pre-Oprah Interview Confession

No matter how young or old you are, dating can be exciting and exhilarating. At times, it can also be unnerving and challenging. I began my mid-life dating quest with the belief that I was going to find the woman of my dreams; but for my own sanity, I also approached this adventure with the belief that dating could be fun. Consequently, I enjoyed myself much of the time, and I had fun writing about it.

Most of what I have written in this book is true. This is the story of an actual middle-aged American man who got divorced after many years of marriage, dove headfirst into the dating pool, and learned how to swim like an Olympic medalist. But in an attempt to make my personal story more entertaining, I *might* have exaggerated a bit here and there. So please don't sue me or get all outraged about it.

I have changed the names of everyone in this book, including me. Just for fun, I gave myself a pseudonym that sounds like one a Babe Magnet might have.

One advantage of using a pseudonym is that my mother won't know that I have written this book. She has enough to worry about without knowing the details of her son's romantic adventures before he met the new love of his life. Another advantage is that much of this book is personal in nature, and using a pseudonym spares me from tarnishing my reputation as a famous brain surgeon in Silver Spring, Maryland. Plus, NASA doesn't appreciate it when the sex life of a former astronaut is posted all over the Internet. And if the Nobel committee ever found out who really wrote this book ... well, let's just say that I would forever kiss my chances of a Peace Prize goodbye.

-- Chad Stone

Hello, and Welcome to My Life: An Introduction

Here I am, middle-aged and single—again.

Sound familiar? It should.

According to the U.S. Census Bureau (2011), there are more than 15.7 million divorced Americans between the ages of 40 and 64. Add in those who are separated and those who never married, and you have a total of more than 30.8 million single men and women in their middle years.

To put that into perspective, 30.8 million people is more than the populations of Maine, Maryland, Massachusetts, Minnesota, Mississippi, Nebraska, Nevada and Oregon—combined. That's a lot of chronologically challenged single folks.

When I got married at the relatively tender age of 24, I assumed that I'd be married for the rest of my life. In fact, I *was* married for more than 25 years, most of which were happy ones. My wife and I (make that my *ex*-wife and I) raised two fine boys into young adulthood. But like so many baby boomers, I did not stay married to the same spouse until death intervened. In my case, I was the one who wanted out of the marriage.

So, after a quarter-century of being a husband, I suddenly found myself single again. In addition to lots of money, my wife got virtually all of our married friends in the divorce, which forced me to start a new life from scratch.

I have to admit that I was totally lost. Even if I had remembered how to be a single man, I was now nearly three decades older and the world had completely changed. When I got married there was no Internet, no satellite radio, no reality TV. Nobody in his right mind ever thought an aging bodybuilder-turned-movie star would be elected governor of California, and then be embroiled in an extramarital paternity scandal. And nobody thought the epidemic of divorce would create entire new industries to serve millions of single adults.

As a newly single middle-aged man in the 21st century, I was faced with new concepts such as "Match.com" and "speed dating." I had to figure out what I was supposed to do on a Saturday night. I had to relearn the rules of dating. Had they changed? Did men still ask women out? When was it acceptable to kiss a woman without risking a sexual harassment lawsuit? Would women even want to go out with me? Was it possible for a young-at-heart middle-aged man to fall in love again?

Without giving too much of the story away, suffice it to say that, yes, happy endings are still possible for single men and women of all ages. During my second singlehood, I learned how to make new friends and engage strangers in playful conversation. I sought out opportunities to try new things, even when there was the distinct possibility that I might look like a fool—or fall down and break something.

With my advancing years has come an indifference to what other people think of me, especially when I might miss out on something fun. So I took dancing lessons. I bought a mountain bike. I discovered the joys of shopping on eBay, bought an electric guitar, and found myself a guitar teacher. I joined a men's support group and met guys I never would have hung out with before, but who have since become some of the best friends I've made since college. I sought out opportunities to meet wonderful women; some of them became friends, and a few became lovers. In the process, I learned how to be comfortable with myself and embrace every step in the journey of life.

I learned that it's never too late to start again, and that it's never too late to meet your soul mate. Along the way, I gained valuable insights about humanity—and had a really good time.

Lest you think that I was able to reinvent my life and find happiness because I am somehow special or fantastically handsome, let me describe myself. Trust me: no woman ever mistook me for Brad Pitt or Pierce Brosnan.

I am in my fifties, making me too old to be young and too young to be old. My hair has thinned in some places and vanished in others due to the curse of Male Pattern Baldness. Consequently, I gave up on having hair at all and shaved my head in resignation. Given the choice of little hair, fake hair, or no hair, I decided to proudly follow in the footsteps of other courageous bald men and flaunt it.

You know the old saying that goes, "If life gives you lemons, make lemonade?" Well, my head looks like a giant lemon, and I'm proud of it. I don't own a comb or a blow dryer. When the wind gusts and everyone else's hair goes ballistic, I make a joke about how much I hate it when that happens (while trying to fix my imaginary hair). Lemonade, baby.

I stand six feet tall on size 12 feet, and I tip the scales at about 180 pounds. I am vain enough to consider myself reasonably handsome, but realistic enough to know that I have never had the striking good looks that turn a woman's head when I walk into a room. My nose is too big and my chin is too small, but I strive to make up for that with a frequent smile, a positive attitude, a friendly demeanor, and an insouciance that makes me appear confident even when I am not.

I enjoy good health and take care of my body. I joined a health club, and work out faithfully three times a week. I live by my own personal 95 Percent Diet: 95 percent of the time I eat sensibly so I can indulge in desserts, cheeseburgers, fries, alcoholic beverages, and other treats the other five percent of the time when so inclined. I dress in nice, conventional clothes, most of which I bought on sale. As this tale begins, I live alone in a tiny apartment and drive a pickup truck; later, I'll move into my own heavily mortgaged house and switch to a used BMW sedan.

In a room full of people, I do not stand out because of my looks, my behavior, or my attire. I am, in virtually every way, an unexceptional middle-class, middle-aged divorced American man.

And yet, somehow, I became a Babe Magnet.

This is my story.

Chapter 1: Alone Again

I'm sitting on the bed in my one-bedroom apartment. The walls are completely bare. I just moved in yesterday, and boxes are stacked everywhere. My clothes are hung up in the bedroom closet, but everything else is in disarray.

The walls are painted a light gray, like a drizzly January day in Seattle. The carpet is gray, too. I thought it was going to be the same beige color as the carpet in the model apartment I toured on the day I signed my lease. The carpet in my apartment wasn't cleaned like it was supposed to be, and it smells like cigarette smoke with a hint of stale beer and empty pizza boxes.

From my bedroom window I have a scenic view of the parking lot and the drainage ditch beyond. My front door faces a swimming pool filled with dead leaves and windblown debris that, hopefully, will be cleaned out when the weather warms up. My upstairs neighbors are four male college students who are blasting death metal music loud enough to shake my walls.

I don't want to live in this crummy apartment. I already miss my old house and my old life. The enormity of what I have done is just now beginning to hit me.

I left my wife of 25 years when it became painfully obvious to both of us that I didn't love her any more. My wife tried everything she could to keep the marriage together. She insisted we go to counseling. I went, but my heart wasn't in it, just as my heart was no longer in my marriage. I found out firsthand that it takes two people to build and maintain a marriage, but only one to bring it down.

So instead of the "perfect" life I had in a spacious suburban home with a wife who loved me and a 17-year-old son who respected me (plus a grown-up son living out of state), I am now living here, in this crappy little apartment that smells like a Seattle ashtray.

I am self-aware and well-read enough to quote platitudes from a dozen self-help books. I accept full responsibility for what I have done. I could have worked harder to save my marriage. Now I must deal with the consequences of my decisions, and I must reinvent and rebuild my life.

As depressed as I am right now, there is still a faint murmur of hope. I am an optimist. I expect things to work out for me, and they usually do. I'll follow that murmur of hope until it grows louder and louder and leads me to a new lover and a new life.

Once, several years ago, I drove my father to a shopping mall. He wanted me to take the first available space in the parking lot. I didn't, opting instead to drive to the best spots closest to the mall entrance to check for an open space. Only after not finding an up-close spot would I settle for a faraway parking place.

My dad chastised me for trying to get a primo spot, saying that I shouldn't have bothered. "That's what you get for trying too hard," he said, after it was clear that all of the closest spaces were already filled.

I remember thinking how sad it was to have expectations that low. Finding a parking space—or rather, expecting NOT to find a good space and settling for a distant space—was a microcosm of the way my father had lived his whole life. He never took risks—even little ones. He worked for one company his entire life and never considered that another job might give him new opportunities. He never strived to be extraordinary, so he never was. Competent, yes. Comfortably successful, yes. But he never pushed out of his comfort zone or followed his intuition or blazed his own trail.

Walking out of my marriage was an enormous risk, with consequences that are still unfolding. Divorce is nothing short of an earthquake that can shatter lives and scatter families. There is no question that my life would have been better *today* if I had stayed married to my wife. For one thing, I wouldn't be feeling sorry for myself in this crummy apartment. But what about next month? What about next year and five years from now? How long could my spirit have survived unbroken in a marriage that was slowly draining the life from me?

In order to survive the coming weeks and months, I have to believe that things are going to get better for me. I have to believe that, while I have made the most painful decision of my life, it was the right decision. I have to believe that my heart will heal. I'm not feeling like a Babe Magnet right now, but I have to believe that I will meet interesting women, who, like me, are middle-aged and single and looking for companionship.

And I have to believe that, when the time is right, I will find someone to love.

Chapter 2: Now What Do I Do?

What's the best prescription for a mid-life crisis and self-induced personal turmoil? For me, it's keeping my head and my hands busy. I have jumped headfirst into work, spending as many hours as I can at the office. I am giving my clients extra hours of my time, for which they will not be billed. I am going through piles of correspondence that have been sitting around for weeks. I am throwing out stuff that I've saved just in case I might need it someday.

Screw *someday*. I need something to do right now.

I am cleaning, filing, discarding, shredding, and organizing. As I get rid of the clutter in my outer world, I feel my mind getting uncluttered, too.

When I'm not busy, my heart feels raw and damaged. But sometimes I'm hopeful and energized. I see couples laughing and enjoying their togetherness and I say to myself, "That's going to be me. I'm going to fall in love again!" Other times, I am disgusted with myself, and I shuffle back to my apartment, depressed. Then I venture out alone to see a movie or attend a lecture, and I congratulate myself for my courage. It's not easy to venture out into public alone and lonely. Sometimes I feel like I'm wearing a sign around my neck that says LONELY, HORNY, AND THOROUGHLY PATHETIC. Then something small but wonderful happens. I hold the door open for an attractive woman, and she gives me a big smile. Or I have a pleasant conversation with a stranger in line at the bank. Through it all, I constantly remind myself that I have *chosen* a completely new life for myself. I am boldly going where I have never gone before.

One thing is consistent: I hate living in a Spartan little apartment. I haven't lived in an apartment building since I was just out of college. I have grown comfortably accustomed to life in a four-bedroom suburban home. Living in a crummy apartment feels like failure.

Through the thin walls of my bachelor apartment, I hear rock music and wrestling from the upstairs neighbors. Sometimes it really does sound like they, full of testosterone and recreational drugs, are body slamming each other onto their floor (my ceiling).

I can tell when the couple next door is having sex, because their bedroom is just a thin wall from mine. They turn up their stereo really loud, but in the gaps between the songs I hear them moaning and shouting "Oh, baby!" to each other. At first I laid in my bed, listening. I tried to remember what it was like to have sex that was so *vigorous*, so loud. Then it started to feel like they were taunting me. "We're having sex over here and YOU'RE NOT!" Now, when they really get going, I grumble and sleep on my living room couch.

As a married man, I tried not to pay too much attention to the women who passed through my life anonymously. Sure, I'd notice a stunningly beautiful woman at the bank or at the mall; I was married, not dead. But for the most part, I didn't look at women passing by because 1) staring at other women is not something that endears you to your wife, and 2) I didn't want the temptation and/or frustration. Why visit a Porsche showroom to look at cars you're never going to drive?

Now my female radar is on hypersensitive. I notice every pair of double-X chromosomes of legal age. I'm not ready to do anything about it yet, but I *have* noticed that there are lots of women out there in the world. In fact, there are far more than I thought. Women are everywhere.

The grocery store is full of women pushing shopping carts through the aisles. They're so cute with their little lists and their no-nonsense expressions as they scavenger hunt for enough ingredients for dinner. I notice women filling up their cars at the gas station, struggling with that fill hose that never behaves itself. The sexual imagery is just so obvious, as they try to slide the huge male nozzle into the just-big-enough female fill tube. I wonder how many of those women are thinking about their husbands and boyfriends as they fill up their gas tanks.

There are women strolling through the bookstore and at the bank and at the cleaners and in the bagel shop and...everywhere.

Granted, not all of these women are single. Already, I've gotten skilled at spotting rings on women's left hands. I look for the glint of a gold band or a telltale flash from a diamond. Just as an eagle can spot a mouse from a thousand feet in the sky, I can spot a ring on the fourth finger of a woman's left hand from across a crowded department store.

I have more free time now than I did as a married man, so I am deliberately reconnecting with friends. One of the mistakes I made over the years was not maintaining my friendships. Looking back on it now, I spent too much time as a husband and not enough time as a man with friends and interests outside of his marriage. So now I'm calling old friends and making the time to see them.

I meet Craig for beers after work. I have known Craig for 15 years, and I have known all four of his wives. I was there to support him during his three divorces. Now he's there for me as I ride the emotional waves of *my* divorce and begin a new journey as a single man.

As I sit across a table from Craig, each of us sipping a fine craft beer, I realize how important it is to have someone to talk to about the things that are on my mind now: women, sex, relationships, divorce, marriage, dating, alimony, loneliness, sex, women, where to meet women, how long it takes to have sex with a woman after you've met her, what makes women attractive even though they're such pains in the ass, sex, and (of course) world peace.

Craig has opinions on all these matters, and his opinions are based upon extensive personal experience. Craig is one of those lucky men who is charming, confident, and financially successful, plus he has rugged good looks that women find irresistible. He's not movie star handsome, exactly, but he has wide cheekbones that women love and, unlike me, he still has every hair that ever grew on his head. All he has to do is walk down the street and women start following him. He tells me that after his last divorce, he immediately started dating three women simultaneously just to fill the void in his life.

"I used to call each one on the phone every night and talk to her for an hour," he says. "I didn't want to be all by myself in my house with nobody to talk to."

I know the feeling. Unfortunately, I don't have three women to call every night. "Wasn't it hard to keep three women straight?" I ask. "Didn't you have trouble remembering what you talked about with each of them?"

Craig laughs. "I did for a while, until I realized that I should talk only about current events—you know, things that had happened that day. I called each one and had the same conversation so I wouldn't get anything mixed up."

Right now, that's a problem that I wish I had.

Chapter 3: What Do I Want?

Now that I'm single again, I've been thinking a lot about what I want in my next relationship. Theoretically, I can choose from any woman in the world. Even if I narrow down the potential pool of women to those who are currently unmarried and over the age of 18 (okay, over the age of 40) and under the age of 55, that's still an impressively large group of available women.

For my entire adult life, I have set goals and written affirmations. For many years I had a sign taped to my bathroom mirror that said TODAY IS THE GREATEST DAY OF MY LIFE! I read that sign out loud every morning just before I shaved. So I figure I should probably start listing the qualities and attributes I'm looking for in a woman.

I get out a yellow legal pad, park myself on the couch, and start to think. This could be a fun exercise in creativity. It's brainstorming time, and I'm going to write down anything that pops into my mind. It's too early to edit myself. Anything goes.

I write WHAT I'M LOOKING FOR IN A WOMAN across the top of the page, then wait for inspiration.

The first thing that pops into my mind is breasts. I swear to God. So I write BREASTS on the paper. But what kind of breasts? Double Ds? Round with large nipples, or small with cute little nibblets? Silicone bombers big enough to have their own zip codes? A matched set of perfect natural specimens?

I told myself that I wasn't going to edit my thoughts at this point, but I'm not happy that BREASTS was the first thing I thought of. After BREASTS I write, "nice, C or D cup," and move on.

Next I write A NICE SMILE. To me that means white, straight or fairly straight teeth, and soft, full lips.

A NICE FIGURE is next. I adore the natural hourglass shape of a woman's body. I love a smallish waist that flares out into distinctly female hips. I love a woman's curves, so I write the word CURVY.

I realize that I am behaving in a typical male way, thinking of physical looks first. But maybe if I just finish the physical wish list I can get to the more important internal beauty.

HEIGHT—5 FEET, 6 INCHES TO 5 FEET, 11 INCHES. I'll leave the short women for shorter men. At the same time, I don't want a woman who is taller than I am. It's a male ego thing, for sure.

HAIR COLOR—ANY, BUT PREFERABLY LONG HAIR. There is something very sexy about a woman with long hair, especially to a bald man.

EYES—BLUE or GREEN. This isn't a deal breaker, but my ex-wife had big brown eyes. When I gaze adoringly into the windows of my next lover's soul, I would like the shades to be a different color.

I review my list so far. There are no surprises here at all. What I have described so far is a Playboy Bunny. Clearly, I have been thinking with the little head in my pants.

All right, it's time to delve deeper. It's time to use my real brain and my heart. What are the inner characteristics I am looking for? How would I describe my dream woman's personality and disposition?

KIND. LOVING. PASSIONATE. GOOD SENSE OF HUMOR. OPEN-MINDED. SPIRITUAL. HEALTHY. EMOTIONALLY MATURE.

Great! I'm making some real progress here.

HORNY.

Whoops. There goes the progress. I cross out HORNY and write HEALTHY SEX DRIVE. I sit and wait for my next thought.

FRIENDLY. OPTIMISTIC. INTELLIGENT. PROSPEROUS. HONEST. DOWN TO EARTH.

I review the list and it's clear that my standards are high. But I'm not done yet.

COLLEGE EDUCATED. Being intellectually compatible is important, especially when the first flush of passion has subsided.

DIVORCED. OLDER KIDS OK. I don't want a woman who has made it to her middle years without ever having committed to a marriage. That's a red flag for me.

I sit with my pen hovering above the pad, but I can't think of anything else to write. And yet, it feels like I'm not done yet. After a few minutes, my pen starts moving again.

I WANT A WOMAN TO LOVE AND CHERISH.

I WANT TO BE SO HAPPY WITH MY LOVER THAT BEING APART IS AGONY.

I WANT TO FIND A SOUL MATE WHO CAN SHARE MY DREAMS.

I WANT TO FIND A SEXUAL PARTNER WHO EXCITES ME AS MUCH AS I EXCITE HER.

I WANT TO FALL IN LOVE AGAIN.

I read through my list a couple of times. It occurs to me that I am looking for the perfect Middle-Aged Babe. In order to attract this perfect Middle-Aged Babe, I will have to become a Middle-Aged Babe Magnet. I do not know how to do this yet, but I have read enough self-help and power-of-positive-thinking books to know that I must start thinking of myself as a Babe Magnet.

I flip to a blank page on my legal pad and write:

BABE MAGNET RULE #1
To be a Babe Magnet, you must believe you are a Babe Magnet.

I look at the words I've just written, and I feel empowered and inspired—as if I've just watched a "new thought" lecture on PBS during pledge week, and I'm making my phone call to the toll-free number with credit card in hand.

With this small step, my journey to Babe Magnethood begins.

Chapter 4: Shopping for Condoms

It's been a while since I purchased condoms. I'm not exactly sure how long, but I know it's been more than two decades.

I'm not sure if it shows up in any Top 10 Benefits of Marriage surveys, but not having to wear condoms is on my list. Monogamy and birth control pills have their advantages.

Back when I was in college, a guy told me that wearing a condom was like "screwing with a sock on your penis." But in a dating world filled with unwanted pregnancies and sexually transmitted diseases, condoms are a necessity.

The first time I was ever brave enough to buy condoms was at my college bookstore. Even way back then (in the 1970s!), the good people who ran the college bookstore were smart enough to realize that 1) college students *wanted* to buy condoms, even if all they did was leave an indelible imprint in a guy's wallet; 2) some college students *needed* to buy condoms, because they were actually going to use them; and 3) college students *hated* buying condoms, because it was an excruciatingly embarrassing experience.

So, the kind and wise college bookstore people actually put a condom display on top of a counter. You didn't have to ask where they were, and you didn't have to ask a clerk to get them for you. All you had to do was pick out the package you wanted and take it to the cash register. An attractive young college student (female, of course) would ring up your purchase. You just knew that she was trying to figure out if you were actually going to get laid, or if you were going to stick a condom in your wallet for the next several years while you waited, in vain, to get lucky.

During my entire marriage, I did not for a moment miss having to buy condoms.

But now that I'm officially single, I need to be prepared for sex. And by sex, I mean Safe Sex. I don't have any prospects at the moment, but I do need to be ready in case I'm perusing the aisles at the grocery store and a *Sports Illustrated* swimsuit model catches my eye and smiles. We'll chat for a while, and I'll be very charming, and one thing will lead to another and pretty soon we'll be naked at my place. With her face flushed with passion and her breasts heaving, she will say to me, "Do you have a condom?" I will whip one out of my wallet, and we will have passionate sex that will last for at least one full minute.

Hey, it could happen.

I go to Wal-Mart, where America shops...for condoms. In the 21st century, Wal-Mart has an entire section of condoms. The condoms section is, thankfully, tucked in a quiet corner of the store next to the pharmacy and behind the adult diapers. I guess this would be the Coming and Going Department. There are dozens of condom choices, all packaged in colorful, appealing boxes and all making claims about pleasure! and sensations! and lubrication! I'm getting excited just looking at the boxes.

There is only one brand I recognize—Trojan. But there don't seem to be plain Trojans anymore. Now there's the Trojan Pleasure Pack (36 lubricated condoms) and

Trojan-Enz Lubricated and Trojan Magnum Large Size Condoms and Trojan Twisted Pleasures Lubricated.

Twisted Pleasures—at Wal-Mart?

There are other types of condoms from other brands. Lifestyles Ultra Sensitive and Durex Natural Feeling Condoms. And on and on. The choices are overwhelming.

But wait, there's more! In a bright red box is a Trojan Vibrating Ring Duo. I don't even know what that is, and I'm afraid to pick up the package to read the description. What if someone walked by and saw me reading the Trojan Vibrating Ring Duo box? And what if that person told the *Sports Illustrated* swimsuit model? She'd think I was some kind of pervert.

With no scientific research or previous buying experience to assist me, I use the logical method of "eenie, meenie, minie, mo" and decide on a dozen lubricated Durex, because I really like the purple box.

I can't buy *just* condoms, so I pick up a few things that I don't need right now but will need eventually—shaving cream, sunscreen, toothpaste, *Sleepless in Seattle* on DVD, aspirin, deodorant, a motorcycle magazine (I don't have a motorcycle, nor do I plan to get one), Fig Newtons, and 59 cans of dog food. I feel like I'm 17 years old all over again, hoping that the clerk won't even notice that I am buying condoms.

As I wait in a long line at the cash register, my mind plays an awful trick on me. I envision the box of condoms not scanning properly. Before I can protest, the sweet young thing behind the cash register gets on the intercom. "I need a price check on Durex Lubricated Condoms!"

There is a long pause during which the store goes completely silent. My face starts to feel warm. The manager finally responds. "What brand?"

"Durex. Durex Extra Sensitive."

"Is that the 36 count or the 12 count?" the manager's voice asks.

"He only wants 12."

My face turns a deeper shade of red. "That's a three-year supply," I joke, lamely.

The 30-something lady behind me chuckles. The old lady in line at the next register, who has been craning her neck all over the store to find out who the sex maniac is who's buying the condoms, finally spots me. She glares and shakes her head.

The manager's voice booms again. "Is that the flavored or the unflavored kind?"

My face turns a shade of red so dark that a marketing guy from Crayola, who has spotted me from two cash registers away, dashes over, snaps a photo of my face, and hands me his card.

Before the manager can respond with a price, my head explodes and I'm finally put out of my misery.

Whew. I didn't know that buying condoms could be so traumatic.

So, out of sheer will, I envision another scenario. This time I am Mister Cool, Mister Middle-Aged and Sexually Active, buying condoms like it's no big thing because I go through a dozen a week. I have tried them all, *many times*. For me, buying condoms is like buying bottled water.

Whenever I buy condoms, the sweet young clerks look at me and think, "Wow. That handsome middle-aged man must have sex a lot. He must be a freakin' love machine. I'll bet the women he sleeps with have multiple orgasms *all the time*. I wish he would have sex with me. *Tonight.* I better give him my phone number. Better yet, I'll get his phone number and send him a photo of myself naked."

Yeah, that's much better.

So here's what really happens. I roll my shopping cart to the checkout stand and there's a 40-something woman who rings up my purchases without even noticing me at all. Her life is hard enough without caring about my purchases. Everything scans just fine, and if she thinks anything at all about what I'm buying, it's "Why the hell is this guy buying so many cans of dog food?" Especially since my ex-wife got the dog in the divorce.

So I've got a dozen condoms. Now all I need is a reason to use one. But I'm ready, and that is an important part of being a Babe Magnet.

BABE MAGNET RULE #2

Babe Magnets are always prepared for Babe-related activities.

I was never a Boy Scout, but they nailed it with the whole "be prepared" thing. And baby, am I ever prepared.

Chapter 5: My First (Almost) Pickup Experience

I just did something amazing. I approached a beautiful woman in public and had a nice conversation with her.

I was sitting alone at the Jupiter Moon Café near my apartment, eating at the counter where it's okay to read the magazines without buying them. I was reading a radical environmental magazine and eating a dinner of fish and chips. In walks a well-built fiftyish woman all by herself. I catch her eye as she sits at a table and quickly surveys the room.

In the most casual, not-too-obvious way possible, I watch her to see if anyone is going to join her. Apparently not.

All right, it's pretty obvious that she *knows* I'm watching her. She takes off her denim jacket to reveal a black tank top and breasts that were not original equipment. They are perky and considerably younger than the rest of her body. But she's in good condition, despite the mileage. Her hair is frosted blonde and her skin is pleasantly tanned. She gets up from her table and walks right in front of me, pretending that she needs extra napkins RIGHT NOW before her food is delivered to her table. I watch her walk back to her table, and she looks over to make sure I'm watching her.

Nice. Very nice.

Well, we're both checking each other out from a safe distance. Now what? I scan the restaurant again to see if anyone is going to join her.

In my youth, I was never a great pickup artist. Actually, I was never a pickup artist at all. Approaching a beautiful woman I don't know is not something that comes naturally to me. It's the worst, most frightening sort of cold call there is. I can make a business-related cold call, because I have a purpose and I have confidence in my business skills. But a cold call to pick up a beautiful woman? That's completely out of my comfort zone.

Just after I graduated from college, I lived in an apartment in Santa Monica near Wilshire Boulevard. I shared this bachelor pad with Pete, a friend from college with whom I also shared my appreciation for the female gender. We were both 21 or 22, single, and we had WAY more hormones than we knew what to do with.

Pete and I used to walk to the supermarket on Wilshire Boulevard every Tuesday after work because we knew that a drop-dead gorgeous woman shopped there at the same time every week. She was tall and blonde and dressed smartly in a business jacket and a tight but not too-tight skirt. We surmised that she was a lawyer, and Pete and I both had fantasies about ripping her clothes off in her private office and having sex with her on top of her desk.

We used to follow her around through the store, hanging back so she wouldn't notice us. I always felt she was out of my league, so the closest I ever got to actually having a conversation with her was the one time I walked beside her and noticed that she had bought some fresh fish from the meat counter. I couldn't think of a thing to say. Finally I said, "Fish. I like fish." She looked at me strangely, like I had just dragged myself out of the ocean and was attempting to walk on land for the first time. I had no follow-up line, so I slunk away, dragging my tail fin behind me.

That was the first and last time I ever talked to the Lawyer Babe.

Another time when Pete and I were grocery shopping, he deliberately put everything in the cart that he could find that cost 69 cents. I told him we didn't need a Catholic prayer candle or chewy treats for cats. We weren't Catholic (or religious in any conventional way) and we hadn't owned a pet since his parrot had died in a tragic marijuana mishap.

"Just wait," Pete assured me. "This is going to be great."

Pete pushed the cart to the checkout stand, where the most beautiful Babe was working. This was in the days before bar codes and electronic scanning, so every item had to be rung up separately by hand. The store policy required the checkers to call out the price of every item.

The Babe started ringing up our purchases, and with each item she would say, "69." She stood there saying 69, 69, 69, 69, while Pete's smile got bigger and bigger. At the end of all the 69s, Pete says to her, "So, what do you like to do for fun?"

The Babe was not amused.

So, my history of picking up Babes is not long and impressive. If I had a dollar for every time I've seen an attractive woman that *I didn't* talk to, I'd be listed right under Bill Gates in the Fortune 400 list of gazillionaires.

Well, what the hell. I'm more than 50 years old and I've never heard of anyone dying from talking to a beautiful woman. Humiliated, sure. But there is no known case of lightning bolts zapping a poor, unfortunate, lonely man who dared to talk to a woman he didn't know.

I have observed many Babe Magnets over the years. These studly men reek of self-confidence and never seem at a loss for words. When they see a Babe, they pounce. That's because they know...

BABE MAGNET RULE #3

Babe Magnets always make the first move.

I take a deep breath. I'm going for it. I get up and walk to the Blonde Babe's table. As I walk across the restaurant, the room keeps getting larger. A little stroll that should have taken me just seconds is stretching longer and longer. After an hour, I am still walking.

Then I am standing next to her, and I am forced to speak. "Excuse me, are you dining alone tonight?"

"Yes."

"Me, too. Do you mind if I join you?"

She smiles. She has perfect white teeth that are no older than her breasts. "Not at all," she says, in a pleasing tone of voice.

I go back to the counter, grab my plate and glass, and walk them over to her table. As I set them down I say, "Well, this is kind of weird, but I didn't want to eat alone."

If it's weird for her, she doesn't admit it. We start talking. Her name is Laura. She is a zookeeper. In my entire life, I've never met a real zookeeper. Her job gives us lots to talk about, and I ask her a lot of questions because I'm genuinely interested. I feel a little like the late Mr. Rogers, asking the zookeeper to describe the fascinating things she does because he needs to fill a whole segment of his TV show.

Laura takes care of the large animals—everything from rhinos to antelopes. From what she says, it's a bizarre and wonderful job. She even taught the animals to stand on a huge scale. It took months of patient work, but she did it. That's the kind of story that would make a great quirky item on the local news.

But while I am talking to her, my mind is filling with inappropriate questions:

"Do you ever use whips at work? How about at home?"

"What's the biggest snake you've ever gotten your hands on?"

"Just how big IS a rhino penis?"

"What do you do with the peacock feathers you find?"

"How many times have guys used a 'Me Tarzan, you Jane' line on you?"

"How often do zoo animals have sex?"

I have to focus *really hard* on our conversation to make all of the wild-animals-having-sex images leave my head.

I tell her a little bit about me and my work. I have a marketing business, and most of my clients sell home and garden products. It's not as exciting as two massive rhinos going at it, but Laura seems mildly interested.

We talk for a while, and in my mind I wonder what she looks like naked. Her arms are well toned and she is clearly vain enough to take pride in her body. And there are those wonderful, young, perky breasts just waiting for a chance to breathe fresh air. Breasts must really hate to be trapped in bras all day where they can't see the light of day.

Set them free, Laura. Set those young boobs free.

How old is she? Somewhere in her early 50s. She has two kids, ages 33 and 31. If she had the first child when she was 18, she'd be 51 now.

She tells me that she's expecting a friend to join her. I assume that it's a female friend. I am dead wrong. Carl, a nice-looking bearded man, arrives and suddenly I go from feeling confident to feeling like I have invaded another man's territory. Crap.

"We were both dining alone and decided to sit together," I explain.

Carl is very gracious—probably more gracious than I would be in his situation.

The conversation at the table dies. It's an awkward moment. Carl gets up to go to the counter to order food, and I get up to find a take-out box to pack up what's left of my fish and chips.

Laura and I chit-chat lightly while I package my food to go. I say "Nice meeting you," and I leave them to their regularly scheduled rendezvous.

I don't get Laura's last name or phone number, so there is no way for me to contact her again.

I think about her later in the evening, when I'm back in my bachelor apartment. We had a pleasant conversation, but we didn't spend enough time together to know if there could have been any magic between us.

It's not like I closed the deal, but I made my first Babe Cold Call, and I feel good. I am proud of myself for having the guts to get up from my comfortable spot in the restaurant and join her. I actually approached a beautiful woman and proved that I could have a pleasant conversation. Sure, I bolted when her male friend showed up, but I still made first contact.

For the first time as a newly single man, I feel like I'm going to do just fine in this brave new world of meeting new women.

Chapter 6: Barleycorn's

Many years ago, when I was in Boston on a business trip, I made a pilgrimage to the Bull & Finch Pub. Not familiar with that name? The Bull & Finch was the real bar that the *Cheers* TV show bar was modeled after. Just like on the TV show, the Bull & Finch Pub is located down a flight of stairs from street level. And the shots of the exterior of the building from the TV show are shots of the actual Hampshire House building at 84 Beacon Street in Boston.

For someone who faithfully watched *Cheers* on TV, walking down the stairs from the Beacon Street sidewalk into the Bull & Finch was a case of déjà vu all over again. When I walked through the door, I expected to see Norm sitting at the bar and Sam Malone serving him a beer. Of course, the real Bull & Finch isn't exactly like the set of the TV show. But the architectural elements are all there—from the style of the benches and the Tiffany lamps to the friendly wooden Indian that stands at the front door.

(By the way, the TV show was such a huge hit that the name of the bar was eventually changed from Bull & Finch to Cheers on Beacon Hill.)

I've always wanted to find a real-life *Cheers* bar where I could hang out with a great cast of characters like Norm, Cliff, Frasier, Lilith, and Sam. Not that I ever wanted people to yell out my name when I walked into the bar, like the "Norm!" greeting that you-know-who always got. But the concept of a friendly neighborhood bar appeals to me.

Well, I found my Cheers. It's called Barleycorn's, and it's within walking distance from my apartment.

I already knew about Barleycorn's, because my ex-wife and I had been there for lunch. The pub food was good, but I seldom went back. When I was married, going to a local pub wasn't a priority. I had more important things to do, like keeping my wife happy by mowing the lawn, scrubbing floors, vacuuming, cleaning toilets, going to the grocery store, painting the house, saying "Yes, Dear" several hundred times a day, and giving away all of my belongings that she didn't think I needed anymore—including my extensive vinyl record collection that would probably be worth about $14 million right now. (But I'm not bitter.)

After I moved into my apartment, I realized that Barleycorn's was literally the closest business establishment to my bachelor pad. I can walk there in five minutes or less. So, on a Friday night when I have no plans and I refuse to spend the evening alone at home, I stroll over to Barleycorn's to see if anyone knows my name.

Wearing a decent pair of jeans and a Hawaiian shirt, I walk through the entrance and nod to the bouncer. He actually asks me for I.D., bless his heart. I'm double his age with a few years to spare. Hell, I have shirts older than he is. But I must have a youthful smile—at least, that's what I tell myself as I enter the bar.

Barleycorn's is essentially one large room with an island bar in the middle and a row of built-in booths against the back wall. The décor is Basic Barroom—mirrored beer signs for Sam Adams, Sierra Nevada, Dos XX and Miller Lite line the back wall. Wine glasses hang upside down in wooden racks above the bar. Off to the far left is a small alcove tucked against a red brick wall where a tiny stage offers just barely enough space for a four-piece band to play. Scattered throughout the bar are TV screens that silently show an assortment of sporting events. Pub tables and chairs fill every available space, except for a tiny dancing area in front of the stage and an aisle that offers passage to and around the bar.

It may not have the ambiance of Cheers, but Barleycorn's is comfortable and unpretentious—like a favorite pair of shoes.

On this Friday night the place is packed. I'm guessing there are somewhere between 250 and 300 people here, and if the Fire Marshall came through the doors right now, some of us might have to go back outside. I scan the crowd as I walk slowly toward the bar. It looks like men outnumber women at least two to one, which does not bode well for possible Babe Magnet activities. But I am glad to be out and about in the real world.

The truth is, I'm not exactly sure what to do. I haven't cruised a bar alone in a long time. I am not comfortable walking up to a group of women and starting a conversation—at least, not yet. So I buy myself a beer and stand near the back of the room with a bunch of other men who are standing around with beers in their hands.

We are all facing the general direction of the band while pretending to enjoy the music, but what we are really doing is looking around to see if there are any Babes to talk to. Actually, it's pretty pathetic. We're like vultures, gawking at women who glance at us with expressions that range from mild interest to thinly veiled contempt. There is no possible way that any of the women seated comfortably at nearby tables are going to approach us. But still we stand at the back of the room, with our left hands in our pockets and our right hands holding beers. If Salvador Dali painted a picture of us right now, he would call it Pocket Pool Tournament with Beers.

It doesn't take a Babe Magnet to figure out that standing in the Single Dudes Zone is the equivalent of tattooing LOSER on your forehead. So I slowly swim my way out of the sea of single men and troll through the room. I start with the booths in the back, strolling past and checking out the groups of threes and fours who are sitting and chatting. Most of the booths are occupied by mixed groups of men and women. Even when there are three women and one man, I keep walking. My mind is completely blank, and I don't know how to get a conversation started.

I keep cruising. Beer in hand, I walk toward the stage, where a local band is playing covers of classic rock songs. It is so freaking loud that I'm not sure I'll be able to carry on a conversation with anyone, even if I figure out what to say.

Right at this moment I am feeling very old. I'm thinking of changing my name to Stonehenge. Most of the women in Barleycorn's are at least 20 years younger than me. Don't get me wrong, they look great in their tight jeans and crop tops that show off their skinny midriffs. But do they want to talk to a 50-something-year-old man?

I begin to think about what we would talk about. How about these for opening lines:

"Hey, I think I know your father!"

"I just had a funny thought—I started having sex 10 years before you were even born!"

"How old was the oldest man you've ever dated?"

"Do you know who the Beatles are?"

"I was born when Eisenhower was president. Who was president when you were born?"

Yeah, right. Witty conversation starters like those are *not* going to make me a Babe Magnet.

I hang around Barleycorn's long enough to slowly sip two tall beers. I ask a couple of women to dance, and one actually says yes. She's probably in her mid 40s, with blue jeans sprayed onto her ample hips, beautiful eyes, long brown hair, and a nice smile—and she is willing to dance with me. We do the basic freestyle rock dance that isn't really dancing at all; it's more like twitching and shaking to a 4-4 beat, especially when a middle-aged white man like Yours Truly does it. At the end of the dance, I try to engage my new friend in conversation. I learn that her name is Tina, and then she makes a beeline toward her friends seated a couple of tables away.

The evening progresses, but I do not get lots of phone numbers or make lots of new friends. I do not feel like a Babe Magnet. But the good news is, I don't feel like Babe Repellant, either.

As I walk back to my apartment, my ears ringing from standing next to the band's wall of speakers, I am glad I ventured out tonight. I know I've got to get comfortable enough to talk to women if hanging out at Barleycorn's is ever going to be any fun. But I feel good. And I have discovered another truth about Babe Magnethood:

BABE MAGNET RULE #4

Babe Magnets don't sit at home all by themselves on Friday night.

Chapter 7: A "Spring Training" Date on the Road

The captain says we're cruising at 31,000 feet. Who am I to argue? It's pitch black outside the jet's window. I am flying back to Springfield after two long days at the National Hardware Show in Las Vegas.

If you've never been to a trade show at the Las Vegas Convention Center, let me digress from the topic of Babes for just a moment to offer a brief description. The Las Vegas Convention Center just might be the largest enclosed indoor space in the history of civilization. It is big enough to house the entire population of Portugal. The Portuguese couldn't be there this week, so instead the building was filled with every kind of hardware imaginable. Friendly and earnest representatives from every company in the world that makes products that have anything remotely to do with hardware and home maintenance were manning the booths.

When you walked down the 17-mile-long aisles, these happy sales people would smile and try to get your attention.

"Hey, let me tell you about our new miracle paint stripper made from fermented fruit juices!"

"Do you like to screw? Have you ever tried supersonic screws?"

"Grab hold of this miracle hammer with a handle made from carbonited plastic polymers!"

"Hi! Pull down your pants and put your butt cheeks down on our miracle, climate-controlled anti-gravity toilet seat!"

Just kidding about that toilet seat. It wasn't anti-gravity. But there *were* toilet seats in 64 designer colors.

I had spent most of the past two days in an adjacent building that was devoted entirely to lawn and garden products. (Again, it was a good thing the Portuguese weren't able to make it, because the building was filled with more garden tools, ceramic pots, bird feeders, mosquito chasers, lawn-care chemicals, and bags of designer potting soil than had ever been assembled in one place before.)

If you like manly stuff like tools and dirt, the National Hardware Show is like Disney World without the rides—except there are more people and the food is worse.

For me, the highlight of the show was having dinner with Linda Patterson from *Weekend Farming* magazine. I met her at a media event and told her all about my client's products. Then, in an attempt to flex my fledgling Babe Magnet muscles, I asked her if she had any dinner plans. She said no.

"Would you like to get together after this is over and get something to eat?"

It felt like I was asking her out on a date. I was excited and confident, knowing that if she declined or took offense I could always say it was a friendly but strictly professional proposition. P.R. people like me are supposed to buy drinks and meals for media people.

"Sure, I'd love to," she said.

As we walked out to the front of the building, which was approximately 12 miles away, I started to get to know a little bit about Linda. Mostly I asked her work-related questions, and I was a perfect gentleman. Not once did I ask for her bra size or the style of underwear she wears.

Linda took a shuttle back to her hotel, and I headed off in the other direction toward the Sahara Hotel. The Sahara is a grand old Las Vegas landmark that had offered me a fantastic overnight rate because, quite frankly, it totally sucks as a modern hotel. The Sahara dates back to pre-Rat Pack days (Frank Sinatra, Sammy Davis, Jr., Warren G. Harding, Daniel Boone). Today, the hotel is held together entirely by the tar and nicotine from the 218.6 billion cigarettes that have been smoked inside it.

Once I had checked into my room on the Phillip Morris floor, I called Linda on her cell phone. We agreed to have dinner at her hotel so only one of us would have to catch a taxi. I went to the front of the Sahara Hotel and attempted to hail a cab. Apparently, the entire population of

Portugal had decided to visit Las Vegas after all, and they were hogging all of the cabs.

I waited at the taxi stand for half an hour. To the uninitiated observer, it might have looked as though I was simply waiting in line. But I was actually passing the time by watching a steady parade of Babes. If you're going to call yourself a Babe Magnet, you should always be on the lookout for Babes. It's stated clearly in...

BABE MAGNET RULE #5

Always have your Babe Radar activated, and always check out the Babes.

The supply of Babes in Las Vegas seems to be endless. Babes shimmied by in skin-tight red dresses with matching red lips, hair, and fingernails. Babes breezed by in the skimpiest of halter tops, their nipples pushing through the flimsy fabric. Babes strolled past with straight, shampoo-commercial hair down to their butts and skirts that barely covered their sexy parts.

These are Eye Candy Babes. They are not the kind of girls you want to bring home to meet your mother (or your kids), and they are definitely not the kind of women you want to marry. They are the kind of women that you go out with when you have extra money and you want to party. They are Sweet Tarts, not wholesome organic meals. You do not hang out with Eye Candy Babes if you are looking for lively conversation or depth of personality. Eye Candy Babes can only converse about personal trainers, beauty treatments (especially plastic surgery), diets, recreational chemicals, shopping, sex, things they want to buy, ex-boyfriends, and—if you're lucky—Oprah. But they sure are fun to look at. And there are probably more Eye Candy Babes per capita in Las Vegas than anywhere else in the world.

Finally, I was able to catch a taxi down The Strip to Linda's hotel. She was waiting for me in the lobby.

Did I mention that Linda is a real woman, and not an Eye Candy Babe? She's a Midwestern lady who is naturally attractive and genuinely nice. Linda and I had a wonderful dinner and a wonderful conversation. It felt like a date, but it was a very comfortable, no-pressure kind of date. I told her a short version of my professional life history—journalism degree, corporate communications work on the West Coast, moving to Springfield with my then-wife, and doing contract work for advertising and public relations agencies to survive. I told Linda about the big idea that changed my career—inventing a marketing concept for eco-friendly products. From there, I specialized in home and garden marketing and built up a clientele.

Linda told me about her move from upstate New York to Iowa with her husband to take over a dairy farm. It was a disaster. The dairy farm mentor and Linda's husband were not suited to be business partners, and Linda and her husband ended up getting divorced. She has one daughter, who now has two young kids. And that makes Linda a grandmother.

Wow, I've never been out on a date (or even a quasi-date) with a grandmother before. But I've never seen a grandmother as attractive as Linda is, and I told her so. It was a great compliment, and it was also true.

I asked her point-blank how old she was. Forty-one.

"Well, you don't look 41, and you certainly don't look like a grandmother."

She smiled. It doesn't take a Babe Magnet to figure out that all women like to be complimented—even grandmothers.

We talked for more than an hour and a half, and there were never any uncomfortable pauses. I had hopes that the evening would continue. I asked her if she would like to go to a casino for a little while to enjoy the pleasures of Las Vegas' favorite sport—throwing money away. She declined, because she still had to go back to her room and write a story based on what she had seen at the trade show. We walked to the hotel lobby and she shook my hand goodbye. I would rather have kissed her.

No matter. The evening was a delightful practice date. Call it a Spring Training date, and now I'm ready for real dating season to begin.

Put me in, Coach. I'm ready to play.

Chapter 8: Flashbacks

I keep having flashbacks of my old life. Today I flashed back to the last normal moment I had with my son, Jason. It was the day that my ex-wife, Valerie, and I told Jason that we were getting a divorce. I had spent the afternoon at my empty apartment, moving a few things in but mostly cleaning. I wanted the place to be as clean as possible when I moved in. I like for things to be spotless when I assume ownership. I don't want anyone else's dirt on my stuff.

I arrived back at the house about 40 minutes before our scheduled family meeting. I didn't know what to do. Jason, a studious high school senior, had been doing homework in his room. He decided to take a break and ride his new unicycle in the front of the house. I decided to play basketball in the driveway so I could be with him.

While he practiced tricks on his unicycle, I shot free throws. On the outside I looked fine, but on the inside I was a jumble of nerves and emotions. I was less than an hour away from telling my son the worst news he had ever heard in his life: his parents were splitting up. I felt like shit. So I made a deal with God. *If I can make 10 free throws in a row, then everything in my life is going to be great. Right, God?*

I don't think I've made 10 free throws in a row in the last 20 years. So if I made 10 in a row, I decided, it truly would be a sign from heaven.

I made the first shot. The second one was a swish. So was the third. I got a lucky roll and the fourth shot went in.

I choked on the fifth shot, and it clanked off the rim. I ended up making seven out of 10.

So I tried it again. First shot, swish. Second, swish. Third shot went in. The fourth shot brushed the rim and fell through the hoop. Fifth shot, swish. I was halfway there. The sixth hit the rim and almost went in before rolling off. I ended up making nine of 10.

I did the test one more time, and made eight. There would be no miracles today.

Telling Jason that I was leaving was the hardest thing I have ever done. The poor kid never saw it coming. Sure, he knew that his parents were in counseling. He knew that we were having troubles and we were working on it. He knew that I was sleeping in the back bedroom. But he didn't know that the marriage was falling apart.

Jason was stunned. His face flushed, and in the next few minutes he got redder and more upset. Of the three of us, he was the only one to hold back tears, but he looked as if he might erupt at any moment.

We tried to say all the right things. But how can you make the worst possible news for a kid sound less catastrophic? We told him this wasn't his fault. We told him not to feel guilty about this. We told him that we both loved him very much, and that wasn't going to change. "We're both going to be part of your daily life. You will still get to go away to college, and we'll pay for it," we said.

I apologized. I cried. I admitted that this was all my fault.

I was going to read Jason the letter I wrote to him to tell him how much I loved him. But I knew I'd be crying so much that I wouldn't be able to get through it. I signed the letter and handed it to him. He took a look at the first line, and his eyes filled with tears. He folded the letter, telling me he couldn't read it now but that he would later.

Then Jason gave me a gift. He said, "I'm glad this is happening now, and not when I'm away at college." He was glad this happened when we were all in the room to share the news.

There is no good time to tell a child that his parents are getting divorced. But this was the right time.

After we were all talked out, I asked Jason if he had any questions.

"Where will you be living?" he asked.

I told him about Creekside Village Apartments a mile away, with a swimming pool and a racquetball court and a pool table. I told him I would love to have him come visit me sometime soon.

After Jason went to his bedroom to process the bomb that his parents had dropped on him, I sat on the couch and sobbed.

With flashbacks like that, it is no wonder that I am having good days and bad days. Today is one of those bad days. I feel completely hollow. My insides have been scraped out like a Halloween pumpkin. I've been hollowed out and carved up, and now my jack o' lantern face shows the world an emotion that I am not feeling. There is no emotion inside of me. I am numb.

Where did my heart go? Why don't I feel anything? Where is the passion that I used to feel?

In the movie *It's a Wonderful Life,* when George Bailey was ready to return to his old life, he stood on the bridge and prayed, "I want to live again."

Well, I want to *feel* again.

Once, many years ago, my heart leaped when I saw the woman who was to be my wife. Where did my love go? Did it sneak off into the night? Did it evaporate like wet footprints on a hot summer sidewalk? Did it invisibly escape, like air slowly leaking from a bicycle tire?

Where does love go when you can't feel it anymore? Will I ever feel it again?

I've got to get myself out of this funk. "Snap out of it—be a man!" I tell myself.

I know that I will regain my equilibrium, and I will learn how to love again. But for the rest of the day, I give myself permission to feel crappy. I'm going to wallow in self pity and get it out of my system. I will pass through the darkness, and soon I will emerge into the light again.

Chapter 9: The World of Cyber Singles

In the spirit of keeping all of my dating options open (and using technology when it can make my life easier), I have decided to venture online into the world of cyber singles. After all, what have I got to lose? The truth is, I can't get any more single than I am right now. If I am truly going to become a Babe Magnet, then there have to be some Babes involved. It's the 21st century, so perhaps the Babes I want to meet are hanging out online. They might be saying to themselves right now, "Hey, where *is* Chad, anyway?" Or, "I wish there were more middle-aged bald men that I could meet online."

But I don't know anything about online dating. The only relevant website I have heard much about is Match.com, so that's where I go first. From what I have heard, Match.com is basically an online superstore for singles. Well, if that's where single Babes hang out, then I should hang out there, too. Because, according to ...

BABE MAGNET RULE #6
Babe Magnets go where the Babes are.

There is another principle that applies here, too:

BABE MAGNET RULE #7
Babe Magnets (even middle-aged ones) are not afraid to learn new tricks.

My former roommate, Pete, met his current wife on Match.com. Many years after we lived together, Pete had moved back to Los Angeles after his first marriage disintegrated. He was single and looking for love, so he responded to a posting by a woman that read "Dodger Fan Seeks Dodger Fan."

They emailed each other, and then they set up a first date. The woman's name was Margaret, and Pete fell for her immediately. Their first date lasted for hours. After dinner, Pete went back to Margaret's place and spent the night. According to Margaret, he never really left. When I went to Los Angeles to attend their wedding, Margaret told me the story of how they met, with love in her eyes.

Pete and Margaret were married in a luxury suite at Dodger Stadium during a Dodgers game. I'm not kidding—there was a baseball game going on in the background of their wedding vows. It was the perfect wedding for them, and I really enjoyed it.

I'm a sucker for a story with a happy ending. So here I am on Match.com, to see if Pete's and Margaret's love lightning will strike me, too.

From the Match.com home page I fill in the Quick Search box. I am a MAN searching for WOMEN between the ages of 42 and 52 within 10 miles of my zip code. I hit the SEARCH NOW button, and in seven seconds a screen pops up with thumbnail photos of 16 local women. That's pretty cool—16 local single women in about the same time it takes to sneeze. As I look more closely, I see there aren't just 16 women, there are *31 pages* times 16 women. That's 496 single women in my age bracket.

Oh my God, I have hit the mother lode! If I went out every night cruising every bar, restaurant, concert, Starbucks, health food store, library, and special event in town, and I met three single women every week, it would take me 165 weeks to meet the same number of women who just popped up on Match.com in seven seconds. That's more than three years' worth of ladies.

I better get busy.

I check out the photos of the 16 ladies on Page One. Some of them I choose not to click on because they've chosen screen names that are bizarre or just a turn-off. Cat_Lady_13 isn't a bad looking woman, but is there a man alive who wants a woman who has 13 cats? She's going to die alone at the age of 89, and by then she'll have 127 cats. I hope those cats don't eat her dead body before the next-door neighbor comes over to check on her.

In some of the photos the women are holding their pets. Any woman who loves her pet so much that she has to include it in her primary photo needs a lesson in Marketing 101. Ladies, that photo is your calling card, and you've got to look appealing AND available. If you care so much about your little Fifi that you can't put her down and have a decent picture taken, then there really isn't room in your life for a relationship with a man.

Aside from my little "pet peeves" (if I were emailing this story to you right now, I would have to add an obligatory LOL), I am really enjoying the Match.com website. When I click on a woman's thumbnail photo, I am instantly transported to her full profile. In a minute or two I can read everything she wrote about herself and see a checklist of her own attributes and what she's looking for in a man. It's better than a resume, because included in the profile is information that would probably take five dates to extract in person: what foods she likes, what her favorite activities are, what books she has recently read, marital status, does she have kids, do her kids live with her, height, weight (described in general terms such as "athletic and toned, "average," and "a few extra pounds"), political beliefs, age, income, education, turn-ons, and more.

Yeah, baby! This is the menu at The Babe Restaurant. I start clicking and reading.

LoveSeason is reasonably attractive, but in the first paragraph of her bio she says that a "sense of humer" is important. One of the things that's important to me is a sense of spelling.

Springfieldhiker's headline reads "MMMMMMM??????" So, she hikes and she likes M&Ms, apparently. Her photo shows her dressed in a jogging outfit along with her dog. I think I'll pass.

An attractive woman with the screen name Jasimom says she's a "widowed mom ready for passion, romance and fun... be stable and have your affairs in order, because I believe I do and I want the same." A little demanding, don't you think, honey? I'll bet that attitude keeps men away in droves.

As I read the profiles, I notice how many of the women are short. I never realized there were so many short women. When I go out, I don't see scores of 5-foot-tall women. Maybe they don't leave their houses, and they all stay at home cruising Match.com. Those short, stubby little legs must get tired.

It becomes obvious that kids are going to be an issue. A lot of women in their 40s and early 50s have kids living with them, and I am not excited by the prospect of dealing with someone else's young children.

Barbiejo544 has the best funny headline: "Possessive/controlling 49 year old, lives with parents, recently released from prison, 8 children with 9 daddies, looking for 7th husband."

The best single line, the one that makes me laugh out loud, is "I don't have any children that I know of." I love a woman with a sense of humor. (As opposed to a sense of humer.)

The worst line: "I've been single a long time and know what I want. Please don't ask me to make exceptions...I won't." Well honey, maybe you've been single so damn long because you don't know how to compromise. Good luck in Spinster Heaven.

It takes me two hours to go through the first six pages, and I am exhausted. I never realized how tiring it is to shop for Babes. I think I'll go get a good night's sleep and resume my search tomorrow.

Chapter 10: Cyber Babes, Part 2

The next evening, I am back on Match.com. It is very addicting.

Dana_mo99 makes me laugh out loud with her subhead: "More Cowbell." Any fan of *Saturday Night Live* and Will Ferrell knows that sketch, which is one of the funniest things to ever appear on SNL. Dana_mo99 makes the first cut, and I add her to my Favorites folder so I can contact her later.

Beth8899 posted three photos of herself without a hint of a smile in any of them. There is no excuse for three non-smiling photos unless a stray hockey puck took out all your front teeth. Beth's fourth photo was of her Yorkshire terrier. Do you think I'm going to call her?

EmeraldWildGirl says she "has kids and they live at home (none)." Perhaps there's something you don't understand, honey, but either they live at home or they don't. Maybe you've forgotten where you've put your kids and it's time to look for them.

1201AB is suffering from a creative block. Her headline reads: "What kind of dating headline could possibly be intriguing?! Any ideas? ;-)" How about: "Beautiful, Rich, Delightful, Horny Woman Looking for a Mildly Attractive Bald Man." That would definitely intrigue me.

96 SCLJD posted a picture of herself swinging a golf club. Her head is down and her visor covers her face. Plus, she looks like she's not even holding the club right. So, who are you trying to impress, honey? Blind golfers?

6Shooter69 was brave enough to post a photo of herself with curlers in her hair. Not as her primary photo, thankfully, but as one of 12 photos she posted in her profile. I immediately send her a "you go, girl!" email that applauds her bravery and spunk.

Kiss_Will_Tell's headline is "Insert Sarcasm Here." She has a "come hither" look on her face that makes me think she'd be good in bed. But there's too much attitude in her profile. She seems too high maintenance for me.

The choices go on and on. I'm starting to get Babe Fatigue from having too many women to consider. SpringFab says she is "fit, funny and fabulous." She is cute and confident. I'm sold, and I add her to my Favorites.

BBBecky76 doesn't know how to leave good enough alone. Her primary photo looks good. But when I click on it to see her entire profile, I flip through the photos and each one gets progressively worse. She goes from looking like a Babe to looking like a goofball, and in her last photo she becomes the Bride of Frankenstein. What was she thinking? Men are visual creatures. Don't chase us away with photos that reveal just how creepy you really are.

I like pizzaz708, who describes herself as a "great catch!" I agree. She's cute, slender and athletic. She is 45 years old with no kids, plays golf, and she's never been married. (Very little baggage, apparently.) She says she wants kids "someday," but I don't think that's ever going to happen. Maybe someone should explain the whole biological clock thing to her.

I think about writing to her. I entertain myself with the lewd and crude email I compose in my head that contains at least one use of the phrase "hitting balls." Then I send her a pleasant and friendly (and non-threatening and non-sexy) message instead. I get all of the lewdness out of my system before I send the email because of:

BABE MAGNET RULE #8
Being a lewd asshole doesn't impress Babes. If a Babe's first impression of you is "jerk," there will be no second impression.

It takes me hours to look at every woman's profile in my target age group, but like a marathon runner, I am exhausted yet exhilarated when I finally finish the task. In the end, here's some advice I would like to give to women:

1. Smile! Why would you post a dour-faced shot as your primary photo unless you want to remain single? Do you think men are looking for a bad time? Trust me, no one ever wrote, "For a bad time call 555-7609" on a restroom wall.

2. Don't post a photo of yourself and another woman if the other woman is better looking than you are.

3. Write a fun and snappy profile. If you can't do it yourself, consult with your creative friends. Or hire a professional writer.

4. Under the category Best Feature, don't choose "feet" unless you're looking for someone with a fetish.

5. Be creative. Have some fun. Most men aren't looking to date librarians. Or women with no spark of personality. Or cat ladies.

6. Sound enthusiastic, not bored. Men don't seek out boring women.

7. Refrain from bad-mouthing men in your profile unless you are looking for a woman as your next lover.

8. Emphasize yourself, not your adorable little dog or your many cats. No man wants to play "second fiddle" to a furry creature that has to go outside to poop.

Chapter 11: The Waiting Game

I have sent emails to 17 women on Match.com. Because I did my homework and read countless profiles, I know better than to merely "wink" at the women I am interested in. Most women say they don't respond to winks, because they take virtually no effort (just a click of your mouse) to send. Furthermore, winking doesn't demonstrate any real interest, nor does it reveal anything about the sender. I think winking is the equivalent of saying, "Hey, baby" to a woman at a bar and then walking on.

I may be new to dating in this century, but I am not completely clueless.

In my emails to each prospect, I write something that shows I have read her profile. ("I see that you lived in California. Me, too!") I find that many of my emails contain similar information, so I create a template that includes an opening paragraph, a paragraph about her profile, a background paragraph about me, and a paragraph about our similar interests.

It doesn't take me long to get the hang of writing a great email to a woman I have never met. This online dating thing is going to be as easy as ordering a double-shot mocha non-fat latte at Starbucks. Make mine a tall.

So, after a long day at work and with great anticipation, I fire up my laptop and log onto Match.com. I just know that my Match.com inbox is already packed with responses. Out of the 17 women I have written to, I figure virtually all of them will reply, even if some of the responses are "no thank you." For a moment, I worry that I shouldn't have sent so many emails right away. What if I get 12 women who all want to date me?

There isn't that much of me to go around. Let's see, 12 women in one week is two dates every day, with Sunday off. Maybe I could handle that for a week or two.

I sign in and click on my inbox. So how many responses do I have from Match.com Babes? None. Zero. Zippo de nada. I am crushed.

I go back to my profile and try to imagine myself as a Babe who has just gotten an email from me. She is visiting my profile for the first time to see what I am like. She's going to look at the photo first. Even though women will tell you that looks aren't as important as what is in a man's heart, you can't see into a man's heart. At least not right away. So you start with the photo.

My photo looks okay. I am a reasonably attractive man in the right lighting. Granted, if a woman is looking for a man with a full head of hair, she's not going to respond to me. But if a cue ball with a great smile turns her on, I'm golden.

Maybe it's my screen name: PlantPapa. I thought it was clever, since I like to garden. But maybe it makes me sound like a dweeb, especially when paired with my headline: "Passionate Man Seeks Passionate Woman for a Growing Relationship!" Is that too geeky?

I read through my profile. I thought I had hit the right tone of sensitive metrosexual and fun-loving adventurer. I wrote: "I love hiking and biking, sunsets, classic rock, movies with heart (*The Princess Bride* and *Field of Dreams*), laughing, fresh strawberries, good books, red wine, day trips to the mountains, starry nights, thunderstorms, and slow weekend mornings."

Later in my profile I wrote:

"I'd like to meet a woman who is kind and loving and attractive and full of life. You're not afraid to try something new, but you're also comfortable snuggling by the fire when it's cold outside or enjoying a margarita or an iced tea in a quiet spot on a summer afternoon. But most of all, I need someone who I can connect with emotionally and who I can love as a friend and cherish as a lover. I love romancing a special woman and sharing all of the moments that make an intimate relationship, well, intimate. I'm looking for someone who would like to share these things—and more—with me."

Isn't that the coolest description ever of the perfect middle-aged man?

Apparently not, at least not to the 17 women I emailed. Perhaps this whole online dating thing is going to take a little bit longer than I had thought.

But I am not going to give up. I flip through a couple of magazines to get my mind off of women and off the disappointing results of my first batch of emails. I find myself looking at the beautiful women in the magazine ads. Then I find myself tearing out the pages with the photos of beautiful women.

Clearly, I still have Babes on the brain.

The ancient Chinese art of feng shui says that energy flows through homes and offices, and if you manipulate that energy (called "chi"), you can create the results that you want. So I decide to make a Wall of Babes in my bedroom. I take the magazine photos of gorgeous women and I arrange them into a collage on my bedroom wall. Now there are blondes and brunettes and redheads smiling at me, and I feel like the world is full of beautiful women who would love to meet me.

Then I get back onto Match.com and write some more emails. I feel like an unemployed person sending out resumes. All the women on Match.com claim to have an opening for a heterosexual man who can fill the job of friend and lover.

For one lucky woman, that man is me.

Chapter 12: A Couple More Beers at Barleycorn's

After a very pleasant nine holes of golf with Karl, a business associate who has become a very good friend over the years, we go to Barleycorn's for beers and an early dinner. The spring weather is absolutely perfect—clear and sunny without being too warm—so we sit outdoors on the patio and soak up the sunshine.

Going to Barleycorn's is a completely different experience during daylight hours. Somehow it feels friendlier and nicer. There aren't as many people here during the daytime, and the hormone levels aren't surging the way they are at night.

Karl and I check out the other tables for Babes, and we watch people come and go. I tell Karl I've been off the singles market for so long that I still don't know exactly how to behave. Is it okay for a 50-something-year-old guy to talk to a 25-year-old woman?

"If you have enough money, you can talk to anyone you want to," says Karl. He tells me there is was one problem, though: I am too nice. "Chicks like rich assholes."

"Really?"

"Yes, really."

I ponder that for a few moments. "Well, I could learn to be an asshole."

Karl doesn't think so. "You've put in too many years as a nice guy to turn into an asshole now."

Well, shit.

After a couple of beers, Karl and I say *adios* and go our separate ways—him to his expensive house in the foothills, where his wonderful wife waits for him, and me to my empty bachelor apartment. I'm not sure what to do with myself, so I make a couple of phone calls. The staff at the retirement home can't get my dad to come to the phone, though, and Jason has only a few minutes before leaving for an important teenage rendezvous.

So here I am, sitting alone in my apartment. I have no plans, no one to call, and nothing to do but watch TV. This is the worst part of my life right now. Without a wife and kids to fill up my time, I don't know what to do with myself. I don't have a garden to putter in. I don't have any new hobbies to keep me busy. Sitting on the couch alone watching TV is the last thing I want to do. Why? Because that's not what Babe Magnets—or Babe Magnets in Training—choose to do. It is clearly stated in...

BABE MAGNET RULE #9

When in doubt, a Babe Magnet gets his butt off the couch and goes out.

I change my shirt, run a wet washcloth over my face, splash some Old Spice on my neck, and walk back over to Barleycorn's. Only an hour has elapsed since I left, but with darkness falling, the place has transformed from a neighborhood hangout to a bar. I am now arriving alone as a single man looking to talk to single women, and that makes the friendly confines of Barleycorn's seem a bit less friendly.

Babe Magnet or not, it's much more difficult to get comfortable in a bar when you're there by yourself. There is no safe "home base" where you can hang out, and no friends to chat with. You have to grow a huge pair of *cojones* to walk up to a woman and be instantly charming and witty—especially if you have to be charming and witty in front of her friends and whatever other guys are trying to hit on them.

I make one quick sweep of the now-crowded bar for potential prospects. I have my eye on a table of three women in their 40s who have been joined by a man who is working the table very effectively. All three of the women are enjoying his company. I watch for a while, and marvel at the effortless way he jokes and talks and keeps them all engaged in the conversation. This guy is a true Babe Magnet, and he is conducting an in-field demonstration. I wish I could hear what he's saying. I would take notes.

But alas, my *cojones* have not yet grown big enough, and my Babe Magnet skills are not yet so refined. I do not know how to break into the group of one man and three women, so I sit in a nearby chair and watch an NBA playoff game on the big screen TV.

After a while, I make another stroll through the room. A blonde woman at the opposite end of the bar catches my eye and smiles. Very interesting, indeed. She is reasonably attractive and within my target age bracket. (She's probably about 45). A much younger guy is working valiantly to keep the interest of this blonde woman and her dark-haired female friend, but the blonde is clearly not as entertained as her friend is.

For a while, I alternate my attention between the Babe Magnet working the table with the three women, and the younger guy with the blonde and her brunette friend. I am enjoying a great new spectator sport I have just discovered—Babe Magnet Cruising. It's entertaining and somewhat educational. But merely watching other Babe Magnets cruise is not going to help me become a Babe Magnet. I'm going to have to get into the game.

Besides, as I stand near the bar, I realize that I am sipping on one of the worst margaritas I have ever had in my entire life. (Note to self: never order another margarita at Barleycorn's. They don't have a clue how to make them. I could pee in a glass, add sugar and tequila, whip it in a blender with ice, and make a better margarita than this.) While I am drinking this horrible margarita, watching other Babe Magnets in action, I feel my balls starting to shrink. If I keep sipping this crummy drink alone, pretty soon my entire body will shrink until I am completely invisible.

Then I catch a break. The band comes back onstage and starts playing another set of barroom rock 'n roll, and the young guy takes the blonde's friend to the dance floor. The blonde is now sitting alone at the bar with an empty chair next to her.

I summon all of the Middle-Aged Babe Magnet energy in my body, and set that body in motion. I arrive at the empty chair before anyone else.

"Hi," I say, smiling. "Is it okay if I sit here for a minute?"

She smiles and says yes. I slide in and start chatting.

I don't even know what I'm saying. Words are flowing out like endless rain into a paper cup; they slither while they pass, they make their way across the universe (as John Lennon once said). It's not the words that matter as much as the simple fact that I had the nerve to walk across the room and sit down next to this attractive woman and start talking to her. She is glad I am here.

I have just learned a valuable lesson about being a Babe Magnet:

BABE MAGNET RULE #10

A Babe Magnet gets points for trying. The fact that you had the nerve to approach a woman is interpreted by her as a compliment. And that makes you considerably more attractive and more desirable than if you had merely admired her from afar.

Her name is Candice. She is friendly, she smiles easily, and she laughs often. Our conversation covers many light topics, and then we venture into strange territory for a barroom chat. She tells me this is the first time she's been out since her dad died two weeks ago.

I give her my sincere condolences. Then I tell her my dad is in a nursing home. This is quickly turning into the strangest conversation I have ever had with a strange woman. (Let me clarify. She is a stranger to me. I don't know yet if she is strange.) But we keep talking, and we keep finding new things to talk about.

She tells me she was raised in a small town where she was a high school cheerleader. She has a four-year-old son whom she had when she was 42. I was almost dead-on in my guess about her age. She's 46.

She lives in a house on the other side of town. She never married her son's father, but they have a legal decree that gives him custody six nights a month. She works as an administrative assistant for a start-up company that is creating a medical website. An image appears in my mind of a large call center in New Delhi. ("Hello, I am Dr. Raja. How are you feeling today? May I have your user name please?") I do not share this with Candice.

Instead, I tell her a short version of my life story: a long marriage ending in divorce, a one-bedroom apartment within walking distance of this very bar, my own business, and a teenaged son. (I brag about Jason quite a bit, but not enough to be obnoxious.)

Candice is nice, she's fun to talk to, and she doesn't smoke. So I'm thinking to myself, *This woman is reasonably attractive and, even if she's never going to be my dream girl, I can definitely see myself going out with her.* I would love to have a female friend and/or lover with whom I could go to a movie or play golf (she's a duffer but she wants to get better). I look her over and she's impressively fit for a 46-year-old woman. As if on cue, she tells me that she teaches fitness classes at a local gym on Saturday mornings as an extra gig.

I don't want to be her son's new daddy, but I would be very happy to go out with this woman. If given the opportunity, I would even like to have sex with her for a couple of months until I can find someone with more long-term potential. (I am not going to tell her all this, of course.)

These thoughts are going through my head while I'm sitting next to Candice at a bar within 30 minutes of meeting her for the first time. Such are the inner workings of the brain of a Middle-Aged Babe Magnet In Training.

Candice hands me her boss's business card so I'll know where she works, and I can call her if I am so inclined. She makes a point of telling me that she declined to take a business card from the younger dude who is hot for her friend.

"Why should I take your card?" she asked him. "I'm not going to call you."

I pull out one of my business cards, telling her she can not call me, too.

"Oh, I'll call you," she says. And I believe her.

At just after 11:00 p.m., Candice and her friend are ready to leave. I walk them to their cars. Standing in the parking lot, I tell them how nice it was to meet them both.

I am feeling pretty good about life as I walk back to my apartment. I have my first phone number as a rookie Middle-Aged Babe Magnet. I am finally in the game.

Chapter 13: The Follow-Up Call

How much time should elapse before you call a woman you've just met? Are there rules for this? If there *are* rules, where would you find them?

This is the 21st Century, so I decide to Google it. I type in "how long before you call..." and Google gives me the suggestion "how long before you call her." I hit Google Search. I click on the first listing, and it takes me to a forum on eNotAlone.com. Cool. I love the Internet when it gives you information that you can actually use in your real life.

A 24-year-old guy writes that he met a woman at a wedding reception on Saturday. They had a great conversation, and he got her phone number. He's thinking he should call her on Monday.

A woman from England agrees. "I would go with Monday evening. I hate it when a guy is too keen and phones the next day, it puts me right off, but I also hate when they leave it too long as you lose interest."

A 29-year-old woman has a different opinion: "Honestly if a girl is interested she wants you to call right away, however, guys have this macho feeling to them where they feel they need to be in control and wait a couple of days. If you like her call her. I think that whole 2 day 3 day rule is stupid, but you do what you want."

And this from a 27-year-old male: "Bad idea to call on monday ... it hasnt been long enough. Wednesday or Thursday would be good. Dont just talk to her on the phone the idea is to get some personal interaction, go out for some coffee or something very casual."

Another man said he had waited as long as 10 days to call. In response, a very attractive 40-year-old woman (who had posted her photo) said this: "If a guy waited 10 days to call me, I'd probably not even take the call. I really appreciate a show of interest, and think a guy's interest is directly related to the amount of time it takes him to call me. I also like a guy who is confident enough to call me even the next day if he is really interested. I've found most guys wait a day or two before calling."

So there you have it. The answer is...there isn't one answer. You go with your gut. But waiting a couple of days for a follow-up call seems to be the most popular answer. And as it turns out, the soonest I can call Candice is Monday, because I only have her work number. So, not wanting to appear too eager or too desperate, I wait until Tuesday to call.

Just before noon, I punch in the number on the business card that Candice gave me. A female answers the phone, but the voice isn't familiar.

"Global Solutions, this is Candice."

Oh my God, it IS her. I take a deep breath and force a smile. I read once that the person on the other end of the phone can hear it in your voice when you smile. I hope Candice can hear my smile, even if it *is* a bit forced.

"Candice, this is Chad Stone. I met you at Barleycorn's on Friday night."

There is a brief pause, and I can feel her energy level rise. I swear I can feel her light up on the other end of the line. "Hi!"

"Hi! Remember me?"

"Of *course* I remember you!" she says. (It sounds like she is smiling.) "How was your weekend?"

We chat for a few minutes, and she tells me about getting up early on Saturday morning to teach two aerobics classes and coming home to take a nap at 2:00 p.m. Hmmmm, I would have liked to have been part of that nap. But I'm not sure there would have been much sleeping going on...

NO, NO, NO, Chad! Pull your head out of your nether regions and be charming. You are a Babe Magnet, not a pervert!

I tell her I'd like to get together, and she says she would love to see me again. I have already thought about this, so I give her a choice—lunch on Thursday, or doing something together on Sunday afternoon. She jumps at lunch on Thursday because she's going to visit her mom over the weekend.

Perfect. We chat for a few more minutes. I am excited, and Candice sounds equally as excited. I've now scheduled my first official date as a single man.

Oh yeah! I am feeling pretty good about myself. The sun is shining brighter on my part of the world right now. Yes, indeed, I should call myself The Magnet, or maybe The Mag for short. Maybe I should get a tattoo that says *The Mag*.

I just attracted my first Babe.

Chapter 14: A Lunch Date

I am deliberately early for my lunch date with Candice. I am excited, because this is literally my first lunch date since before the Berlin Wall came down and all Germans (East and West) were given equal access to strudel, Volkswagens, Rammstein, and the Autobahn.

Although there is very little about lunch dates in written historical records (and, shockingly, there is no "Lunch Date" entry on Wikipedia), I am quite sure that the lunch date was one of the first inventions of dating. A lunch date is the perfect first date—especially in the modern age. We're all busy people, and after an hour-long lunch date we have to get back to work or get back to whatever we do when we're not working. Either way, everyone knows that a lunch date is not going to be a big time commitment. Conversely, nobody is going to get laid—so there's very little pressure, and you don't even have to wear your best underwear.

Candice and I have agreed to meet at a Mexican food restaurant that is conveniently close to where Candice works. I sit at a table right next to the door so I can see her when she walks in. Candice arrives, sees me, and smiles. We move to a table outside on the patio. It is a lovely day, and what makes it even lovelier is that Candice is clearly happy to see me.

"I didn't think you were going to call," she tells me as we look at the menus.

I was a little surprised myself, although I don't tell her this. More than anything else, I called because I need the practice. I need to find out if dating is like riding a bike.

The light at midday in the great outdoors is much different than in the light in a bar at night. Daylight is much brighter and much less forgiving. Sitting across from me now, Candice looks older than she did at

Barleycorn's. But then again, I'm sure she could say the same thing about me.

Don't get me wrong—Candice is attractive, but nowhere near drop-dead gorgeous. She is 46 years old and she has some wrinkles etched around her eyes and her mouth from years of smiling. Now that I am getting my first really good look at her, she's not a low mileage woman. She is not someone who has been pampered and protected.

Ten minutes into our lunch date, I already know that Candice and I are not destined to have a long-term relationship. She has told me all about her "delightful" four-year-old son, and at my age I've already done enough parenting of young children. However, Candice is nice, she has a nice body for a 46-year-old woman and, so far, she seems to genuinely like me.

So I'm having a mini-moral dilemma. Am I leading her on by even having lunch with her? Is it wrong to pretend that I think there is any future for us? Is it okay to simply enjoy a lunch date? Is there anything wrong with me trying to be charming enough to seduce this woman?

I think that if I do the right things—call her, take her out a few times, visit her house or invite her to my apartment—I can get Candice into bed in two to four weeks of dating.

That's just a guess. I have absolutely no recent experience to go on. I don't know her well enough to know how quickly she operates. But even before I finish my lunch, I think that I can "have sexual relations with this woman" (as Bill Clinton once said) if I want to invest the time in her.

I don't want to hurt her. I don't want to pretend that we'll be together for a long time. But I do like the idea of going out with Candice again.

Candice will be gone for almost a week to visit her mom. I will be out of town the following week to visit my dad. So I won't actually see Candice again for two weeks.

We hug our goodbyes in the parking lot. Neither one of us is ready to commit to even a quick kiss.

A lot can happen (or not happen) in two weeks, so I decide to call Candice during the few days in between her getting back into town and me leaving. I am surprised at how effortlessly the conversation flows. She tells me about her visit to her mom's house, and I tell her what I did over the weekend. We talk about the five aerobics classes she teaches a week. At one point she has to hang up and call me back because her dog has eaten the macaroni and cheese off her son's plate. Ah, the joys of having small children.

I tell her I'll call her back after I return from my four-day trip, and she seems delighted. After I hang up, I wonder what Candice looks like naked. She's got a nice figure, and she's got to be in excellent shape if she's teaching five aerobics classes every week.

On my master To Do list, I write, "See Candice again. If possible, see her naked." That's because of ...

BABE MAGNET RULE #11

A Babe Magnet knows what he wants, and he states his intentions clearly.

(This also works in other, non-Babe Magnet areas of your life.)

Chapter 15: Man-to-Man Advice

It is the day before I fly to California, and I am sitting outside on the patio at O'Malley's Tavern with Craig. We're drinking cold beverages and talking about women.

In uncharacteristic fashion, especially for a conversation between two men, I spill my emotional guts. I tell Craig how I fell out of love with my wife. I tell him that I am battling loneliness, horniness, and fear of the unknown. But it's not all bad news, because I am also excited to be entering a new, uncharted phase of my life. One of the things I don't miss about my old, married life is the sameness from day to day.

Craig is the perfect person for me to pour my soul out to, because he's been through all this—three times. He has been married to two delightful women and one heartless bitch, and he divorced them for entirely different reasons. So, it is quite safe to say that I am not telling him anything he hasn't already experienced for himself.

For the price of me buying him a beer or two, I get to dump all of the angst onto him that I've been stoically carrying around and not sharing with anyone. And he gets to give me advice as the old pro to the newly single middle-aged man. It is the ultimate man-to-man win-win situation.

Craig says he dealt with his last divorce by getting involved with a new woman almost immediately. The relationship lasted, on and off, for about a year.

"That's what I need, a bridge relationship. I need a woman I can be with for a while, but who won't put any pressure on me to commit to a long-term thing."

In other words, as my grandfather might have said, I want the milk without having to buy the cow.

Craig totally understands, but he's lactose intolerant so he doesn't drink milk, and he doesn't know why I would want a cow in suburbia. He doesn't get the metaphor because he is too busy looking at the hooters on the cute blonde waitress. And that is Craig in a microcosm.

I tell him about my desire to become a Middle-Aged Babe Magnet and find the new love of my life. He totally understands the part about becoming a Middle-Aged Babe Magnet, and he gives me this really good advice:

First, visit a few of the nice restaurants in town on Friday and Saturday nights. Order dinner at the bar. There is no point in going to a restaurant and eating dinner alone at a table, because there is no way that you can easily strike up a conversation with anyone. You just look like a lonely, pathetic single man who is eating dinner alone. But if you have a drink at the bar and then decide to eat dinner, the worst thing that can happen is that you'll have a decent meal while watching a ball game. The best thing that could happen is that you might sit next to an attractive single woman who also is having dinner at the bar because she doesn't want to be alone, and you start talking and you get to know her and then you go home with her and you have wild, passionate sex because she turns out to be a hot young woman who is a former Victoria's Secret model. (This, by the way, actually happened to Craig.)

Second, go on a cruise by yourself. Take three novels and plan to do a lot of reading. But tell the maître de to seat you at the table with the single women. You never know what might happen if you are flexible and available and willing to have an ocean-based fling with a moderately attractive divorcee from Omaha who has grown kids in college and just needs to get laid. This also happened to Craig. But he had those paperback novels just in case he needed them.

Third, tell the women you meet that you are going through a traumatic post-divorce period in your life and you don't want to sleep with anyone right away. You're just not ready. They will want to have sex with you even more. In sales, that's called "the reverse close." You act like you're selling something (in this case, yourself), but as soon as the prospect gets interested, you tell her she can't have what you've been selling. We have all seen this approach work from time to time, but in this case I'm not sure I'm that good an actor. I feel like I have HORNY stamped across my forehead. I won't be able to convince any woman that I don't want to have sex with her. Not even an elderly nun with bad teeth and a clubfoot. But Craig says no, this approach really works.

Fourth, beware of the Curse of Saturday Night. If you are fortunate enough to be dating more than one woman at once, you will find out that they each want to be your Saturday night date. Alas, there is only one Saturday night each week. So you have to learn how to juggle, or you have to get lucky enough to find at least one woman who regularly works on Saturday nights.

I laugh. I am so far away from having more than one woman to date that it seems more likely that I will awaken tomorrow morning in a yurt with an unexplainable ability to speak fluent Japanese while balancing a bowling ball on my nose.

Right now, I look forward to honing my Babe Magnet skills enough to attract *one* woman into my life.

Chapter 16: Babes, Babes, Everywhere

Today, there are women wherever I go. I must be giving off the scent of an available single man. Women can smell it—even though I can't.

At the bank, I stand in line right behind a woman who makes a point of turning around a couple of times to smile at me. I say a few friendly things to her, but I don't pursue anything because she's too frumpy for me.

That's just the beginning. This afternoon I have my first Match.com date. She is a fellow plant lover who sent me an email saying she liked my smile. Her photo was, shall we say, less than hot. I never would have initiated contact with her based solely on her appearance. But it's a wonderful ego boost the first time a stranger picks you out on Match.com.

I responded to her initial email, and once she found out that we were both in the Master Gardener program, she was convinced that we were a Match.com made in heaven. Her name is Nancy, and she sent me six emails that first day.

So I go to the City Garden Center to meet her. She is doing a shift on the Garden Hotline, which is a volunteer job that every Master Gardener must do. People call on the phone with questions about gardening, and we attempt to answer them. I figure the Garden Center is the perfect place to meet, since we have the Master Gardener program in common. Plus, it's a sneaky way to meet her without it costing me anything.

I am approaching this meeting as a "practice date." High school students take practice SAT tests. Law school students take practice bar exams. Actors and musicians rehearse their shows. There is no reason why a novice Middle-Aged Babe Magnet shouldn't go on a few practice dates to hone his skills.

I walk into the Garden Center and spot her right away.

"You must be the PlantPapa," she says warmly, referring to my Match.com screen name.

"Hi, Nancy. I'm Chad Stone."

"I kind of like PlantPapa better," she says with a smile. She looks better in person than she does in her online photo, but she is still a big woman, and I have never been attracted to big women. This may sound crass and shallow, but I don't want to date a woman who outweighs me.

We sit outside on a bench in the flower garden. I ask her how long she has been gardening, how long she has lived in town, how many kids she has, how long she has been divorced. Basically, I am conducting an interview. Nancy is a nice woman, and she would be a wonderful friend. But she isn't a brilliant conversationalist, and I don't feel any instant chemistry between us.

When we say goodbye, she gives me a big hug. It feels like I am hugging the Pillsbury Doughboy. I am slightly grossed out and hungry at the same time. Then she insists that I take her phone number, so I do.

Clearly, Match.com is not an instant answer to my dating prayers. But I did have one more date today than I would have had without it.

From my practice date with Nancy, I go to a counseling appointment. I have not always been a big fan of counseling, but during the collapse of my marriage I decided to see a counselor to help me understand what I was going through. I admit that it has helped to have a semi-nonjudgmental male who doesn't know me listen to my problems. In fact, counselors and therapists are fabulous people to talk to when your regular bartender is out of town.

BABE MAGNET RULE #12

A Babe Magnet isn't afraid to get professional help when he needs it.

So I'm in the waiting room at the counselor's office, and I start talking to an attractive woman who is waiting with her two kids. I can tell by the conversation between them that they are here because of a divorce in the family. This woman is clearly attracted to me, and had we not been interrupted by my counselor coming for me, I probably could have gotten her phone number. Sure, it would have been the phone number of a woman in a relationship crisis, but hey, maybe we could be each other's rebound relationship.

After dinner, I go to a store to buy a tablecloth and a set of wine glasses. I have my first nighttime date with Candice scheduled for tomorrow. Just in case I get lucky and she decides to come back to my apartment for a drink after the movie, I want the dining table to look decent (hence the tablecloth), and I want to have wine glasses in case she wants to drink wine.

While looking at wine glasses, I notice a hot single woman looking at dishes. I like the tight fit of her jeans and the way she cocks her hip to the side when she is concentrating on which plate pattern she likes. The Hot Babe is shopping with two women friends, and they are all quite animated. They are clearly enjoying their shopping adventure, in a way that most men are genetically incapable of. Women shop for entertainment; men shop to hunt and gather. For men, shopping is not about fun, it's about getting stuff you need and getting the hell out of the store.

If I had the energy, I could walk over there right now and engage the Hot Babe in a playful conversation about dishes.

"Excuse me, you seem to know a lot about plates," I would say.

The Hot Babe looks at me with an expression that says, *What do you want, dweeb?* Then she realizes that I am attempting to be friendly and charming, and she gives me the benefit of the doubt. (See Babe Magnet Rule # 10.) "Well, not really..."

"I couldn't help but notice the way you were looking at those plates, and I was wondering if you could tell me how to tell the good ones from the bad ones."

"I just know what I like..."

"Exactly," I say with a smile. "I'll bet you have excellent taste."

She grins sheepishly.

"I mean, you picked out that blouse, right? And you look fabulous in it."

BABE MAGNET RULE #13

Well-timed flattery, when used skillfully and in moderation, can sometimes help you get laid. And even if it doesn't help you get laid, women will still love you for it.

"Well, yes. Thank you..." She smiles in spite of herself, and her eyes flash with newfound interest. Inside her panties, she notices a slight tingling sensation.

I hold up two different plates. "So, which of these do you like the best?"

She picks one. Okay, it's time for me to use my razor-sharp wit and get her to laugh. Women dig men who can make them laugh.

"Sure, that's a great choice for you. But what about for a manly man like me? Maybe I should get plates with tanks or bazookas on them."

She laughs.

I sneak a quick, up-close look at her bazookas, and I like what I see. At the same time I flash my best dazzling smile, and her heart warms. But I'm not done yet. I decide to delight her with my Arnold Schwarzenegger impression, which is quite good if I do say so myself. "Ya, I don't want any girly-man, Martha Stewart dishes."

She laughs and twirls a strand of her hair next to her neck. The tingling in her panties grows stronger and wetter.

"Hi. My name is Chad Stone, Babe Magnet. What's your name?"

"Heather. Heather O'Horny."

"Oh, an Irish girl," I say, slyly. "Is it true what they say about Irish girls?"

"That we give great blowjobs?"

"Well, I wasn't going to mention that one right away. But since you brought it up—so to speak..." The tingling in her panties seems to be contagious. Now it's also in my boxer shorts.

"I'm not sure I know you well enough to answer that question," she says.

"Then we'd better get to know each other, don't you think? Why don't you give me your cell phone number and we can go out. I'm thinking dinner, a movie, and a nightcap of some kind," I say, suggestively.

She laughs. "Sure. That sounds great," she says, unconsciously rubbing her thighs together until her jeans erupt into flames.

You see how easy it would be? But I'm tired, and I don't have the energy to talk about dishes right now. Besides, today has proven to me that there are Babes everywhere. Until further notice, I am going to assume that there are LOTS of available women out there for me. I am going to meet cute, middle-aged women everywhere I go.

But tonight I am going home to get some sleep.

Chapter 17: Virgin No More

Tonight is my first nighttime date with Candice. I am trying to be cool and nonchalant, but I am a nervous wreck. My armpits are wet, and my pulse is racing. There is a small possibility that I will get laid tonight, and just thinking about that possibility gives me a woody that Paul Bunyan would be proud of.

I tell myself to relax, just relax. You are a Middle-Aged Babe Magnet—or at the very least, a Middle-Aged Babe Magnet in Training. You have been out with women before. You know how to behave around women. You know how to go on a date with a woman and show her a good time.

I might be a little rusty, but at least I'm not clueless. I have perused enough books and dating websites to know that a true Babe Magnet—of any age—takes dates in stride. That's one thing that separates Babe Magnets from ordinary mortal men. I know...

> **BABE MAGNET RULE #14**
> Babe Magnets are confident and sure of themselves. Even if they have to fake it.

So that's what I need to be right now—cool, calm, collected, and confident.

I am working on it.

Candice and I have decided to do the Most Popular Date Ever—dinner and a movie. At this point, I am not confident enough in my dating repertoire to come up with anything more creative than that.

Candice comes by my office to pick me up just before sex—er, *six*. She is suitably impressed by my office space and décor, which is one of the reasons I suggested that we meet here. At 1,000 square feet, my office space is not huge; but it's nicely furnished, with attractive artwork hung on walls painted in colors selected by a professional decorator. The fact is, my office space is much more impressive than my bachelor pad.

We chat for a few moments while I give her a quick tour, and then we get into her cute little silver sedan and drive to Jupiter Moon Café for dinner. The restaurant is hip and casual, and it sends the right message for tonight's date. We're not on a fancy dinner date, nor are we on a fast food burger date. We're on a "trying each other out but neither of us is making a big commitment here" date. We order our food at the counter, and then we find a nice table for two.

Candice is looking very nice. Her blonde hair is loosely pulled back and it falls gently onto the shoulders of her blue-flowered blouse. She is wearing a pair of lightweight white stretchy pants that accentuate her shapely legs.

I am surprised at how delightful Candice is. She is a joy to be with. We talk easily, and we make each other laugh. She seems to be as cool and collected as a woman can be on a first nighttime date—not that I have anyone recent with which to compare her. Thankfully, her aura of comfort and ease helps me to relax, and I am very happy to be with her. Maybe I should have picked a more expensive restaurant.

After dinner, we drive downtown for a showing of an Indian film that was highly recommended by a co-worker of Candice's. I am not happy about the movie choice, but I defer to her as a sign that I am the kind of real man who can see chick flicks and foreign films and enjoy them if the woman I am with enjoys them.

The movie is the story of an eight-year-old girl whose "husband" is an old man. He dies, making her a widow. In India, circa 1938, widows were shunned and sent off to austere dormitories and put to work in horrible jobs. It is a depressing story, so it isn't exactly what I would call a "date movie." Date movies are supposed to be fun and light, and they are supposed to be about romance and the promise of sex, so a couple on a date can start thinking about romance and sex. A date movie is Hollywood's version of foreplay.

I am sitting in the darkened theater next to Candice, thinking to myself that I am getting no foreplay help from this movie at all. The tortured lives of young girls in India do not make a woman think to herself, "Hey, I'm feeling very amorous right now. I really want to have hot, passionate sex with a man that I barely know."

So here I am, sitting next to this attractive woman who seems to be attracted to me (or she wouldn't have agreed to this date), but we are not touching each other at all as we watch this very artfully done but depressing non-date movie. The thought pops in my mind that I should just be bold and reach over and gently hold Candice's hand. My heart speeds up a little, and I feel like I am 16 years old again.

When I was 16 years old, I would have thought about holding her hand for A LONG TIME before I ever made the move. But now I'm over 50, and I'm not getting any younger as I sit here in the dark. So I just reach over and take Candice's hand in mine. With my other hand, I start gently stroking the inside of her forearm. The physical contact is tender, and it feels nice. It is also my way of telling Candice, "We are on a romantic date here. Get ready."

Candice seems to enjoy the physical contact as much as I do. I hope she understands that it is supposed to be theater foreplay. The movie goes on and on and on. The best part of the movie (at least for me) is me stroking the soft nook of Candice's arm.

We talk about the movie on the way out of the theater. Candice really liked it, which surprises me because I hadn't thought that she was classy enough to like artsy foreign films. Maybe I underestimated her.

Because I took her to dinner and paid for the movie, Candice wants to take me out for dessert. Instead, I suggest that we go back to my apartment for a glass of wine. She agrees, which I take as a very good sign. I feel the blood flow to my nether regions in hopeful anticipation.

Back at my bachelor pad, we settle onto my couch while sipping glasses of red wine. My apartment is small and Spartan, but most of the furniture goes together as if it were purchased with some kind of a plan in mind. It looks reasonably nice. Thank God I hung a few pictures on the wall earlier this week, and bought the wine glasses and tablecloth last night.

The date is going very well. I have successfully taken a delightful woman to dinner and a movie. Even more important, I have successfully gotten her to my couch. But now I am nervous, because I know that the next move is mine. Even though I am new to this, I know there is a Babe Magnet Rule that applies to this situation:

BABE MAGNET RULE #15
You don't "get lucky" by sitting on the couch all night, just talking.

I move closer to her on the couch and lean in for our first kiss. It is soft and wonderful. Our lips meet tentatively, and then I apply more pressure and more passion. She returns my passion with her own, and I know right away that this woman is a great kisser.

Her tongue darts in and out of my mouth. Soon our tongues are dancing the country two-step and then the cha-cha. When the radio plays a slow song, our tongues hug each other and sway to the music.

All right, it's time to escalate. I gently slide my hand across her blouse and massage her breast. She moans with pleasure. I caress the side of her face with my fingers and then reach down to her right breast from above, sliding my hand under her bra until...

Candice comes up for air. She leans forward on the couch and reminds me that she has an aerobics class to teach at 8 o'clock tomorrow morning.

If this was a baseball game and I was up to bat, that little objection would be Strike One. No reason to panic yet.

In response, I lift up her hair and kiss the back of her neck. I love that spot, and every woman I have ever kissed on that spot loves it, too.

"I'm not exactly all cleaned up," she confesses. "Fridays are busy for me, because I teach an aerobics class at noon."

Strike Two! I dig into the batter's box. I am not going to strike out tonight.

I kiss her on the back of the neck again. This time she tastes slightly salty. I don't mind. "I can put you in the shower and hose you down," I say.

"True." She smiles.

I move in to kiss her again, and she responds with passion. I begin to massage other parts of her body through her clothes. When I get to her crotch area she moans with pleasure and leans her hips into my hand. I still have two strikes on me, but I am feeling good about this at bat. I sense that this is my pitch. I take my best swing, and suggest that we go into the bedroom. I take her by the hand and she willingly follows.

Holy crap. This is my first nighttime date with this woman, and we're going to have sex. Tonight. Now. I am rounding the bases and heading for home.

I pull the covers off the bed, and she undresses down to her sexy new underwear.

"My panties are a little too big," she says sheepishly. I realize that she bought them just for tonight, just in case she was going to have sex. She probably didn't try them on until today. Her new panties get my undivided attention for only the few seconds that it takes for me to strip them off of her.

Now I get my first look at Candice naked. She has a hot little body for a woman in her mid 40s. I am very pleased as I strip off my clothes and lie naked beside her.

God, I love making love to a woman. I love everything about it. I love the skin-to-skin contact. I love stroking the body parts that I do not have—the soft, round breasts and the passion-swollen nipples and the moist and mysterious region below.

I see. I come. I conquer. Our lovemaking is hot and passionate. And we are very good together. In the heat of passion she shouts, "Yes, baby. Yes, baby! YES, BABY!"

I have never had a lover call me "Baby" before, and I like it.

I am lying on top of her, completely spent, and she starts laughing. I stroke her face and tease, "I'm not sure that laughter was the reaction I was going for."

"That's joy," she says. "I'm laughing from pure joy."

Wow. That's just about the nicest compliment any lover has ever given me.

We lie naked, her head nestled on my chest. We talk effortlessly in post-coital bliss. I hadn't realized until just now how much I had missed holding a woman in my arms. Sure, the sex felt great. But so does the tender cuddling that so effortlessly follows. Life is good.

Candice leaves at midnight. She wants me to call her tomorrow afternoon and maybe come over to see her house.

I have trouble sleeping. The Halleluiah Chorus keeps playing in my head. My libido has been awakened, and I want more.

For the first time, I actually feel like a Babe Magnet. And also like Babe Ruth. I just hit a homerun.

Chapter 18: Easy Come (Ahem...), Easy Go

I wake up feeling fabulous. The summer sunlight fills my bedroom, and I am aglow with the memories of last night's romance. I have successfully launched my Babe Magnet Era, and it feels great.

There is no reason that Candice should be a one-night stand. She's fun, she's attractive, she's willing, and I like her. Best of all, we had a really good time together. She is a better conversationalist than I gave her credit for, and has a pleasant personality.

As she suggested, I give her a call in the early afternoon. I get her voicemail, so I leave a friendly message. Then I call her two hours later. She doesn't pick up, and I don't leave another message.

Then it hits me. She is blowing me off. SHE is blowing ME off! Even after telling me, while we were lying naked in bed, "This was a GREAT date!"

The way I feel right now must be what it's like for a woman when a man doesn't call. This must be what it feels like to think a connection has been made, and then—poof—it's gone. Unless she calls me back, I have no control over the situation. I hate the feeling of having no control. Of course, Candice might simply be busy. Something important might have come up with her son or her dog or her sweater drawer. But damn, I would have loved to see her again today.

I am still in a funk after dinner, but dammit, it's Saturday night and I am *not* going to sit alone watching TV in the dark. If I did that tonight, I would feel pathetic. There has to be a rule against that. Oh yeah, it's...

BABE MAGNET RULE #4a

Babe Magnets don't sit at home all by themselves on Saturday night, either.

I force myself to drive to Sicily Grill to have a beer. Craig told me that eating dinner at the bar is a great place to meet women. Maybe going there will cheer me up.

Sicily Grill is a chain restaurant that tries very hard to seem like it's not a chain restaurant. The décor and architecture are Early Fake Italian Villa. The waiters and waitresses are friendly, attractive, and eager to please. The restaurant is located in the parking lot of a shopping mall, right across the street from a large hotel.

When I arrive just before 9 o'clock, half of the stools at the bar are empty. I sit next to an attractive 40-ish blonde who is perched on the corner stool. I order a draft beer and watch the baseball game on the screen up above.

Being here is a good idea. Just sitting here in a public place makes me feel better. I am starting to get into the Babe Magnet mode once again. It takes me just two minutes to strike up a conversation with the blonde. Then we talk for two hours, until the restaurant closes.

Her name is Bobbie Fuller. She is 42 years old and she works for a clothing company as a regional sales manager. She spends a day or two in town every month to visit with store managers, set up promotions, and make sure her company's products are being properly merchandised. She likes hanging out at the Sicily Grill bar, and the bartender knows her by name.

Bobbie and I talk about a little of everything—politics, religion, work, traveling, relationships. She never once laughs, and she smiles only occasionally.

There is a sadness about her that I have seen before in other women her age. She has been divorced for many years and she has no kids. She travels a lot for work, and although she doesn't tell me this, I know that she is married to her job. Her biological clock is ticking, and it makes her melancholy. Either that, or she has given up on ever having kids, and the disappointment lives in her eyes even though she doesn't want it to show.

I like Bobbie instantly, but she also makes me sad. I want to tell her that her sadness keeps men out of her life. Men don't want sad women; we want fun, vibrant women. Like Cyndi Lauper said in her '80s hit song, boys just want to have fun. (Oh, wait... Well, you know what I mean.)

After more than two hours of talking, we slide off our bar stools so I can walk her to her rental car. She is shorter than I thought she'd be. But she is quite attractive and she's smart, and there are plenty of men looking for a smart, attractive woman.

But Bobbie walks through life alone.

I give her my business card, and ask her to call me the next time she is in town. I offer to buy her a nice dinner.

I already know that I will never hear from her again.

Later in the week I talk to Candice. She apologizes for not returning my earlier calls. She says her life has been crazy. There is some hassle concerning the visits between her son and his father. I hear the clanging of very loud warning bells in my head. It sounds like I'm standing in a fire station just as the firefighters get a call. The ringing in my ears is so loud that I can barely hear Candice when she agrees to go out with me this Friday. I ignore all the clanging because I am thinking with my little head, not my big head.

I am pumped up for my second nighttime date with Candice. I tell Karl about my date, and he wants to hear all about her. When I tell him she has a four-year-old son, he frowns. He doesn't have to say a word.

I am giddy with excited anticipation. Then, on Friday morning, Candice calls and abruptly cancels our date. "There's something I have to work out with an old boyfriend, who is back in the picture," she explains.

I am devastated. Damn her—and a pox upon all womankind.

I think about Candice on and off during the next week. If I had more Babe prospects, I wouldn't care that much about Candice. But I'm still honing my Babe Magnet skills, so I don't have any other women to ask out on dates right now.

The more I think about Candice, the more plausible it becomes that I have come on too strongly. After having sex with Candice once, I have proceeded to call her as if I were an obsessed weirdo. If Candice is at all normal (and I think that she is), then having an obsessed weirdo calling her repeatedly probably scares her.

After thinking about it way too much, I decide to give Candice one more call. I am going to try a different approach.

She is friendly when I get her on the phone. “You know, I’m really not that scary,” I tell her.

She laughs. “You’re not the scary one, I am.”

Candice has just told me the complete, unvarnished truth. But unfortunately, I do not realize it. With a little cajoling, I convince Candice to go out with me again.

And again, on the morning of our scheduled date, Candice calls to cancel. I remind myself that there are many tuna in the sea, and I swim on.

Chapter 19: Match.com is the New "Friends"

Who needs cable TV when you've got Match.com? I haven't met any new lovers yet from the online dating site, and Nancy is the only woman I have actually met face to face. But I certainly enjoy searching online for women, checking out their photos, and reading their profiles.

When I search for women on Match, I feel like a fox with the keys to the henhouse. All I have to do is pick an age range and a location and POOF—instantly I get dozens of women's profiles to peruse. If I want to narrow the search and eliminate all smokers, conservative wackos, cat ladies, and women with tits that are smaller than mine, I can do that with a few clicks of a mouse. In a few moments, a new Babe Menu pops up and I can read all about them.

So instead of watching TV, I now surf Match.com. I have searched for women in my target age group (from 10 years younger than me to my age). I have searched for women in their 30s, just to see what comes up. I have even searched for women in their 20s, just for the hell of it. Based upon my own personal research, here is what I have observed about women of different age ranges:

- Women in their 50s look old. Yes, they are my age, but they look WAY older than I do. Either I am in complete denial about how old I look, or I look younger than my chronological age. I certainly FEEL younger than the women my age look. The women in their 50s who have let their hair go completely gray look old enough to be my mother.

Women in their 50s know exactly what they want, and they are not afraid to tell you about it in great detail. They want men who are successful, handsome, sexy, independent yet devoted to their chosen woman, monogamous, fun to be with, and handy with a wrench when the faucet breaks. They love going out to nice restaurants but also like to snuggle at home near the fireplace. They like having a gentleman open the door for them, but they want to be respected as equal partners. They sound exhausting.

• Women in their 40s are trying to seem confident, even when they are not. Many of them sound wistful when they describe the man they are looking for. The disappointment of not having men in their lives right now seems almost palpable.

Women in their 40s are looking for companionship and partners. At the same time, some haven't yet given up on the idea of finding a Prince Charming. A surprising number of 40-something women have never married, which bothers me. What's their problem—extreme pickiness, or an inability to commit?

Here's what a typical woman in her 40s says in her profile: "I am a happy and content person. However, I know something is missing. Sharing life and experiences with someone would add that missing piece." Women in their 40s are usually looking for men in their 40s, but some are willing to date men in their 50s.

The good news is that women in their 40s usually look better than women in their 50s. The bad news? They are much more likely to have kids still living at home.

• Women in their 30s are Babes. They are hot, and they know it. They love to show off their still-sexy bodies. At the same time, they want to be taken seriously as career women who are intelligent, ambitious, independent, and still willing to show off their sexy bodies.

These 30-something Babes are women in their prime, and many of them already have kids. The mommies all say that their kids come first, but each is looking for a special man in her life. The women in this age group who do *not* have kids wake up in the middle of the night to the sound of their biological clocks ticking. Most of them still hope to find the right man to father their kids before it's too late.

Personally, I feel bad for 30-something women with kids who are trying to date. Babysitters are expensive, and the sound of men running away from women with kids will sometimes wake up the kids when they are supposed to be sleeping.

- Women in their 20s are Babes, but they are ridiculously young Babes. Based upon their photos, every woman in her 20s has had breast augmentation, and they are really proud of their big, sexy American breasts. I can't say that I blame them.

A shocking number of 20-something women have tattoos. And not just cute little butterflies or unicorns. We're talking dragons, skulls, black widow spiders, and battleships. Some of them seem addicted to tattoo ink.

Women in their 20s all want to have children. Their hormones are surging out of control, and they all want to find a hot young man, have hot passionate sex, and make babies. There is not a single woman in her 20s who is looking for an old fart like me.

Women in their 20s do not listen to the music that I like, and when they talk about their favorite movies they never mention my favorite movies. We have absolutely nothing in common.

As fun as surfing through Match.com for Babes is, checking for emails from Match.com Babes is really disappointing. I send out dozens of emails to women, and I get very few in return.

Most cyber-women simply ignore me. Clearly, there is something wrong with my approach. It's obvious that I do not have the hang of this whole online dating thing yet.

I click through the list of emails I've sent recently. They are well written and grammatically correct, even when sent to women who clearly need a proofreader before they post their profiles. ("I am an electric engeneer by education but I work as healthsurvice provider" or "I am looking for someone to compliment.") In my emails, I always mention something about me that is not in my profile. ("I actually know how to ride a unicycle!") And I always say something that proves I have read their profiles. ("I see that you once worked as a tightrope walker in a circus. Me, too!")

As I look through the photos of the women I have contacted, an obvious pattern emerges. They are all Babes. They are all stunningly beautiful and they are all younger than I am. On the proverbial 1 to 10 scale, they are 8s, 9s and 10s. Just for fun, I click on my profile. I see the smiling face of a 50-something bald man who is mildly handsome—but he ain't no George Clooney. Maybe he's a 6 or a 7. My online profile doesn't convey how charming I am, how fun I am to be with, how intelligent I am, how sharp my wit is, or how I make a woman feel wonderful and special. Not to mention how humble I am.

Maybe I'm aiming too high. Maybe I should lower my standards a bit. Maybe I should broaden my target from women who describe their body types as "athletic and toned" and include those who are "about average." Karl says that "about average" actually means "fat" when you meet a woman face-to-face. All I know is, I am striking out so far on Match.com, so it's time to change my strategy.

I'm going to pick a few women who are about five years younger than I am, and I will send them each a delightful email. They don't have to be stunningly beautiful, just above average. They don't have to be wealthy, just employed. They don't have to be Einsteins, but they must know how to handle their end of a conversation that isn't about shopping.

Based upon what they say in their online profiles, women value a sense of humor. They all want to laugh, and they find a great sense of humor a real turn-on. (I guess that means Jerry Seinfeld and Jimmy Fallon are really sexy.) Well, I have a great sense of humor, and I am going to dazzle these women with my wit.

Okay. Here goes.

T. Watson looks like a nice lady. But she chose TWATSON101 as her screen name, so I can't think of anything to say to her that doesn't start with TWAT.

This is going to be harder than I thought.

Chapter 20: Moby Dick Gets a Tan

I am lying out by the pool on a glorious morning to get a little bit of color on my pale Moby Dick body. I wear sunglasses to protect myself from the glare coming off my white legs and belly. I have 30 minutes out here before I have to move my clothes from the washing machine to the dryer, and I am enjoying every moment of it. *Wish You Were Here* by Pink Floyd is playing on my iPod, and I am content. If there is anything bad happening in the world right now, I don't want to know about it.

But alas, my half hour is soon up.

In the time it takes for me to walk to the laundry room, move my clothes into a couple of industrial-strength dryers, and walk back, my neighbor, Katie, has parked herself on a chaise longue in the shade. She is intently focused on the book she is reading.

I met Katie briefly just after I moved into my apartment. She lives upstairs, two doors down. I have been looking for an opportunity to talk to her ever since.

I know that she drives a sporty red Toyota. From my bedroom window I can see her car parked in her usual spot next to the trash dumpster. Sometimes when I am getting dressed, I look out at the parking lot and see people get into their cars and drive to work. I've noticed that Katie leaves for work at about 7:30. So, in an attempt to say hello and maybe even strike up a conversation with her, I have taken trash out to the dumpster at 7:29. I have also retrieved things from my truck that I didn't really need, just so I could walk back through the gate at about the same time that she is walking to her car. And, I must admit, whenever I see her walk by, I suddenly find a reason to go out for a walk or check my mail or...whatever.

The thought occurs to me that, in the mind of a perverse criminal attorney, it might be construed that I am stalking Katie. Yes, I am watching her. No, she doesn't know that I am watching her. But it is not stalking. I repeat, IT IS NOT STALKING. It's just innocent spying on a young woman in an effort to get to know her, so she will have sex with me.

Just for fun—and to prove that I AM NOT A STALKER—I visit http://stalkingawarenessmonth.org. I learn that a recent report by the Justice Department revealed that 3.4 million people were stalked in one year. (Holy crap, that's a lot of people! That must mean that the definition of stalking is really broad.) All 50 states have laws against stalking, and most stalking victims are regular people, not celebrities. A full 75% are being stalked by someone they know (at least a little bit). Well, I do fit the profile of a stalker, in that I already know Katie a little bit. But come on, that hardly makes me a stalker...

Three things that a stalker does is following, frequent phone calls, and monitoring computer use.

Well, there you go. Sure, I *am* following her (sort of). But I AM NOT calling her on the phone or monitoring her computer usage, because I do not have her phone number or access to her computer. I am only 33% stalking her.

Okay. Now that we've got that settled, I can get back to my story about how I am innocently spying on Katie. Thus far, I haven't been very successful at "spontaneously" striking up a conversation with her. I've managed to say "hello" a couple of times, but that's about it.

So even though I hadn't planned to go back out to pool after moving my laundry, Katie reading a book out by the pool is too good an opportunity to pass up. Even as a married man, I observed over the years that the guys who get the girls always seem to have the time to talk to Babes whenever they (the men) meet them (the Babes) on the street. Or in the aisles of the supermarket. Or in line at Burger King. Or wherever. These Babe Magnets make the time, even if they are in a hurry. I now call this...

BABE MAGNET RULE #16

Babe Magnets take advantage of opportunities to talk with Babes. Even unexpected opportunities. *Especially* unexpected opportunities.

So I walk over to Katie and ask if I can pull a chaise over to share her shade. She smiles and says, "Sure!" But that is the extent of our conversation. I notice that she is reading *The Great Gatsby* by F. Scott Fitzgerald and taking notes on a lined pad. She seems to be in a studious, not a talkative, mood.

I settle in and read my book. I really want to get to know Katie, because she's cute and she seems bright. From what I have observed, she is single and available. She appears to be about 35, and if she thinks of me at all it's probably as someone from her father's generation. But what the hell. The worst thing that could happen is that I could go after her and be rejected and humiliated. Any Babe Magnet worth his subscription to Playboy TV is willing to risk a little rejection.

Katie reads her book silently for 15 minutes. I finally decide to strike up a conversation. "That's not exactly light summer reading," I quip.

She smiles. "I am taking a summer literature class at the university."

"Yeah, I didn't think you were reading *The Great Gatsby* for fun."

We talk for 45 minutes. She is very articulate and can converse on topics ranging from current events in Africa to pop culture. She already has two college degrees (Apparel Design and something related to that), and she's working on another degree so she can teach. Her green eyes light up when she smiles, revealing perfect white teeth. She has lovely straight dark blonde hair that dances atop her shoulder blades.

I ask her about the dark tattoo that circles her right bicep like an armband. It's a motif of South American images. She doesn't explain why she chose those symbols to wear permanently on her arm.

I don't know why Katie doesn't have a boyfriend. I don't know why she spends so much time alone. (I have been watching.) I do know that my laundry has been dry for a quite a while, but I don't want to leave. I have been waiting a long time to have a real conversation with Katie, and I don't want it to end.

We talk some more. Then she reads for a few minutes before I entice her back into a conversation. This goes on for two hours, and then we walk back toward our building. Katie tells me she is going to be moving out of her apartment because her rent is going up. Crap! I don't have much time to get to know her.

How can I keep this encounter going? I have to think fast.

"Would it be all right if I peeked into your apartment?" I ask. "I have never seen an upstairs unit with a vaulted ceiling."

She frowns. "It's kind of a mess."

Yeah, but everyone always says that. I didn't just fall off the Babe Magnet truck. I know that's a very soft excuse.

Sure enough, she walks me upstairs and into her apartment. Her place is so full of furniture and stuff that it looks small, even though it is the same size as my apartment. The difference is she's lived here for five years and I've only been in my apartment for a few months. The high ceilings are great, and she also has a small fireplace.

I look past her living room into her bedroom. Her bed looks very comfortable, piled high with an assortment of fluffy pillows in bright colors. Katie is telling me about her passion for clothing design.

Katie has turned her dining area into a sewing room with an industrial work table. On one wall is a large bulletin board, upon which are tacked drawings of her original clothing designs. And they are good—impressively good.

She tells me she is moving in three weeks. I look around at all of the stuff and offer to help her move. "I even have a truck."

She looks surprised, but she also seems to appreciate the offer.

I have just three weeks to get to know this woman. It's not going to be easy, because despite the past two wonderful hours, I know that Katie lives like a hermit. I've got some serious Babe Magnet work to do.

"Now that you know me a little better, you have to answer the door when I come knocking to take you to Starbucks for a chai."

She says she will.

Three hours later, I decide to test her. I knock on her door to ask her to join me for an impromptu dinner. There is no answer. I walk around to the parking lot, and there in Katie's regular spot is her red sports car.

She blew me off. Dammit, she blew me off. Well, Katie, I am not going to give up that easily.

I'm not going to get my Babe Magnet Merit Badge by giving up.

Chapter 21: No Chemistry

A week later, I am finally able to run into Katie again. I stake out the parking lot at her regular morning departure time, and this time she has a few minutes to talk. I ask her out and she accepts. (NOTE TO KATIE'S ATTORNEY: It is NOT stalking if the object of your attention agrees to go out with you.) I suggest that we go to Jupiter Moon for an early dinner on Friday evening. I make sure Katie knows that it will be a casual dinner, so as not to put any pressure on either of us.

As I knock on Katie's door to pick her up, I am not completely sure if this is a real date or a "friends" date. Katie is at least 15 years younger than I am, so I don't know if we're in the early stages of being platonic friends or if she would ever consider something romantic with someone my age. I want this to be a date, but I also don't want to get my hopes dashed.

Katie opens her front door and greets me with a smile. She is wearing "date clothes." Her cute little high-collared black top has a semi-revealing cut-out on her chest that shows just a hint of cleavage. It is very sexy, and so is her slim young body poured into a pair of black jeans. She's wearing black wedge shoes that make her four inches taller and, to me, quite a bit sexier. This girl cleans up real nice.

I should tell her how great she looks, but I don't. I guess I am kind of stunned into silence. It's not very Babe Magnetish of me, but I totally miss the chance to give her a great (and honest) compliment. I am surprised that she is ready to go, and disappointed that she doesn't invite me in while she's making her final getting-ready touches. There is something delightfully intimate about being present while a woman does her last-minute beauty and wardrobe preparations.

"You ready to go?" she asks.

"Sure."

All right then. Since she is wearing date clothes, I quickly decide that I don't want to go in my pickup truck, which is definitely not a date-mobile unless you're driving to a rodeo or a tractor pull. I know that I am the man and I should drive, and I should open doors for her and be gentlemanly, but my brain has temporarily turned to mush. I suggest that she drive, and she seems fine with that. We zip over to the restaurant in five minutes, during which time Katie demonstrates some pretty impressive driving skills.

We order our food and settle in for our date. I am beginning to find my "date legs," and I am pleased to be with Katie, who is young and attractive. In fact, I am now more relaxed than during my last date with Candice, and I am oozing with charm. I immediately set out to be a light and amusing conversationalist.

My first topic is movies. Everyone likes movies, right? And no matter who you talk to, there is always some common ground in the movies you have both seen. The most recent movie I have seen is that Indian film I saw with Candice, so I tell Katie all about it. I'm thinking that anyone who reads *The Great Gatsby* out by the pool is a fan of foreign films, right?

Wrong. "I don't like foreign films. I especially hate subtitles, because I don't like to read when I'm watching a movie. I don't want to work that hard."

I didn't expect that answer, but I am a brilliant conversationalist, and move on. "So, what movies do you like?"

She mentions a few that I don't care for because they are sarcastic or mean-spirited or just plain bizarre. She likes *The Big Lebowski* and *Resident Evil.* She thinks *The Exorcist* was a comedy. "I never laughed so hard in my life," she tells me.

I decide not to tell her that *The Exorcist* was the scariest movie I ever saw in a theatre. Scary movies give me nightmares, and I do not find them funny. Instead, I tell her that sometimes I'm a sucker for good sentimental movies, and I watch *It's a Wonderful Life* every Christmas. She frowns and says she hates that show. She pretty much hates every black and white movie ever made. Well, shit. I'll try another subject.

"Are you an outdoorsy person at all? Do you ever go hiking on the trails in the foothills of the mountains?"

"I'm not a big fan of walking unless it's in an air-conditioned mall."

Okay. Time to shift gears again.

"So, how is your class coming?" I ask.

"It's killing me. I don't know why I thought I could work full time and take a literature class during the summer."

"Well, at least it will be over soon."

"Yeah, but what a waste of a good summer. Reading until your eyeballs bleed."

Whoa! What is going on here? Katie is making me work way too hard. No matter how hard I try, I can't seem to hit upon a subject that we can agree on—or even chat lightly about. It's time for some conversational brilliance to turn this date around.

In my head, I try out a few lines to see if anything sounds usable.

"What's up with that whole string theory thing? Do you really think there are invisible strings everywhere? Wouldn't we trip over them?"

Or maybe...

"Here's a strange fact for you. Did you know that the law that prevents the interstate transportation of *women* for immoral purposes is called the Mann Act? It's true—you can look it up."

Or how about...

"Tell me more about your tattoo. And are there tattoos hidden anywhere else on your body?"

Or, I could throw a Hail Mary and ask a provocative sexual question like...

"So, where were you when you had the best sex of your life?"

Oh, God, I have visions of this date crashing and burning right here in the restaurant. This is not going the way I had hoped. With each passing moment, Katie looks less and less attractive. It doesn't matter how great a woman looks if you don't enjoy being with her.

Is it possible that Katie is doing this on purpose? Is she actually *trying* to be disagreeable and hard to talk to? Or maybe she thinks it's humorous in a post-modern, ironic kind of way to express general disdain and not like anything. Maybe it's her deep-seated lack of self-esteem. I don't know, and at this point I don't really care. If this how she behaves on first dates, then it's no wonder she is perpetually single. What man would volunteer for another date with Katie if she does to them exactly what she's doing to me right now?

Or, of course, it could just be me. It could be that Katie and I just don't have any chemistry together.

Nah. It's her.

I start chewing faster. The quicker I can chew and swallow, the quicker we can get out of here.

It's still ridiculously early, but there is no point in trying to extend the date. Katie drives us back to our apartment complex. I walk Katie to her door and leave without even trying to kiss her.

In another week Katie will be moved out of her apartment to another complex down the street. If I don't get her cell phone number before she moves, I will probably never talk to her again. And the way I feel right now, I'm okay with that.

But tonight's date was not a total waste of time. At this stage of my Babe Magnet career, I am learning valuable lessons with every new experience. Tonight I learned:

BABE MAGNET RULE #17

A Babe Magnet knows when to hold 'em, knows when to fold 'em, knows when to walk away, and knows when to run like hell.

Chapter 22: Back at Barleycorn's

Another workweek has passed, and it's Friday night. I have no plans. Craig is out of town and Karl is at home with his wife. But I am not going to sit on the couch all night, watching TV. So I walk over to Barleycorn's to drink a beer and talk to some Babes.

Nobody calls out my name as I walk through the door, but the bouncer smiles and doesn't ask to see my ID. I am now a semi-regular.

The evening starts out slow. Men outnumber women by at least two to one. I stand in the back and scan the place. I look around to see if Candice is in the house. I am not sure if I want to see her, or if I want to *not* see her.

Candice isn't here, and I am relieved.

I spot two women at a table across the room. They are probably in their late 30s or early 40s. One is a total Babe, but her friend is unattractive. I walk over to say hello.

The women seem friendly and glad that I came over to talk. The pretty one, Nicki, does most of the talking. Her homely friend, Cheryl, is vapid and has nothing to contribute. Poor thing. Cheryl didn't get good looks *or* brains. I hope she's a great cook, knows how to sew, or has other skills that aren't obvious in a barroom setting.

Nicki says she lived in Las Vegas for a few years, and that gives us something to talk about. In my short time as a Middle-Aged Babe Magnet, I have learned that it's always easier to converse with a woman about a topic that she's interested in, and it's almost always a mistake to talk about yourself until she asks about you.

BABE MAGNET RULE #18

When talking to a new Babe for the first time, choose a topic of interest to her and try to keep the conversation light. Don't talk about politics, religion, or ex-lovers. Especially ex-lovers.

I know that asking for Nicki's phone number in front of Cheryl would be fruitless. It's an honor thing among honorable Babes: the attractive one never lets herself get picked up in front of her not-so-attractive friend. Now, if I wanted Cheryl's phone number, Nicki would be thrilled for her friend. But why would I want Cheryl's phone number unless I needed my socks mended? So I move on.

I walk to the end of the bar closest to the band and enjoy the live music. The guitar player, a young guy named Ryan McAdams, is incredible. I have seen Pete Townsend and the Who in concert. I have seen Jimmy Page and Led Zeppelin. I have seen Eric Clapton, B.B. King, Derek Trucks, Joe Satriani, and countless other great guitar players. I swear, this kid is in their league—or he soon will be.

Here's the most amazing thing. In chatting with the folks next to me in between songs, I learn that Ryan McAdams is only 19 years old. His dad has to accompany him so he can get into the bar to play his gigs.

I strike up a conversation with Lenora, a short Hispanic woman with a head full of curly brown hair. Lenora's girlfriend is dating the bass player in the band. Lenora and I hit it off, and we dance. We take a break to sip our drinks, and then we dance some more. We repeat this pattern a few times, and we both marvel at Ryan McAdams's ability to cover classic rock songs, play the blues, and even dazzle us with a few original songs.

This kid is going to be a big star some day, and I'll be able to say I saw him play in a little neighborhood pub and blow the place away. At the end of the show, I swear he is channeling Jimi Hendrix during a rendition of *Purple Haze* that morphs into *Voodoo Child*—with lots of guitar acrobatics, including playing his Stratocaster over the back of his neck and also picking the guitar strings with his teeth.

If I were still married, I wouldn't be here to see this. I would be at home with my wife, watching something stupid on TV. That's one advantage of my life as a Middle-Aged Babe Magnet: I get out a lot more.

Sometimes you just have to get out of the house so you don't miss what's going on in your own town.

So Lenora and I are enjoying the music, and our dancing gets more physical and more sexually charged as the night wears on. While we are dancing, I can't help but notice two very attractive women in their 40s who are dancing next to us. One is Asian, the other a classic Caucasian blonde. Both are Babes, but I am already committed to Lenora for the evening. It's too late and I've spent too much time with Lenora to bail on her now. That's just the way it goes out there in Babeland, as expressed by:

BABE MAGNET RULE #19
Don't switch Babes in midstream.

Lenora and I exchange cell phone numbers, and I also agree to meet her downtown tomorrow night for a free concert. As we say goodnight, I try to kiss her. She turns her head and gives me her cheek instead. She's a good Catholic woman with two grown kids, and she's not going to give it up right away.

I arrive downtown the next evening at Civic Plaza for the concert. Lenora said she'd meet me by the stage, but I don't see her. As I get closer, I see a middle-aged, moon-faced Hispanic woman waving to me with a big smile on her face.

Shit. Barroom lighting strikes again. I swear, Lenora looked at least five years younger last night, and she looked way more attractive through my beer goggles.

BABE MAGNET RULE #20
Beware of barroom lighting. Really.

And the important corollary, which is:

BABE MAGNET RULE #21
Don't get too excited about someone you just met. Especially if you just met her in a bar.

I sit beside Lenora and she introduces me to her friends. They are all Hispanic women, and they are all older than Lenora. I feel very, very white. Plus, I am the only penis in a gaggle of vaginas. It doesn't take Scooby Doo to figure out that this is going to be a very long evening.

Lenora and I seemed to hit if off so well last night. But now we chat about the weather and some of the places we have lived, and then...silence. We can't think of anything to say. I consider myself a talented conversationalist. But this evening, my mind is as empty as a spinster librarian's social calendar. I just don't care to expend the energy it would take to keep the conversation going.

After waiting for the longest hour and a half of my Middle-Aged Babe Magnet life, the Pancho Sanchez Latin Band takes the stage. They are fabulous, and it is almost worth the pre-concert boredom. Lenora and I join the crowd of dancers in front of the stage and we shake our booties. At the end of the concert, Lenora gives me a quick hug and leaves with her friends.

On the walk back to my car, I process the events of the past 24 hours. I met a woman, I got her phone number, and I went out on a casual group date with her and her friends. And although tonight did not go well, I learned several things that will prove valuable in my future Babe Magnet activities. I learned that a first date should probably be a one-on-one meeting where the two of you can talk. Meeting a bunch of Lenora's friends right away was too much for a first date, especially when I was so completely outnumbered.

On the other hand, meeting her friends and being so thoroughly unimpressed with them probably saved me some time. When you date someone, you will ultimately be seeing her friends. So if you don't like the friends or find them boring, you have to take that into account when you decide if you still want to keep seeing her.

I have already decided not to call Lenora again. But hey, it's been an interesting weekend.

Chapter 23: I Say a Little (Vulgar) Prayer

On a quiet evening, I sit down to a lovely meal that I have prepared for myself and say a little prayer of thanks. "Thank you, God, for this wonderful food. Thanks for all of the many blessings I have, and for all of the adventures I get to experience.

"And God, please send me a new lover, because I really need to get laid."

I realize what I have just said, and I laugh out loud. I'm not sure it's okay to ask God for a lover. I wait quietly for a moment to see if I get struck by a lightning bolt. Nope, nothing. So maybe it's all right, after all.

I'll bet God is up in heaven, having a good laugh at my expense. I think He probably finds me quite entertaining.

"The joke's on you, dude," says God. "You thought being single was going to be so simple. You thought finding the next love of your life was going to be as easy as falling down drunk. Well, it can take a little time to reinvent yourself, Mr. Hotshot Babe Magnet. You'll be fine, and I've always got your back. But you still have a lot to learn."

Touché, God.

I've only been living on my own as a single man for a few months, but I am starting to get impatient. I know it will take time to build a new life and hit my stride as a Middle-Aged Babe Magnet. I *am* making progress, and for that I am thankful. Most of the time, I am happy that I have embarked on this adventure. But the process of making new friends and meeting new people—especially women—is taking longer than I had hoped it would.

I am tired of spending so much time alone. It eats away at you, gnawing at your self-confidence. If you spend enough time alone, other people start thinking that you are a loner. They can start to see the holes in you, and they think you're creepy and they stay away from you. And that means that you will spend even more time alone.

See what I mean? Loneliness can get to you and start warping your brain.

One of the biggest mistakes I made as a married man was not cultivating enough of my own friendships. I didn't take the time to go off away from my wife and hang out with the guys or play golf or just go drink a beer with a buddy in front of a ball game on TV. I didn't develop a life of my own that didn't include my wife. We hung out with the same friends—almost exclusively couples. And she got almost all of "our" friends in the divorce, which is something I didn't see coming.

So part of me is really pissed at my ex-wife. Part of me is really pissed at my ex-friends, for choosing to drop me in favor of my ex-wife. And part of me is really pissed at myself for letting all of this happen.

I talked to a friend of mine today, who gave me a great piece of dating advice: "Be open to everything. You never know when you might meet someone." If you are not open to meeting new people and having new experiences and adventures, you might miss an opportunity to meet the next love of your life.

You can meet people who become your friends. You can meet people who become your lovers. You might meet someone (male or female) who introduces you to someone else who could turn out to be THE ONE.

That's good advice, so I make it...

BABE MAGNET RULE #22
Be open to all opportunities to meet someone new.

Actually, I have already begun to incorporate this bit of advice into my life. I've gone to lectures, book signings, and business mixers and conversed with the women I've seen there. I've made casual conversation at Whole Foods and at the public library. I renewed my fitness club membership primarily so I can get to know some of my fellow exercisers better.

I have also made a mental list of other activities that offer opportunities to meet people and make friends of both genders. I can take a continuing education class. I can volunteer for Habitat for Humanity or another charity. I can join a book club or a hiking group. I can join a new church, join a bowling league, or take dancing lessons.

One of my favorite—and most productive—activities is going for a bike ride around the nearby park. The physical exercise and sunshine do me good, and so does chatting with the people who are at the park to exercise or relax.

So instead of moping around feeling sorry for myself on this gloriously sunny summer day, I put on shorts and a T-shirt and ride my bike to the park. I cruise around the perimeter of the park to get my blood flowing, all the while scanning for Babes.

I spot one on the far side of the park sitting on a bench. I ride around and stop nearby, pretending to check my front tire so I can check her out. She's cute, athletic, and probably in her early 40s. I can't tell if she's wearing a wedding ring, but her boyfriend suddenly materializes with a golden retriever. I move on.

Riding my bike gives me plenty of time to think. One of the things that I have already learned about the single life is that meeting women is a numbers game. You have to be scanning for them wherever you go and whatever else you are doing. Women are always out there, but finding the perfect woman (for you) is a matter of locating lots of women and then weeding out the ones who are:

1. Too old
2. Too young
3. Not attractive enough
4. Married or in a relationship
5. Weird in an obvious way (too many tattoos, too frumpy, too nerdy, carrying an "I Believe in Faeries" book bag, has B.O., looks like a virgin, looks like a slut, wears men's clothing, is dressed in an outfit that looks like a costume and it's not Halloween, and/or looks like she might be criminally insane)

Depending on how picky you are, the above list weeds out a lot of women.

Then there's the other factor—some of the women you meet are going to weed *you* out. Maybe they don't like bald men. Maybe young-at-heart 50-something-year-olds are not what they're looking for. Maybe you look too much like her ex-husband or ex-boyfriend. Maybe she wants someone with the looks of a male model and the money of Donald Trump.

So you've got to cast your net in the dating waters frequently and with gusto. Then, to make it all work, you have to believe that sooner or later you're going to catch the Babe you want.

That's what I keep telling myself—especially on days like today. I WILL FIND THE PERFECT WOMAN FOR ME. Otherwise I get depressed.

I take another lap around the park. Almost immediately I spot a truly Babe-alicious woman up ahead walking a dog. Dogs are the best icebreakers ever invented. You can go up and talk to anyone about his or her dog. All you have to do is say something nice about the dog, ask a couple of questions, and—bingo—you've got a conversation going.

I pull up beside the Babe and ask her if I can say hello to her dog. She gives me a quick look from my head to my toes, the way I have seen men check out women. I bend down to pet her little hairy rat. Normally I would comment on what a lovely dog she has, but this dog looks like it just stuck its tongue in an electrical socket. If Rod Stewart did something really, really bad, and was forced to be reincarnated as a three-pound dog, he would look like this.

"I miss my dog," I say. "My wife got him in the divorce. I miss my little Zippy."

"My fiancé lost his dog in his divorce, too," says the Babe.

Easy come, easy go—yet again.

Okay, I'm going to make one more pass around the park. The ride is pleasant, but there are no more Babes. I make the last turn around the far end of the park before I head back home, and I spot a nice-looking 40-ish woman jogging up ahead. Mmmm, promising.

I ride my bike past her, and then I pull over to take a swig of water. As she passes by I say "hi" and ask her if she knows what time it is.

She stops long enough to dig a cell phone out of her pocket. And that is all it takes to start a conversation. We chat for a few minutes, and I am enjoying myself. I am pretty good at this now—asking non-threatening questions and volunteering some of my own information along the way.

This woman is very attractive. Beautiful, in fact, if you like the completely natural look (and I do). She has a nice face, a great smile, a tall athletic body, and a good vibe. She wears her dark blonde hair in a simple, shortish haircut that tells me she has a job and doesn't have time to fuss with long hair.

Her name is Vanessa. She lives nearby in a house with her two kids, ages 10 and 15. She is divorced. She has a dog but doesn't always take him when she jogs.

I ask if I can take her out for coffee sometime, and she gives me her phone number. I write it down with the pen and pad I always carry with me when I am trolling for Babes.

My short conversation with Vanessa lifts my mood, and my funk is a distant memory. All this Middle-Aged Babe Magnet needs is a little hope, and today Vanessa is all the hope that I need.

Chapter 24: Where Everybody Knows His Name

Here I am at Barleycorn's. Again.

I am not particularly proud of myself for hanging out at my neighborhood bar. Never in my life have I spent so much of my free time in a darkened room filled with people whose passion is consuming large quantities of alcoholic beverages. But I have to admit that Barleycorn's is a happy place. The people who hang out here are in a partying mood, and when I don't have anything else to do, it's easy to walk through my apartment complex, push open Barleycorn's door, plop myself on a stool, and talk to some happy people.

Right away I spot P.J., my 30-something neighbor who lives upstairs (next to the four college-aged testosterone-fueled males). P.J. and I say hello to each other as we pass on the sidewalk, but we have never really had a long conversation.

P.J. invites me to sit at his table. With a wave of his hand, a young, scantily clad waitress materializes, and P.J. orders a beer for me and another beer for himself. In a few minutes I learn a lot about P.J. He has never been married, and he doesn't have a girlfriend. P.J. tells me that he works as the sales manager for the largest local beer distributor. And, judging by the number of people who come by his table to say hello—including every person who works at Barleycorn's—P.J. knows everyone in Springfield who drinks beer.

"It's my job," he says with a coy smile.

I was beginning to think that Barleycorn's was my own personal hangout, and people were going to start knowing me when I came in. Now I realize that this has been P.J.'s place all along.

Because P.J. works for a beer distributor, it's part of his job to be out in bars to schmooze with the folks who place large orders of alcoholic beverages with his employer. But P.J. lives in fear of getting pulled over for a D.W.I., because he knows that the local media would crucify him. And based upon what passes for news on the local TV stations, I am sure he is right.

P.J. likes to hang out at Barleycorn's because he can walk here, so he is in no danger of driving while intoxicated. He is both brilliant and practical. I like this guy.

So P.J. and I are sitting at a table for four, and he is holding court like he is the Godfather of Beer. As each waitress stops by to say hello to P.J., I get introduced to them all. There is Stacey and Amber and Brittany and Heather and Bambi and Airhead and Vulva and… I have no idea what their names are after a couple of beers. My new best friend P.J. keeps the alcohol flowing, and he keeps getting me to try the different brands that his company sells.

Two women ask if they can join us at our table. I say, "Yes!" without checking with P.J. Their names are Lynn and Roxanne. Lynn is wound a bit tightly and has trouble sitting still, but Roxanne is friendly and nice. We chat for a while until they spot some friends and dash off to the bar.

P.J. tells me all about the alcohol business as we drink our beers. He makes calls on the biggest retail stores, making sure that they have plenty of cases of beer. He helps them create humongous displays that feature cases and cases of beer stacked up in creative depictions of football stadiums or sand castles on the beach—depending on the time of year. He visits restaurants and bars and encourages them to sell the many brands of beverages that he represents.

Basically, beer is P.J.'s life. I don't know whether to toast his luck or bemoan his career choice. I don't think I could devote such a large part of my life to encouraging the consumption of alcohol. But right now, P.J. seems to be having a wonderful time as Don Beerlioni.

Meanwhile, the chairs at our table remain empty for about 20 minutes, until I invite two women to join us. They have just arrived at Barleycorn's, and they are clearly looking for a place to sit. I generously welcome them to our table because I am a true humanitarian, and because they are both Babes.

The blonde Babe with big boobs and an easy smile is named Jackie. She is tanned, fit, and well-manicured, right down to her hot pink nails with accenting little decals. In the high-pitched voice of a cartoon character, she tells us that she is a flight attendant. She is a living, breathing cliché. I can't help but typecast her as the kind of woman that men see, and instantly all they can think of is getting her into bed. I know this because I felt a "schwing" sensation in my jeans the moment I saw her, and all I could think of was getting her into bed.

Her friend, Sally, is attractive in a much more real, less flamboyant way. Sally's hair is also blonde, but the color is more natural. Her skin hasn't been darkened by regular visits to a tanning salon, and her body gets a bit generous at her hips.

In the world of singles meeting singles at a bar, Sally is clearly overshadowed by her friend's dripping sex appeal. But Sally is easy to talk to; there is an honest sincerity about her. She works for a medical records company, which is far less sexy than Jackie's airline job. But I give her my full attention when she talks, and I give her as much eye contact as I give her lusty, busty friend. As a result, Sally warms up to me right away.

Sally has enabled me to prove the wisdom of...

BABE MAGNET RULE #23

Your odds are better if you go after the less-attractive Babe.

I am sure that when she goes out with Jackie, Sally must feel invisible—or just plain unattractive. That has to suck, big time. So even though part of me would love to fawn over Jackie like every other man, I decide to treat Sally with respect and interest—even to the point of ignoring Jackie. Besides, that leaves P.J. to talk to Jackie. It's the least I can do for him after he has bought me so many drinks.

Sally lives in a house not far from Barleycorn's. She has been divorced for 11 years, which sounds like a really long time to me. How can an attractive woman with a good job and a friendly personality remain single for 11 years? What's wrong with her? Does she snore like a truck driver?

Does she have 17 cats? Is she looking for perfection in her next husband, constantly disappointed when men turn out to be, well, men?

Sally says falling in love isn't that easy. "I think a lot of people are getting married even though they're really not in love."

I tell her I am newly divorced, living in an apartment within walking distance. Being single is new to me; and yet, it's like déjà vu all over again. She laughs.

Fueled by the alcohol in my system, I decide to regale Sally with my thoughts on love. I tell her that humans have a tremendous capacity for love. I don't believe there is only one special person for each of us. It's not like your soul mate is in Argentina and you are in New Jersey, and unless you miraculously meet at an airport you're never going to get a chance to fall in love.

"You can just as easily fall in love with your next door neighbor," I tell her. "In fact, you probably WILL fall in love with your next door neighbor if you spend enough time with him or her."

Sally is silent for a while, and I fear that my pomposity has put her in a funk. But then she tells me that she is taking salsa-dancing lessons.

"I have always wanted to learn that!" I reply, which is actually true and not just barroom banter.

"The classes are on Wednesday evenings. You should come to the next class."

"Okay, I will."

She seems delighted. We exchange business cards, and on the back of hers she writes the directions to the health club where the dance lessons are held.

I leave Barleycorn's in a particularly good mood. I'm going to start taking salsa-dancing classes because of a woman named Sally.

Chapter 25: Let the Dancing Begin

Today I will call Vanessa. It has been five days since I met her at the park. Five days is probably too long to wait for the first phone call, but I just haven't felt motivated enough to call her until now. Dating takes a lot of energy. It's not a spectator sport. It requires the participant to be mentally sharp and fully engaged. I don't want to be put into the dating "game" without warming up a little, taking a few practice swings in my mind, rehearsing how I want a conversation to go. All of that takes energy, and sometimes after a long day of work I don't have the energy for dating-related activities. I hate to admit it, but being middle-aged might having something to do with it.

Besides, waiting five days proves that I am not too eager. I just hope Vanessa still remembers meeting me.

When I get her on the phone, Vanessa seems nervous—which I find cute and endearing. I can't help but wonder how long it has been since a strange man (make that a man she does not know) tried to pick her up. Vanessa is a single mom with two kids, and I don't know if dating has been a part of her life at all. This is just speculation, of course, but by the sound of her voice she is excited and flattered that a new man is interested in her. We set a date for lunch on Saturday.

Excuse me while I take a few more practice swings.

I am on my way to meet a friend for lunch when Sally calls me. I know it is Sally before I answer the call, because I have put Babe Magnet Rule #24 into practice. I have already programmed Sally into my cell phone.

BABE MAGNET RULE #24

Use technology to your advantage. Cell phones, emails, IMs and text messages are a Babe Magnet's best friends.

Remember the story about when my friend Craig was dating three women simultaneously? He said programming their numbers into his cell phone saved his dating life on several occasions. Knowing who was calling before he answered the phone kept him from the embarrassment of having a woman call and say, "Hi! It's me!" and him not knowing which "me" she was referring to.

"Sally, I was just thinking about you!" I say, trying to sound both casual and bubbly.

"You were?" She sounds pleased.

I was going to call her after lunch. No, really I was. But her calling me is a good sign. "I wanted to remind you about the dance lesson tonight," she says.

"And I was going to call you to let you know that I would be there."

We agree to meet in the lobby of the health club at 6:00 o'clock. I arrive a few minutes early, and she is already waiting for me. We say hello and chat for a moment. Then, at my suggestion, she shows me the basic salsa dance moves that they learned in last week's class.

Sally is not a very good dance instructor, but a woman named Stephanie, who is also in the class, comes over to assist. Then Lisa, the actual instructor, comes over and gives me a real lesson. All this is before the class begins. I feel like a genuine Babe Magnet, with three women all giving me a personal dance lesson.

When the real class starts, there are four men and five women. It turns out to be a very good beginning class, covering the basic steps of Salsa, Cha-Cha and Meringue. By the end of the hour-long class, I feel like I have made some real progress. I think I have just discovered a wonderful way to meet and interact with women.

After the class I walk Sally out to her car. I ask her if we can get together before the next dance class, and she is noncommittal. "I might be going out of town this weekend. I have a house in the mountains, and I haven't decided yet if I'm going to go up there."

Hmmmm. If that's how she responds to a potential suitor, then it's no wonder she has been single for 11 years.

On Saturday I am in my truck, driving to my lunch date with Vanessa. She calls me on my cell phone to let me know that she's on her way. She arrives at the restaurant 15 minutes late, looking beautiful but just a tad frazzled. I, however, am cool, relaxed, and confident. I have used the extra 15 minutes to compose myself and get into an almost meditative dating zone. I am the Zen master of dating, and I greet her with a friendly smile.

"You must be Vanessa," I say, coyly.

"And you must be Chad."

That's Chad Stone, Middle-Aged Babe Magnet. I am feeling very much like a Babe Magnet right now, and that is largely due to my attraction to Vanessa. She really is a Babe. She has a nice face, a beautiful smile, and a fit, attractive figure. She stands about five foot nine in the running shoes she is wearing. Her sleeveless white top reveals well-toned arms, and her jeans are just tight enough.

We order salads and fancy pizza and take a table in the corner where we can talk. Vanessa has just come from work, so that's where our conversation starts. She's been working on a series of special events to commemorate the city's anniversary. I tell her a little bit about my work, and I give her a business card. She looks at the address and says she knows the building. She took commercial real estate classes there, but she ended up never working in real estate.

Maybe Vanessa is a little nervous, but she seems pretty serious. She is easy to talk too, but I am having trouble getting her to laugh or even smile.

Our lunch date lasts one hour and 15 minutes, and there are no uncomfortable silences or pregnant pauses. From my perspective, it goes really well for a first date, even though I can't get Vanessa to lighten up. In her serious way, she seems to have a good time, too. I tell her that I'll call her in the middle of the week after I get back from my business trip.

"I'll look forward to your call," she says, sincerely.

I walk Vanessa to her car. We say goodbye without kissing and without touching. She is clearly operating on First Date—Daytime Rules, so I do not attempt to violate her personal space.

Of the three women that I have had encounters with this week, Vanessa is on my mind the most. It is Vanessa who intrigues me. It is Vanessa I think about when I drift off to sleep at night.

Chapter 26: Mixing Babes and Business

I am in Providence, Rhode Island, standing on an open-air deck at the Biltmore Hotel. I am surrounded by well-dressed, happy white people. The glass in my hand contains single malt scotch and ice. The weather is clear and gorgeous, and it is simply a delight to be basking in the late afternoon sun with a faint smell of ocean water in the air.

It may not sound like it from the above description, but this is strictly a work gig for me. I'm attending a trade association conference, networking with clients and potential clients. It is similar to networking at a social event in search of single women to date. Many of the same rules apply: Be friendly. Don't be afraid to walk up to someone you don't know and start a conversation. Look people in the eye when you meet them. Remember their names. Smile. Ask questions and listen carefully to the answers. Try to learn something. Talk about them more than you talk about yourself. Have business cards in your pocket that you can whip out at a moment's notice.

> **BABE MAGNET RULE #25**
> Practice your Babe Magnet skills even when you are not trying to pick up a Babe. Some people call that "being friendly and easy to talk to."

A man comes over to say hello to me. He clearly knows who I am, even though I do not know him. We chat for a few minutes about cocktail party subjects such as the weather, sports, and business. He sees a young woman he knows and calls her over. She is tall and attractive, with long dark hair and green eyes. She is young, probably about 25, but she carries herself with a confidence that most 25-year-olds haven't yet developed.

"Heather, this someone you need to meet," says the man, whose name I have already forgotten. Damn.

"Chad Stone," I say, and I put out my hand.

She grasps it firmly. "Heather Brown." She smiles.

This is the nicest reception I've gotten all day. I am definitely going to remember Heather's name. I will have to thank what's-his-name for introducing me.

"Chad is *the* man to talk to about advertising and marketing in this industry," says my nameless new friend, sounding like I need to slip him a crisp Andrew Jackson.

"Yes I am," I say, in my best fake sincere voice. But my smile says, "I might be joking, so you're going to have to talk to me for a few minutes to find out the truth." Even while I am doing this, I am amazed at how quickly I have shifted gears from casual business networking to full-on Babe pick-up mode.

Heather's eyes light up and her smile spreads across her face. Now I have her undivided attention.

I am not really trying to hit on 25-year-old Heather, and she is not interested in me in a dating way. But as I talk to her, I realize that so many of the Babe Magnet skills and techniques can work in almost any social setting. Being a person who is fun to talk to and who can skillfully participate in and direct a conversation just might be the most valuable social skill a person can possess.

Heather is just getting her career started in communications. She lives in Providence, but rides the train an hour into Boston every workday. She has a low-level job at an advertising agency, and she wants to learn fast and get her career established.

During the next 15 minutes, Heather asks me questions about how I got started in marketing, what the most important skills are, and how I started my business. She listens carefully to every word I say, and her eyes never stray from mine. I am drinking in the attention and interest of this beautiful young woman, and it feels wonderful. This must be what it feels like to be Brad Pitt, except he gets this 200 times a day, and all of those women want to strip him naked.

Just when I am running out of my best work-related stories and anecdotes, my cell phone rings. It's Sally. She is on her way to salsa dancing class and is sort-of returning my call. I had left a message, telling her that I wasn't going to be able to make today's class, but I was looking forward to seeing her at the following class.

I walk over to the other side of the deck and look across the city. Sally is quite chatty, and she wants to know where I am and what I am doing. I tell her I am enjoying a lovely early evening in Providence, but I am sorry to miss today's dancing class.

When I met her at Barleycorn's, Sally said she wasn't looking for a relationship. I think that's what she says to convince herself that it's perfectly fine to be single for 11 years. Now I get the vibes that she is really warming up to me. I think deep down she wants some companionship. When it comes right down to it, don't we all?

Chapter 27: Attractiveness and the "Eeewww" Factor

I am having some success meeting women the old-fashioned way—in the wild, in person. I am growing much more confident in my Babe Magnet abilities. I can almost always think of something to say to a stranger. But I am having far less success online.

I thought it would be just the opposite. After all, Match.com and other dating websites are filled with single women. By simply joining an online site, they are advertising their willingness to meet and date men. In fishing terms, they are practically jumping into the boat.

Well, maybe they are jumping into somebody else's boat, but they haven't landed in mine yet.

Despite my lack of online success, Match.com continues to be very entertaining. I love cruising for chicks online in the privacy of my home, while in the comfort of my bathrobe. I still love reading the profiles and checking out the photos. But what is getting old is the lack of response I am getting.

So far, the only person I have gone out with from Match.com is Nancy. And I'm treating Nancy as a friend, not a date. We have a couple of things in common, particularly gardening and golf. But I am simply not attracted to Nancy. She thinks she has a good sense of humor, but she doesn't laugh much and I don't think she has ever made me laugh.

Nancy is just learning to play golf, and she isn't very good. She lifts her whole body up during her backswing, and when she hits the ball she never knows where it will go. (Can you say, "Fore!"?) Because I am willing to play the Par 3 golf course with her, she fancies us as golfing buddies.

I meet her at the golf course this morning, and she's dressed in a black pullover that's way too warm for today's weather. Her brand new golf clubs are gleaming in the bright sunlight. She greets me with a smile and a hug. My involuntary reaction is "Eeewww!" I am simply not attracted to this woman, even though she is a very nice person.

This whole issue of physical attractiveness has me thinking. After playing golf with Nancy, I consult the world's authority on everything in the 21st century: Wikipedia. Yes, there is a lengthy article titled "Physical attractiveness" that has more than 100 footnotes and references to other writings and studies on what human beings find attractive in other humans. Evidently, I am not the only person intrigued by this topic. The article begins with a statement from the "Duh!" file:

> Physical attractiveness is the perception of the physical traits of an individual as being aesthetically pleasing or beautiful. The term often implies sexual attractiveness.

The story goes on to talk about how physical attraction is a combination of three factors: 1) universal perceptions common to all human cultures, 2) specific aspects of one's own culture, and 3) individual preferences that can be completely subjective. So, in many ways, the traits that we find physically attractive have been programmed into us by society and eons of human experiences.

That makes me feel a little better. It's not all my fault. Blame my father, my grandfather, my great-grandfather, and every other human male all the way back to Adam. There's no way Adam would have bitten that apple if Eve hadn't been a total Babe.

According to David Buss, author of *The Evolution of Desire*, men place a significantly higher importance on physical appearance in a romantic partner than women do. That's probably because, historically, when it came to reproducing the species, a healthy female with symmetrical features was a better bet than a lumpy, ugly woman. A male's ability to provide for his offspring was less likely to be signaled by physical features alone, so women aren't as consistently picky about attractiveness.

According to the sources cited in the Wikipedia story:

- Heterosexual women and homosexual men prefer faces that show masculine traits associated with testosterone—heavy brows, prominent chins, broad cheekbones.
- Women tend to be attracted to men who are taller than they are and who have broad shoulders and a relatively narrow waist.
- Men are attracted by women who are slightly shorter than they are, have a youthful appearance, and have a symmetrical face, full breasts, full lips, and a low waist-to-hip ratio.
- In studies in China, New Zealand, and the USA, women have rated men with no body hair as the most attractive.
- Symmetrical (physically attractive) men and women begin sexual intercourse younger, have more sexual partners, and have the most reproductive success. (So, being physically attractive really does help get you laid.)

Here's a shocker: penis size matters. Studies in China, England, Italy, the United States, Sweden, New Zealand, France, and Spain have revealed that women really do consider men with longer, thicker penises to be more attractive than little-dick men.

But alas, a woman doesn't know how big a man's penis is until she has essentially agreed to have sex with him. Ever since clothing was invented, and men started hiding their penises in their pants, male sexual size has been the Big Grab Bag of dating. If you ask me, it's totally unfair to women. I wonder if clothing was invented by some little-dick dude thousands of years ago who was tired of the "big boys" getting all the Babes.

From the TopDatingTips.com site, I learn: "The basis of any courtship, date, or relationship is basic physical attraction. If you are not attracted to someone and they are not attracted to you, you have just become friends." That certainly sums up my feelings (or lack of feelings) for Nancy.

While surfing the Internet, I come across a story on livescience.com entitled, "The Bikini Effect Makes Men Impulsive." It states: "Bikinis and other sexy stimuli can make men more prone to seek immediate gratification—leading to blown diets, budgets, and bank accounts.

"In the study, detailed in the *Journal of Consumer Research*, men alternately fondled T-shirts and bras (which were not being worn during the test). After touching the bras, men valued the future less and the present more, said lead researcher Bram Van Den Bergh of Katholieke Universiteit Leuven in Belgium. Viewing ads with women in bikinis had the same effect.

"It wasn't that men were simply distracted by their sexual arousal, which caused them to choose more impulsively. On the contrary, they exhibited improved cognition and creativity after exposure to sexy stimuli."

I am not quite sure what to make of all that. The fact that men are distracted by bikinis is common knowledge. That's why women wear bikinis, after all. But the apparent fact that a man's brain shows improved cognition and creativity after bikini exposures? Perhaps they should hand out the *Sports Illustrated* swimsuit issue to male musicians before they tune up their instruments, so to speak.

Um, excuse me for a few minutes. I'm going to get a bikini magazine and stimulate my creativity.

Chapter 28: Going, Going, Gone

Ever since our first lunch date, Vanessa has been on my mind. I don't know her well yet, but I like her. A lot. I already feel a kind of chemistry between us. I'm definitely attracted to her, and that physical attraction makes me want to get to know her better.

When I call her on the phone, she sounds happy to hear from me. We effortlessly talk for half an hour. Our conversations are now more relaxed and more comfortable.

I thought she had two kids—a boy and a girl. She actually has three boys: ages 10, 15 and 19. The oldest is living away at college, and today is the first time she has mentioned him.

Vanessa says she thought of me this week when she and her boss were talking about getting someone to do local publicity for the city's upcoming tricentennial events. I could totally do that, and I tell her so. I slip effortlessly from Babe Conversation to Work Prospecting Conversation, then back again.

Vanessa is going to Arkansas in a week to visit her mother and other family members, so I suggest that we get together and do something fun before she leaves. We pencil in Sunday for a fun date. I will call her on Friday and we will firm things up.

I start thinking about possible Sunday afternoon dates. We could do dinner and a movie, although I think that sounds pretty pedestrian. I want to impress Vanessa with my creativity, so I flip through a bikini magazine to stimulate said creativity, and then I read the weekend section of the local newspaper. There's an outdoor bluegrass concert that sounds fun. Another possibility is driving to a park and then going for a short hike. I start making a list. By the time I call Vanessa two days later, I have five great ideas for a Sunday afternoon date.

Her voice sounds friendly but frazzled when she answers the phone. She says she has been really busy, plus her air conditioner broke again. There is also some problem with water leaking from her hot water heater.

"That's not good," I say, trying to sound sympathetic.

Then the news gets worse.

"I don't think I can do anything with you on Sunday."

Oh, crap.

"I really like you and all..."

Okay. Here it comes. She's dumping me already. She's dumping me even before we get started. I brace myself.

"...but I've got so much to do before I leave for Arkansas..."

She's canceling. That's all; she's just canceling. But is it just this one date, or is it a permanent goodbye?

"...so can we just wait and get together when I get back?"

Damn. I really want to see Vanessa. But as long as she is just postponing our date, I can live with that. In my mind, I was already looking forward to having a picnic lunch with her and then...

But I can be patient. I tell her I am disappointed, yet I try to be as gracious as possible. We chat for a few more minutes, and Vanessa sounds truly sorry for having to cancel. I take the sound of remorse in her voice as a good sign.

A week goes by, and I don't hear from Vanessa. She said she was going to call me when she got back from Arkansas, but I have already discovered that women don't call men. It doesn't matter how far Western society has come in "liberating" women, most dating rules haven't changed much in the past 10,000 years.

If you are a man, you must think of yourself as the hunter.

BABE MAGNET RULE #26

Make the phone calls. Send the emails. Initiate the contacts. It's what Babe Magnets do, and it's what women want.

So I wait two days after Vanessa is supposed to be back in town, and I give her a call. I get her voicemail, so I leave a friendly message. "I hope you had a great trip! I'm looking forward to hearing all about it."

Two days later, when I haven't heard from her, I call again. I leave another voicemail. "Hey, I wanna hear about your trip. What are you doing this weekend? Let's get together."

When she doesn't call me back, I give her one more try. She doesn't answer her cell phone again, so now I think she is deliberately avoiding me.

I once knew an insurance salesman who told me that some people just don't like to say no. They never say no to your face, and they don't even like to say no to you on the phone. They just avoid the conversation by never calling you back. He called that a "slow no."

Well, I just got a slow no from Vanessa. And no self-respecting Middle-Aged Babe Magnet is going to keep pursuing a woman who doesn't want to be pursued.

In dating, as in baseball, three strikes and you're out.

Chapter 29: Call Me a "Couch Shark"

Today I am a shark. I have to keep moving. I have to keep searching, because I know that my next woman is out there somewhere. But I won't find her unless I am trolling the waters, looking constantly.

Okay. I'm not really a shark. I am a man in a T-shirt and a pair of ratty-looking cut-offs, cruising on Match.com. I am a Couch Shark. I am cruising, but I am cruising in the virtual world, and I am cruising in comfort. I have my laptop and I'm searching through pages and pages of Babes and Babe-wannabees.

Couch Potatoes watch TV. Couch Sharks cruise for Babes. As a Couch Shark, I feel far superior to lowly Couch Potatoes. And yet, when I actually think about it, cruising for Babes online is like talking to a woman in the same way that playing Guitar Hero is like performing in a band.

So I don't think much about it, and I keep checking out women's profiles online.

There is one woman on Match.com that I am in love with. She is a BABE. She is 44 years old and she is drop-dead gorgeous. Based upon her online photos, she is a Perfect 10. She has blonde hair, blue eyes, and the figure of a dancer. She is so hot looking that most men, me included, wouldn't even bother to talk to her at the supermarket because we'd figure she was:

1. Already in a relationship
2. Way too attractive to talk to me
3. Not interested in being "picked up"
4. Tired of hearing stupid things said to her by strange men
5. Etc.

What do you say to a gorgeous woman without sounding dumb? How about, "Wow, you are the finest thing I have ever seen on two legs." I tried that line once, and it didn't work. Maybe, "Did it hurt?" (Did what hurt?) "Did it hurt when you fell from heaven?" No, that's even worse.

Coming up with a great opening line in person requires quick thinking and great timing. But as a Couch Shark, I can think about what I want to say. I can write it all out and read it to see if it sounds good. Plus, there's all this great material in a woman's online profile that you can comment on.

I don't know this Babe's real name yet. Her screen name is ZuuZuusPetals. She is artistic, and she has her own business selling handmade fashion accessories. The headline on her profile says, "I want to be with someone who will let me love and adore him, someone who's not afraid to try new things." She goes on: "I'm actually interested in meeting a man who would like to have an intimate relationship." She likes "kissing, the beach, snorkeling, shopping, cooking at home, listening to music, and laughing."

I like all of those things, too! We are perfect for each other!

Unfortunately, she must not think I am perfect for her. I sent her a clever email using my standard format: I commented on something she said in her profile, and I told her three things about me that aren't in my profile. I even told her that I know how to ride a unicycle because I thought that might impress a woman who she says she likes to try new things. But alas, she did not respond to my first email. So now I send her another one. This time I ask her a specific question about her business, and tell her that I would love to see her creative work.

The rotten thing about online cruising is that you have absolutely no control over whether someone is going to respond to your emails. So I start thinking. ZuuZuu has given me quite a few clues in her profile. She made a reference to working out of her house, and she mentioned the cafés that she likes to hang out in. They are all down in the funky part of town by the university. I'm thinking she lives down there.

ZuuZuu is a funny name for a woman. I wonder if that's a reference to her business. I start entering search terms on Google that include ZuuZuu and keywords such as "art" and "fashion accessories." It only takes a few minutes to find www.zuuzuufashions.com.

Bingo.

There are photos of her handmade scarves and accessories. In one of the photos she is modeling her own creations. As I poke around on her site, I find her real name. Then I go to whitepages.com and find her address and her phone number. Sure enough, her address is down by the university.

I am delighted that it was so easy to track ZuuZuu down. Now I have to figure out what to do with this information. I can't just call her on the phone. She hasn't responded to my emails on Match.com, so I can't imagine that she would respond kindly to me calling her cold. "Hi, ZuuZuu. This is Chad Stone. We've corresponded on Match.com."

"Chad who?"

"Chad Stone. Actually, I've sent you a couple of emails, but you haven't responded, so I thought I'd just pick up the phone and call."

"How did you get my number?" Her voice sounds suspicious.

"Well actually, that's a funny story. I did a Google search using clues I deciphered from your online profile."

"How did you know my name?"

"It was mentioned somewhere on the website for your business."

"I'm really not comfortable with this..."

"I know this is a bit strange, but I really wanted to talk to you. I loved your profile. I feel like I know you already."

"Are you the guy who rides a unicycle?"

"Yes! Yes! That's me!"

"Only clowns, weirdos, and perverts ride unicycles."

"I don't ride a unicycle all the time. I just said that so you'd..."

"...so I'd think you were a pervert? Well, you're really scaring me. I have Caller ID, and I know what number you're calling from. I am going to hang up now and call the police. Goodbye, Chad Stone. Enjoy your night in jail."

Click.

No, that's not going to work.

I wonder if I could go down to her neighborhood and just hang out at one of the cafés she likes. No, it could take forever before she showed up. How about if I drive past her house a few times to see if I can catch her coming or going. I could walk past her house...no. If I walk by her house too many times she might think I am stalking her. Unless I am walking a dog. Then I can walk by her house just as she is leaving, and smile and say "Hi!", and she'll tell me what a cute dog I have.

Except that I don't have a dog anymore. Maybe I can borrow one.

Crap. I'm going to have to give this some more thought.

Chapter 30: Yoga for Babe Magnets

It's Monday morning at 7:55 a.m., and I am unrolling a thin black foam mat on the floor of the exercise classroom at the gym. I am going to get intimately involved with this thin mat in the next hour. I will place my body in positions that it probably has never been in before. I will attempt to bend and contort my body in ways that are illegal in at least 27 states.

I am in this class because of a woman named Eileen. Last week, I noticed her leaving the exercise classroom at the gym, and I struck up a quick conversation with her. She was very friendly, and she wasn't wearing a wedding ring. She told me she had just been in the yoga class, which meets Monday and Wednesday mornings.

Hmmmm. I took a yoga class once, about 25 years ago. It seemed kind of woo-woo, but it was also physically difficult in a surprisingly delightful way. When I mentioned yoga to Karl, he told me a story about a guy that he knows who took a yoga class when he was newly single. He was only mildly interested in yoga, but he heard that yoga classes were a great place to meet Babes. When he arrived at his first yoga class, it was him and 15 attractive women. He had his pick. The woman that he picked ended up becoming his wife.

There is a lesson in this for all Babe Magnets In Training:

> **BABE MAGNET RULE #27**
> Embrace social opportunities in which males are likely to be outnumbered by females.

So now I am in the back row of the yoga class next to Eileen. (And yes, of the six students, I am the only man.) I am having trouble concentrating, and my eyes keep wandering off in Eileen's direction. She has one of the nicest bodies of any woman I have ever had the pleasure of meeting in person. Through her tight yoga pants, she looks firm and toned and perfect.

The yoga class starts out mercifully slowly. We do a couple of spinal twists, and we do something called "Mountain Pose," which involves standing up straight and not moving. That I can do.

When we start to do positions that involve stretching, that's when it gets difficult for me. I have never been physically flexible. I suffer from Male Muscle Syndrome. I can workout with weights and bulk my muscles up, but I couldn't touch my toes without bending my knees if my life depended on it. In 99.5% of my life, I am okay with that. But in yoga class, my lack of flexibility makes me feel like a dweeb.

The instructor tells us to bend into a "Forward Fold," putting our palms on the floor. The five women students do this with no problem. I laugh. "I can touch my shins, does that count?" I quip. I get a chuckle out of the women. Already I have found my place in this class: comic relief.

During the next hour I learn and relearn many yoga positions. "Downward Facing Dog" is basically making yourself into an upside down V with your butt in the air. "Cobbler's Pose" is sitting on your butt with your knees bent and legs spread, looking at your genitals. "Cat" and "Cow" are alternating positions in which, on your hands and knees, you flex your spine one way and then the other. There are Sanskrit names for everything, which I do not understand. So I try to remember the English slang names.

An hour-long class proves to be an excellent workout for me, and I am glad when we end the class lying flat on our backs in the dark for a few minutes of quiet meditation.

After class I try to time it so I can leave the room with Eileen so we'll have a chance to talk. I put my shoes on very slowly. I do a couple of unnecessary stretches. I leisurely walk out of the room and get a drink of water, with Eileen right behind me. My plan is going perfectly. I am about to exit out the front door of the gym, and I will hold the door open for Eileen and strike up a conversation with her.

I hold the door open for Eileen, smile, and say "Hi!" as she walks out. But what's this? Two more women are right behind her, so I have to hold the door open for them, too! And these aren't young, spry, fast-moving women. These are slow, disabled women who have no business taking up valuable space in a gym.

Oh no! Now Eileen is a good 20 paces ahead of me as she walks into the parking lot. Either I make a bold move right now, or I have to wait for the next yoga class.

What should I say? Something yoga related, and it has to be light and breezy. Out of my mouth pops: "That was some impressive head stand in there!"

In my head a voice yells, "That's it? That's the best you could do? You are going to start a conversation with 'That was some impressive head stand in there!?'"

Fortunately for me, most Babes appreciate being engaged in a pleasant conversation by a man. Besides....

BABE MAGNET RULE #28

Sometimes it's not what you say to a Babe that matters, it's the fact that you had the guts to say anything at all.

And sometimes you actually do say the perfect thing at the perfect time.

Eileen stops, turns, and smiles. God bless her. "I've been working on that pose for a whole year—ever since I started taking yoga," she says. "Getting into that pose was one of my goals, and I did it for the first time today."

Well, there you have it, sports fans. Sometimes the dumbest thing is the perfect thing to say. "Yes! I really enjoyed it when you stuck your firm, perfect butt into the air." Of course, I don't actually say this out loud, but I think it.

We stand in the parking lot and talk about yoga, exercise, and our drinking and eating habits—both now and in our younger days. She admits to "drinking like a sailor" in her youth, though now she rarely drinks.

Maybe I should have met her sooner.

She asks me why I decided to take yoga.

"So I could get to know you," would be the most truthful answer. Instead, I tell her that I hurt my hip several years ago, and I was hoping that yoga would help.

Eileen tells me that she has a 16-year-old son, and she doesn't like movies that are dark and depressing. She has a house with a deck. She has a job that gives her some flexibility in her schedule. And judging by the way she talks to me in the parking lot for 30 minutes, waving her naked ring finger in my direction, she doesn't have a man in her life.

If there's an opening, I would like to apply for the job.

I toy with the idea of asking her out for coffee right there on the spot, but it seems too soon. Besides, now I know how to see her again. I have just decided to be a regular in the yoga class.

"See you on Wednesday," I tell her with a smile.

Chapter 31: Whole Lotta Nothing

Alas, ZuuZuu the Online Babe still hasn't contacted me. My Babe Magnetic personality must not be coming through in the emails I have sent her. Maybe she thinks I am too boring and conventional for the creative spirit that she is. I may never know for sure. I have yet to be brave enough or stupid enough to drive down to her neighborhood in an attempt to "accidentally" meet her.

I have kept going to yoga class often enough to be a regular. I still can't touch my toes, but my fingertips are ever-so-slowly inching toward them when I do my very best "Forward Fold."

I have seen Eileen several times in class, but we have never had a conversation that even approaches the connection I was feeling with her the first time we talked. Since then she has been aloof and not especially friendly. Whatever spark I felt at the outset has not been fanned into any kind of flame. We never even went out for coffee, and now I don't see any point in asking her out.

Oh, and Sally from dance class? She fizzled out, too. I went to the final two salsa-dancing classes, and Sally didn't show up for either of them. I called her on the phone a couple of times, and she never called me back.

So to recap, I got a "no go" from ZuuZuu, a "slow no" from Vanessa, and a "slow no" from Sally. Oh, and I got a "you bore me now" from Eileen.

It would appear that I am in the midst of a lull in my dating life. It's not my fault, of course. These things happen in dating, in business, in sports, and in all areas of life. There are all kinds of clichés that support this:

"To everything there is a season."

"Into every life a little rain must fall."

"If it weren't for bad luck, I'd have no luck at all."

"Women are like hurricanes—warm, wet, and wild at first, but in the end they take your house and leave you with nothing."

Okay, I am really starting to depress myself now. That's not something I want to experience, so I am going to take a little break from dating. I am going to forget about women for a little while, and I am going to do something else. I am going to enjoy my singleness, and the opportunities it gives me to do whatever I please.

So I sign up for a golf class through the local university's Continuing Education program. It meets on Saturday afternoons for the next seven weeks. I have always enjoyed the game, but I have never been very good at it. Still, it's a good sport for a middle-aged man because it's thoroughly civilized and no sweating is involved. It's the perfect sport for a Middle-Aged Babe Magnet who wants to get his mind off Babes.

I arrive at the first class with my golf clubs slung over my shoulder and a smile on my face. This is going to be fun. The instructor is a charming man in his mid 30s who clearly loves the game. His name is Skip, and I like him instantly. Skip gives a very long introduction about golf and how he got into the sport. Then he walks us to the huge practice putting green. He says putting accounts for about 40% of your golf score, and it's the easiest part of the game to improve.

For the next hour we putt. We get lessons in how to hold the putter and how to swing it in a pendulum motion so the stroke is always consistent. Instead of hitting the ball toward the hole, we mark off 10 feet with a piece of string and we strive to hit the ball exactly 10 feet. "Distance is the Big D, direction is the little d," says Skip, and it makes perfect sense.

If I were in Babe Magnet mode, all this talk about putters and the Big D and holes would have me thinking of women. But I'm not here for the women, I'm here to learn something about golf and enjoy my Saturday afternoons.

I leave the class feeling as if I've gotten more than my money's worth. Who needs women when you have a hobby?

The next week I arrive early for class. This time it's all about pitching and chipping. I have been playing golf on and off for years, and I never knew there was a difference between pitching and chipping. I thought they were two words for the same thing. But Skip puts us through some drills that teach us how to swing the club in a controlled, pendulum motion without much wrist movement that creates a consistent chip shot. (A pitch shot is longer.)

After his demonstration, Skip positions us in an arc about 30 feet away from the practice green. Because space is an issue, he tells us to pair up and take turns with a partner. I notice that a woman in the class has deliberately positioned herself so that we will be paired up.

She is an attractive, 50ish woman. I wouldn't call her a Babe, exactly, and she might be a few years older than me. She has her dark blonde hair pulled back in a ponytail, and she smiles easily and often.

I enjoy being her chipping partner, and we encourage each other when we hit good shots. We even offer each other friendly advice.

There is something just so *familiar* about her, and finally I figure it out. She is the perfect woman to be cast in a TV sitcom to play the next-door neighbor or best friend of the female star of the show. Not only does she look the part, but she has the perfect quirky voice. She sounds just like what you want the best friend to sound like.

Her name is Arlene, which is also the perfect name for the quirky next-door neighbor. Here I am in golf class, minding my own business and working on my golf swing, and Arlene the quirky neighbor starts getting friendly with me. It's not just my imagination. Arlene is getting all chatty and laughing at my jokes. By the end of the class she is standing closer to me and putting her hand on my forearm when I say something mildly witty.

I think I am getting a message here. I think the universe is telling me to just relax. I don't have to be "on" all the time. I don't have to try to be a Babe Magnet all the time. I can just relax and be myself.

Maybe Yoda, the green dwarf known throughout the galaxy as a Babe Magnet, said it best in the second Star Wars movie, *The Empire Strikes Back*. (By the way, for reasons still not completely understood, the second

Star Wars movie is now referred to as Episode V). Anyway, Babe Magnet Yoda said, "Do or do not...there is no try."

Or as I would say right about now:

> **BABE MAGNET RULE #29**
> Don't try so hard to become a Babe Magnet. Just be one—by being yourself.

So I take golf classes to get my mind off of women, and as soon as I relax, a woman is attracted to me. And, while still quite relaxed, I go home and I discover that a woman from Match.com has winked at me.

Chapter 32: A Fish Jumps in the Boat

I turn my computer on, launch Internet Explorer, and login on Match.com. Much to my surprise, I find a "wink" from a woman with whom I have not corresponded. While I was out deliberately not chasing women, a fish jumped into my online dating boat.

In my time on Match.com, I have received a few winks from women. Apparently, it's okay for a woman to wink at men online, in much the same way it's okay to smile at a man from across the room at a coffee shop. It's safe, and it sends a message of interest without being overly forward.

Unfortunately, the few winks I have received have been from women who did not interest me. I am sure they were all wonderful human beings, but the women who winked at me looked, well, *middle-aged.* None of them were Babes. And when I read their profiles, they all sounded middle-aged and boring.

Perhaps I am not facing reality here. I am clearly a middle-aged man. I am not the most attractive man in town, so it's unrealistic to think that Babe-alicious women are going to be camped outside my door or sending me unprompted emails. Especially young Babes. But I find myself, despite my advancing age, still attracted to women who are younger than me. And it's not just the way they look. Younger women seem to have so much more life and energy. They describe themselves in more active terms, with more spark, more adventure, more passion, and fewer cats and/or small dogs.

I check out the profile of the new winker. Of all of the women who have winked at me, she is by far the most appealing. She calls herself TravelBug22, and she is 49 years old. She is divorced, doesn't have kids and doesn't want any, has light brown hair and blue eyes. She says her best feature is her hair.

In the little checklist of 25 categories, she matches what I am looking for in 24 categories. (At five foot four, she is just a tad shorter than my ideal woman.) I match her in 23 categories. For some reason, I don't match her in "Plan child" even though neither of us wants more kids. Neither of us perfectly matches each other in the Politics box because she is "middle of the road" and I am "liberal." Not a deal breaker at all.

This sounds very promising. I read on.

"I have a warm heart and like to make people laugh. I also have a wicked sense of humor. At times I can be assertive and other times somewhat shy. I am a professional woman who works hard and also likes to play hard, but try not to take life too seriously. Love to travel and have been blessed to visit many places in the world, which makes me want to see more."

Like every woman who has ever filled out a dating profile online, she likes going out, staying home, movies, music, reading, and spending time with family and friends. She is also content to spend time alone on the couch reading a good book. Oh, she's a romantic and loves to romance and be romanced.

I grow more intrigued as I learn that she likes to hike, kickbox, listen to blues, and rock out to the classics. She makes a good living as a sales manager. And then she seals the deal with a great last paragraph that only needs minor editing:

"I would enjoying (sic) finding someone who also would love to travel. An ideal companion is a lover and best friend who is strong, stable, honest, humorous, intelligent and also independent person. I tend to like people with a positive outlook on life, and really love to laugh."

Well, hot damn. She has just described me *perfectly*.

I send her an email thanking her for the wink. I compliment her on her profile and tell her she sounds wonderful. I mention a few of the places I have traveled recently for business, and mention that I will soon be visiting my mother in Kentucky.

The next day I get a response from her. She is traveling in the southern part of the state on business. Her work territory covers parts of three states, and she mentions again how much she likes to travel for fun. Then she tells me that her 79-year-old mother lives in town, but her father has passed away.

She ends with, "Thanks for the email. Keep in touch. Maddy."

I reread her email, just to make sure I have gotten it all. This sounds very promising indeed. I write her back, commenting on her email and adding a few details about myself.

She responds the next day. She is still on the road. "Thanks for your email. It is nice to come back to my hotel room and have email other than business." She tells me more about her sales manager job, and she comments that we both like golf. "I am trying to hit with more power. When I go to the driving range, my shots run from 2 feet to 100 yards." She tells me again how great her sense of humor is and that she loves to laugh. For a fleeting moment I consider setting her up with Will Ferrell or Jon Stewart.

She signs off with, "I fly back home tomorrow. Take care. Maddy."

For the next couple of days, Maddy and I exchange more emails via Match.com. It is amazing how one ongoing email exchange has lifted my spirits. I am beginning to feel more like a Babe Magnet with each passing day and with each email. As the weekend approaches, Maddy gives me her cell phone number and invites me to call. She says she's available to meet me this weekend.

Two days later I am at a Starbucks in an upscale part of town waiting for Maddy to arrive. I get the perfect table inside, and choose the chair that faces the door. Thanks to her photos online, I am confident that I will recognize her when she arrives.

At least, I *think* I will recognize her. Her photos were clear, and she looked pretty good. But what if she posted old photos? What if that's what she looked like 10 years ago? What if old age has roughed her up, and now her face is all wrinkled and lumpy? What if she has been bingeing on chocolate éclairs and is now four sizes bigger? I have heard of people lying about themselves in their online profiles and posting photos that bear no resemblance to present-day reality. What if she walks in the door looking like the Bride of Frankenstein, and she walks straight up to me (because I posted recent photos), and she smiles with rotten teeth and blocks the exit and I have to sit with her for an hour while she drones on about how much she loves dressing up her hamsters for Halloween?

Relax, Chad. This is just first date jitters. Even Babe Magnets get first date jitters sometimes. I have no reason to assume the worst about Maddy. Besides, I have given myself the home field advantage by arriving first, as expressed in...

> **BABE MAGNET RULE #30**
> Be the first to arrive for a date—especially a first date. Give yourself a few minutes to claim the place as your own. This will give you extra confidence and help put you in command of the date. And Babes *love* a confident man.

Maddy arrives and spots me right away. My smile is part relief and part "I am happy to meet you." She looks exactly like her photos. Her hair is indeed light brown, long in the back with short bangs in front. Her blue eyes sparkle when she smiles, which she does easily. Her body could be described as pleasantly, womanly pear-shaped. We shake hands and sit at my table for a few minutes before ordering coffee.

I don't pretend to be an expert on the First Date—at least, not quite yet. But I do know that Starbucks and similar coffee stores are great places for a "meet and greet" date. They are safe, public places where a woman doesn't feel intimidated. "Laptops and lattes" stores are conveniently located, and every neighborhood has one. In an age of hyper-efficiency and time-crunched schedules, a coffee shop offers a very businesslike approach to meeting someone you aren't ready to commit to for an entire meal. Easy in—and if need be, easy out.

For about 10 bucks you can buy two beverages and perhaps something to munch on, sit across the table from each other, and talk for as long as you want to. That's exactly what Maddy and I do.

Maddy is pleasant and enjoyable. She is reasonably attractive and she knows how to keep a conversation moving. We talk about work to start the conversation off. Maddy is a sales manager for an office products company. She oversees sales reps who visit stores, so sometimes she has to make store visits to supervise her reps.

When we tell each other short "date" versions of our personal lives, I can tell that Maddy would have been happy to have had kids. But the timing of her divorce and subsequent relationship just did not make that feasible. Now she seems at peace with her childlessness because it gives her the freedom to travel.

I like Maddy. She is a very nice woman. She is professional and well mannered. She appreciates my sense of humor right away. I find it easy to make her laugh, and her laugh explodes out of her mouth in a rapid-fire giggle. I would be happy to be seen with Maddy, and I would be happy to introduce her to my friends and family.

Maddy tells me that she is looking for a lover and a best friend. Aren't we all? I think what she is really telling me is that I have already passed the audition.

An hour and a half goes by before I look at my watch. I don't want this date to go on so long that we run out of things to talk about. My butt is getting tired from sitting so long in the same position on an unpadded chair. Plus, I need to go to the supermarket and buy food for the coming week. As we walk to our cars, Maddy gives me her business card and I give her mine.

As I drive away, I already know that I will be seeing Maddy again.

Chapter 33: Keep Your Eye on the Ball

The next morning when I check my email, I have a message from Maddy thanking me for the tea and pleasant conversation. I send her a response telling her that I had a great time, too, and I would love to see her again. I don't ask her out, I just prep her for it.

She sends me an email back, suggesting that we meet at a nearby golf course on Thursday afternoon and hit some balls at the driving range.

I pick up the phone. It's nice that Maddy is so willing to go out with me again. That's a real ego boost. At the same time, it's my job as a manly man to regain control and be the one who moves things forward.

I know this because of the extensive research I have done online. I Googled "Man asks woman out" and the first hit of 18,100,000 relevant websites is an answerbag.com question:

> Should women ask men out or wait until the man asks her out? What do we think? Should a woman ask a man out or wait and let him make the first move?

I love this man's answer:

> Not unless you want to hear "I had to make the first move" from the woman for the rest of your life.

One woman had a very practical (albeit jaded) response:

> I prefer a man to ask me first, but I would be a crotchety old hag by the time men get off their asses around here...

A man well versed in humorous sarcasm says:

> Yes, I mind. I hate it when a woman finds me attractive and then wants to spend time with me! Yuck!

That's a funny response, and there is a lot of truth in it once you get past the fake sarcasm. There is no doubt that being asked out is a wonderful ego boost—whether you are a woman or a man. But the consensus (from both regular dating people and relationship experts) can best be summed up like this:

> I'm old school and believe the man should ask out the woman. I am all for women's rights, but in this case I believe it should be left up to the man.

Why? Because dating behaviors are partly learned and partly encoded in our DNA. The DNA part is old-old-old school, and there is something very masculine about being the one who chases down a woman and pulls her to the ground by her hair. Not literally, not in the 21st century, of course. But even though we are now completely civilized and enlightened, the primal act of a man finding and choosing a woman is still very appealing to men and women alike.

So now it's time for me to call Maddy and reclaim some of my caveman legacy. I run through a possible conversation in my head.

"Hello, Maddy. This is Chad Stone, and I would like to thank you for helping me to feel like a Middle-Aged Babe Magnet. You have made it quite apparent that you would like to go out with me again. I appreciate your receptiveness, which is quite sexy to someone of my male gender.

"Therefore, I would like to officially ask you out again. I suggest that we do something physical, something that involves balls and a stick. Let's see how far we can hit little balls with a long, hard stick, because in doing so I can prove my manliness to you. I will strike a little ball with such force and with such accuracy that it will fly directly to the heavens. I will prove my worthiness on the battlefield of the Driving Range, where I can use my superior muscle strength to win your admiration and favor."

Instead of all that, I just call her up and say, "Sure! I will be happy to meet you at the driving range on Thursday afternoon."

When I arrive at the golf course, Maddy is in the clubhouse looking at the cute stuffed animal club covers. I get us a large bucket of balls, and we walk to the driving range. Up until now, I have never considered that a golf driving range would be a good place for a date. But as we find two open spots at the range and get settled in, I realize that this is perfect.

Most men (myself included) get bored with just talking. When the average man talks to the average woman, the man runs out of things to say long before the woman. So the man uses up his word quota for the day and ends up with nothing left to say while the woman is just getting her talking motor running. While the woman goes on and on about how she felt when she saw her first sunset over the Pacific Ocean on a tropical island, and how the air smelled of hibiscus flowers and the breeze blew in from the southwest along with a flock of seabirds and the colors of the sun lit up the billowing clouds in every shade of gold, peach, and persimmon that has ever been captured by every great painter since the invention of paint, reminding her in some ways of summers as a little girl that were spent on her grandparents' idyllic farm in the green countryside that she thought at the time was the closest to heaven she would ever get, the man thinks to himself, "Whoa, I got *so* wasted the first time I went to Hawaii. It was awesome."

Women like to talk and men like to do stuff. So the driving range offers something for both of us. I get to prove my manhood by hitting golf balls as far as I can, and Maddy gets to talk to me in between swings.

The weather is simply glorious, and it is a fabulous afternoon to be outdoors. I put on my golf glove and take a few practice swings. Maddy is already apologizing for her lack of skill. My impressive manly man muscles are getting warmed up, and I am looking forward to putting on a show. The last time I hit balls, I was connecting really well. It felt like I was successfully incorporating my golf class lessons into a swing that was going to catapult me onto the PGA Tour. (Or at least the Champions Tour, for the 50-and-over golf pros.) But today I have left my swing at home, and I am hooking almost every shot. I thought I was going to be showing off for Maddy, but instead I look like a duffer who is still learning the game.

Fortunately, Maddy hits like a girl. She wasn't kidding when she described her golfing skills on her Match.com profile. Sometimes the ball goes 75 to 100 yards. Sometimes she tops the ball and it dribbles forward about five feet. But she's got a great attitude. She doesn't expect to hit a perfect shot every time because she knows she is still learning.

If this were a date movie, I would take this opportunity to help Maddy with her swing. I would show her how to grip the club, and then I would reach my arms around her and, very slowly, guide her club back. I would hold her arms up in a perfect backswing, gently giving her words of encouragement. She would turn her head toward mine and look up toward me. Our eyes would lock, and there would be that moment of pleasurable tension when time stops and thoughts are racing through your head. Is he going to do it? Is he going to move his head closer to hers to test her response, or is he going to chicken out and pretend that the moment never happened? And then I would move in and we would kiss for the first time—a long, romantic kiss that would make us both forget all about golf.

But this ain't no romantic comedy. I let Maddy worry about her own damn swing. Mine is so inconsistent that it's pissing me off.

BABE MAGNET RULE #31

Don't expect every date to be perfect. This is real life—not some romantic comedy at the Cineplex.

We hit balls for an hour, and then we walk back toward the parking lot.

"I don't know if you have any plans for this evening, but I have two tickets for a preview screening of a new movie for tonight..." she says, not phrasing it as a question.

I think for a moment. I think about going home alone to my barren bachelor apartment. I think about cooking dinner for myself and eating it alone in front of whatever dumb show is on TV tonight.

"Actually, I don't have any plans, and I would love to go with you to the movies. That would be nice."

Her face lights up like a concert stage. Score one for willing to be flexible.

We have just enough time for a casual dinner before the movie. We talk throughout the meal, and there aren't any long awkward pauses or tense moments. We tell each other more episodes of our respective life stories. We are both smart enough to not talk about the single worst topic of conversation for a first or second date: ex-lovers.

The movie is a pleasant diversion. I sit next to Maddy in the dark, not talking. (I have used up all of my words for today and all of my words for tomorrow, too. I may not have anything to say until next week.) We do not touch each other at all. I am not trying to prep her for any further activities tonight. It has been a good date, and I am satisfied at leaving well enough alone.

On the drive back to get her car, Maddy mentions that she will have guests staying at her house this weekend, but they will be leaving on Sunday at noon.

"Let me know if you want to get together and do something," she says.

Chapter 34: Role Models

A week goes by before I see Maddy again, because I leave town to visit my mother in Kentucky. My mom lives alone in a townhouse that she bought after she divorced my father. My parents are one of those couples who stayed married for the sake of the kids. It was during the Cold War, when Russia and the USA did a lot a posturing as they got ready to launch missile strikes that never happened. At my house, my parents did the married couple's version of the same thing.

My mom and dad had loved each other at first—I could tell from the silent 8mm movies that were shot when my brother and I were little. But by the time we got to be teenagers, my brother and I didn't see our parents behave in a loving way toward each other very often. There was an underlying sense of unrest, and a palpable tension hung in the air, like the stale smell at a fish fry. It was as if the kitchen staff (my mom) was going to go on strike against The Man at any moment. Not only did my parents act as though they didn't love each, they didn't even seem to *like* each other.

I watched my parents' relationship, and I learned from it. Mostly, I learned what not to do. I watched my mom, and I learned that it's better to be happy than to try to be right all the time. My mom was so intent on being right that she bad-mouthed my father during their entire marriage and then long after the divorce. I watched my dad and learned that staying in a bad marriage eats your life force away. Pretty soon, you forget how wonderful your spouse was when you fell in love with her. From there, it gets easier and easier to resent her.

I knew there had to be a better way. Today, I would put it in these terms:

BABE MAGNET RULE #32
When you find a Babe that you want to be with, the one who makes your heart and soul sing with joy, treat her like the goddess that she is. Love her, respect her, defend her, and appreciate her.

If you can do that, you can maintain a cherished love relationship forever. That's what I am looking for—a cherished love relationship. My goal is not to be Babe Magnet. That's just a means to an end. The real goal is to find the new love of my life.

Just as my parents demonstrated for me what a marriage should not be, my mom's current life is the perfect example of what I do not want to become in my old age.

After she divorced my father, Mom moved back to her hometown and tried to make time stop. She didn't date anyone because she set her standards so high that no man could possibly measure up. In doing so, she deliberately chose a life of celibate aloneness. I guess she thought that a relationship just wasn't worth the trouble. She didn't want to compromise anymore, and she didn't see the value in partnering with someone "for better or for worse." Quite simply, my mother will die unmarried because that's the life she has chosen for herself.

I have made a different choice. I chose to go out into the dating world and find a delightful woman to love and cherish. To make it more likely that I will meet and win the heart of a new love, I am learning everything I can about women. Fortunately, I am enjoying the education.

While visiting my mom, I do my best to retain my positive outlook. Staying with Mom is a lot like spending a week working for AmeriCorps. The pay is awful and the living accommodations leave a lot to be desired, but the work is rewarding. I clean windows, I do yardwork that she can't do anymore, I fix things, and I keep her company. I even take her to the electronics store and buy her a new television. I get it all set up just in time for her to watch the evening news. She just isn't happy unless she's watched enough news to make her miserable.

While she is watching the mayhem and violence, I sneak off to find an Internet café. (Mom doesn’t have an Internet connection, and she doesn’t know how to use a computer.) I fire up my laptop and send an email to Maddy.

“Want to get together on Sunday when I'm back in town?” I ask.

I don’t need a reply. I already know the answer.

Chapter 35: Wait for it.... Wait for it....

I arrive at Maddy's house in the early afternoon for our date. This is the first time I have seen where she lives, and Maddy gives me the grand tour. Her house is nice and cozy. Not cozy in a frumpy grandmotherly way—cozy in a comfortable, lived-in kind of way. On one side of her living room are large display cases filled with toys. She gives me an overview of her toy collection, which includes valuable antiques as well as some modern collectibles. Maddy does not have any pets or kids, so apparently she gives herself permission to indulge in a very expensive toy collection.

The sliding door near her dining table leads out into a back yard that is plain and boring. There is an island of lawn surrounded by decorative rocks, with a couple of sad trees in the corner. *Better Homes and Gardens* it ain't.

Maddy offers to walk me upstairs to see her bedroom, but I decide to save that for another time. We hop in my truck and drive to the nature center down by the river. It's a lovely place for an afternoon hike amidst the cottonwood trees and the birds. We walk along the pathway and chat amicably as the sun shines brightly in the western sky.

Talking to Maddy is definitely a great ego boost for me, because she gets my jokes and laughs freely. Her giggle erupts quickly and bubbles out like a mountain spring. I find myself saying silly things just to get her to laugh.

We stand behind the bird blind and watch the ducks and geese frolic in the pond near the visitor center. We try to count the turtles sunning themselves on logs, but lose track. I haven't done this kind of hanging out since I embarked upon my quest to become a Babe Magnet. Having a goal or a mission is a wonderful, manly thing, but maybe I've been taking it too far. Maybe I've been trying too hard. As I sit with Maddy, neither of us saying anything, I realize that I have stumbled upon an elusive but important principle:

BABE MAGNET RULE #33
Relax, Mr. Babe Magnet. Just friggin' relax.

We have walked around the entire nature park and have seen everything there is to see here. I am starting to get hungry, and I don't want this date to end.

"Would you like to go somewhere and get an early dinner?" I ask.

Her smile is the only answer I need.

Dinner is casual and fun. We talk and we do some people-watching. But soon, we are finished eating and neither of us is done with the date. So we go next door to the bookstore and just browse. This is only our third date (counting the Meet and Greet at Starbucks), and I never would have planned an interlude at a bookstore for a third date. But like everything else today, it's working. We show each other interesting books and little gifts that we find, and in the process I get to know a little bit more about Maddy. She has a soft spot for animals, and she laughs easily at the humor books.

We drive the scenic route back to her house, past the stately mansions that back up to the open space along the river. I have always entertained fantasies of living in one of these mansions, and we point out the homes that we like the best. She picks the sprawling horse farm, while I choose the Tuscan-style house with the vineyard in front.

I pull into her driveway. It's still early, but we have been together for almost six hours. "Want to come inside?" she asks, without a hint of sexual tension.

"Sure. I'll come in and visit with you for a while."

We watch TV on the couch while sipping mediocre white wine. We snuggle a little. I kiss her, but receive a lukewarm response. I am content anyway. I do not need for anything else to happen tonight. It has been a very pleasant day.

The movie on TV is washing over me, lulling me into the perfect trance that advertisers love because it makes you more receptive to sales messages. Maddy is still snuggled up against me, and now I notice that her hand is resting lightly on my thigh. So after a while I lean over to kiss her again, and this time the smoldering coals erupt into flames. Gently and carefully, I start giving her a full body massage through her clothing. It begins with arms and shoulders, then moves to her back and migrates slowly to her girl parts. I deftly slide my hand up inside her blouse and unfasten her bra.

"I'm going to get my breasts done next month," she announces. "It's my gift to myself for turning 50."

I do not know how to respond to this. I have not yet seen her breasts, so I cannot say, "Your breasts are wonderful just the way they are." I also cannot say, "That would be great! You can't be too thin or have breasts that are too big!"

So I say, "That's nice," and leave it at that. We will have to discuss her breasts at greater length some other time.

Our kissing and rubbing grows more passionate. We are both old enough to know what tunnel this train is about to pull into. Suddenly, Maddy pulls back and looks into my eyes. "Do you think it's too soon for this?"

Okay. This is the moment. Do I behave like a Babe Magnet with his eye on the prize, and respond with a well-rehearsed line like, "It's never too soon for love"? Or do I play it cool, showing my chivalrous and gallant side?

I go for cool and relaxed. "It's totally your call," I say softly. I give her a gentle kiss. "Whatever you want."

I can see from the expression on her face that she is conflicted. Her body is all primed for action, but her mind…

"I don't want you to think I'm…." Her voice trails off before finishing the sentence.

I smile. "I promise not to call you a slut."

The honesty of the moment cracks us both up.

"Do you have any condoms?" she asks.

Are you kidding me? I have one right here in my wallet….

Chapter 36: Easy Come, Easy Go (Again)

The first thing I see when I open my eyes early the next morning is a ceiling fan. Hmmmm, that's weird. I never noticed there was a ceiling fan in my bedroom before. I stretch a little, and the sheets against my skin feel somehow different.

I realize there's a warm body sleeping next to me. Even in my grogginess, I know that this is not normal. Then the previous night comes rushing back to me in glorious waves of memory.

I have woken up in Maddy's bed. Holy Cow!—as Harry Caray (the great Chicago Cubs radio announcer) used to say. I have not woken up in anyone else's bed since my middle-aged singleness began. It is a strange and exhilarating experience.

I remember making love to Maddy last night. I remember hearing lots of moans and squeals of delight. And Maddy was pretty happy, too. I remember leaving a trail of clothing on the way up to the bedroom, and I remember falling into a deep sleep after we wore ourselves out. I won't need to go to the gym today.

It feels strange to lie here in Maddy's bed, but it also feels wonderful. I did not expect this to happen so soon, which makes it all the more delightful. I lay still, listening to the sounds that Maddy's house makes. The water in her toilet runs a little bit to fill up the tank. A car drives by outside.

It's Monday morning, but I don't feel any hurry to rush into work. I will savor this moment. I will savor the feeling of lying naked in bed with a woman as long as I can.

Wait a minute. Maddy is waking up. She snuggles next to me and looks to see if my eyes are open. Then she reaches over and gently caresses me.

Here we go again.

****

Two days later I wake up feeling ill. It has nothing to do with Maddy. My head hurts, my stomach is queasy, and I feel like crap. I've got some stupid virus working on me, and I don't like it at all.

I guess even cowgirls get the blues, and even Babe Magnets get the flu.

I get up just long enough to take some Echinacea and 1,000 milligrams of Vitamin C. Then I go back to bed. Three hours later, I suck it up and go to my office.

Out of sheer willpower, I manage to keep working until mid-afternoon. Then I make the short drive back to my apartment, where I quickly fall asleep on the couch.

When I wake up it is dark and I have no idea what time it is. My cell phone is ringing—or, rather, it is playing its ringtone. I hear the Red Hot Chili Peppers sing "The Zephyr Song," and I know it's time to answer my phone.

It's Maddy, calling during intermission at the Chippendale's show. Yes, the Chippendale's show that features scantily dressed, stunningly handsome men dancing suggestively for an audience full of women. The show is having a predictable effect on Maddy. She is in a very friendly, amorous mood. By the sound of her voice, she and her girlfriends have already consumed an impressive number of alcoholic drinks.

"Hey, big boy," says Maddy. "How are you doin' tonight?"

"Not so great, I've got the ..."

"I'm doin' great," she says. "The show is FABULOUS, and the dancers are really HOT."

"Have you been drinking?"

She just laughs. "These guys are AWESOME, and they are really making me horny."

"Well, that's great, except..."

"You know what? I think you should come over to my house after this show is over, and I GUARANTEE you will have a WONDERFUL time."

"That's a very tempting offer, and normally I would jump on it."

"No, I will jump on it!" She shrieks with laughter. "I will definitely jump on it."

So that's what she meant in her Match.com profile about having a great sense of humor. Well, she certainly appreciates her own wit when she's drunk.

My head throbs. What a horrible time to be sick.

"I'm sure you *would* jump on it if I gave you half a chance tonight," I say. "But I really feel sick. I couldn't even work today."

"You're sick? Well, I'm SURE I can make you feel better." She laughs.

I do not want to disappoint a very horny woman, but I don't think I can manage it tonight. Even though I feel like crap, I don't turn her down altogether. I tell her to call me after the show is over to see how I am feeling.

She hangs up to catch the last half of the Chippendale's show, and I get into bed. I promptly fall asleep. At some point, I awaken just enough to hear my phone ringing in the other room. It is dark and my body will not move. My phone stops singing, and in a few moments it makes the little chirp that tells me I have a voicemail message. I do not have to get up to know who just left me a message.

As I drift back to sleep, I imagine seeing the headline of tomorrow's newspaper:

MIDDLE-AGED BABE MAGNET TURNS DOWN
SEX WITH HORNY WOMAN

That's how sick I am.

Chapter 37: The Gentle Art of Seduction

It is two more days before I feel up to seeing Maddy. I still don't feel 100% healthy, but I feel well enough to go over to her house for dinner and a movie.

Maddy isn't much of a cook. She's a thoroughly modern woman who buys semi-prepared food that requires minimal work and a small amount of skill to turn into a meal. She fixes me broiled salmon with teriyaki sauce from Trader Joe's, green beans, and French bread. It isn't fancy, but it is wonderful to have a woman cook dinner for me.

When dinner is over, we sit up on the couch and watch the movie. Well, we sit next to each other on the couch, shoulders and legs touching, and we sort of watch the movie. It doesn't take me long to lean towards Maddy and give her a gentle kiss. I gently reach my hand up to stroke the hair behind her ear while I nibble on her lower lip.

There is a gentle art to seducing a woman. A Babe Magnet has to know when to make his move, and how much warming up his woman needs. It's an art more than a science, so the man has to constantly interpret cues from the woman to determine if he is moving too fast or too slowly.

It doesn't matter how old you are or how many times you've done it before, there are dozens (maybe even hundreds) of cues to pay attention to during the seduction. When you move in for the first kiss, does she greet your advance with a tentative peck on the lips and then pull away? When you kiss her again, this time with a little more passion, does she lean into you or does she keep her body position neutral—neither advancing or retreating?

In the vast majority of cases, it's the man who plays the role of the amorous aggressor. That's the masculine role, and any self-respecting Babe Magnet is going to play the odds and play the masculine role. So the man is gently but firmly reading the woman's cues and pushing the seduction forward.

Meanwhile, the woman is blissfully enjoying the kissing and tender physical foreplay, completely oblivious that the man's brain is processing 100,000 thoughts per minute and his pulse rate is off the charts.

According to my own anecdotal research, inexperienced Babe Magnets, due to their own nervousness or lack of confidence, often break the mood by talking instead of seducing. (All right, most of this "anecdotal research" is my own experience, back in the days when I was a total dweeb.) But trust me—you are much better off following:

BABE MAGNET RULE #34

Pay attention to your woman's non-verbal and involuntary physical cues when it comes time for seduction. Stop talking and listen to her body.

So I pay close attention to Maddy's signals. This is, of course, much easier the second time around. I seduced Maddy last week, so tonight I am quite confident of my Babe Magnet seduction abilities. But still, you never know for sure.

I lean in for a passionate kiss. She returns my passion. This signals the pleasure center in my brain, which coaxes me to gently stroke a more erogenous part of her body. My Babe Magnet Mental Command Center (BMMCC), located deep inside my brain, is running at full capacity. Inside the BMMCC, the computers are buzzing with data. The surface temperature of Maddy's skin has increased 6.3%. Her respiration is up 9%, and her involuntary primal vocalizations have gone from zero per minute to 12. Meanwhile, blood flow throughout my body has increased 14%. Blood flow into my crotch area is up 166% and rising. Literally.

When Maddy lifts her blouse over her head in a single motion and then flings her bra across the living room, the BMMCC sends out an all-points bulletin: CHAD IS GOING TO GET LUCKY TONIGHT!

Chapter 38: The Delights of a New Relationship

Why is sex so good at the beginning of a relationship? Why is it that when you are still getting to know someone romantically, the sparks fly and you physically just can't seem to get enough of each other? How is it possible for a man to suddenly become a Sex God, capable of superhuman feats of lovemaking—including "personal bests" in frequency and duration—when he is in the throes of a new passion?

Experts say that exciting sex is the result of many physical and emotional factors. Although the physical part of a new sexual relationship is inherently exciting by itself, it is the combination of the physical enjoyment with the stimulation of the mind that helps make it so incredible.

With a new lover, there is also the excitement of discovery. Everything with this new person is, well, new. A new lover brings a novel freshness to every touch and every expression of love. There is also something wonderful about feeling physically attracted to someone new. It can literally make your body tingle and feel more alive. The energy of attraction is palpable as it flows from you to your new lover and back again. There may be nothing quite as satisfying, in an utterly primal way, as being the object of your new lover's attraction. The ego boost alone is a powerful aphrodisiac.

In the late 1960s, Dr. Skyler P. Dobbstrobben took advantage of the dawn of the modern sexual revolution (and a loophole in government funding) to go where very few researchers had ever gone before. He began to study the science of sex. Using an ingenious combination of psychology, physiology, chemistry, and anthropics, Dr. Dobbstrobben conducted carefully designed experiments that actually measured the mental and physical changes that occur before, during, and after a man and a woman have sexual intercourse for the first time.

Some of these physical occurrences had been already documented. During sexual arousal and sexual activity, body temperature rises and pupils dilate. Skin sensitivity increases, and the body "opens up" its receptors to touch by flooding them with blood. Pleasurable hormones are released throughout the body. None of this information was new, because Babe Magnets from the Middle Ages (as opposed to Middle-Aged Babe Magnets) documented their knowledge of the physiology of seduction in books such as *Amor Vincit Omnia* (*Love Conquers All*) and *How to Pick Up Wenches*.

But Dr. Dobbstrobben was the first to document and isolate the specific hormones that make sex so sensual. He discovered that erotic physical stimulation releases phytohormones that create sexually oriented thoughts and suspend normal inhibitions. And he identified the specific receptors in the hands, breasts, genitals, and ankles that respond to the exogenous chemical compounds released by a human body in the midst of sexual passion. In short, he codified the male arousal mechanisms (which quickly became known by the slang expression, "The Boner Syndrome") and the female sexual response to erotic stimuli (which, likewise, was crudely referred to as "Happy Wet Cat in Heat."

Dobbstrobben found the longer the physical relationships, the more likely it was for levels of the "pleasure" hormones to be significantly reduced. Yes, some couples married for 30, 40, or 50 years were still "getting it on" with regularity and registering impressive hormonal rates. But on average, the longer the relationship, the more likely the spark of romance had long since died. And without exception, every couple whose relationship spanned more than 90 years was no longer having sex because both partners were dead.

According to Dr. Dobbstrobben:

> "The thrill of a new sexual experience is nature's way of bonding a man and a woman, much like Super Glue can bond your finger and your buttock if you are careless enough to scratch yourself while in the midst of a gluing project that

> you are, for no particular reason, doing in the nude. Not that I have any direct experience with that or anything."

So, what can we learn from Dr. Dobbstrobben about new relationships?

Nothing at all. I just invented all that stuff about Dr. Dobbstrobben to see if you were paying attention.

That's right. There is no Dr. Dobbstrobben. I made him up. (A Google search for Dobbstrobben reveals zero results. ZERO!) I don't know anything about the science of sex. But I do know what any self-respecting Babe Magnet knows:

> **BABE MAGNET RULE #35**
> Enjoy the rush of a new sexual relationship, because there is no telling how long that rush is going to last.

So my inquiring mind probes deeper. I ask a few married friends, and each of them says they had more sex with their wives before they became their wives than after they were married. I also talk to a guy at Barleycorn's while I am there eating lunch. This guy, I think his name is Ed, claims to be married and having sex every day. But I don't know if I can believe a guy who spends his days hanging out at a bar.

On www.askmen.com (which, unlike Dr. Dobbstrobben, really exists), I find this:

> While physical attraction was probably what gave you the courage (or motivation) to initiate a conversation with your woman in the first place, it is important that you show her that sex need not come first. If you want to make this relationship a serious one, don't think of sex as a top priority. This is a great move on your part, as you are showing her how smitten you are with her mind.

Oh God! I am not smitten with Maddy's mind AT ALL! This does not bode well for a long-term relationship.

Maybe I should just enjoy the sex while it lasts.

Chapter 39: Welcome to My Bachelor Pad

Tonight is a milestone in my single life. Tonight I am cooking dinner for Maddy. It's the first time I have cooked dinner for a woman in my bachelor pad. I straighten the place up, clean the kitchen, vacuum the floor, and generally try to make a crappy one-bedroom apartment look like a 4,000 square foot house overlooking the Pacific Ocean. There is only so much I can do with Windex and Pledge. But I do what I can.

I must admit that I am excited to have Maddy over for dinner. This is a big step for me as a dating man. My friend Craig says that when he is hot for a woman, he always invites her over for a home-cooked spaghetti dinner. "My spaghetti is the world's best aphrodisiac," he says. "It has never failed. Ever."

Sounds like a testimonial to me. Maybe he should sell his own homemade spaghetti sauce on eBay. If it's half as good as he says it is, he will be a millionaire.

But I am not cooking spaghetti. The menu for this evening is one of my favorite dinners—grilled flank steak, rice with teriyaki sauce, fresh green beans, and fresh raspberries over vanilla ice cream for dessert. I even make the teriyaki sauce from scratch. It's not a fancy dinner, but it is very tasty—and it's impressive even though it is not difficult to prepare. In other words, it's the perfect Middle-Aged Babe Magnet home-cooked meal.

BABE MAGNET RULE #36

Any time a man cooks a meal for a woman, he gets relationship points. The more impressive the dinner, the more points he gets. These points can be redeemed for

> things like sexual favors or a "Night Out with the Guys" pass. Earn enough points and sometimes you can even cash them in to erase something you've done that was really stupid.

Maddy arrives with a smile on her face and an inexpensive bottle of wine in her hand. I have already opened a nice bottle of Cabernet Sauvignon, which is breathing on the kitchen counter. I thank Maddy for bringing wine, place her bottle on the counter, and pour two glasses of my wine.

With wine glasses in hand, we step outside to grill the flank steak. I show off my manly man grilling skills, which turns Maddy on. (Women respond to the prehistoric combination of man and fire.) I deftly get the grill hot and suavely flip the meat at the perfect moment. She doesn't even notice when the grease from the steak sends the flames racing skyward, burning off my eyebrows.

"You smell really good," says Maddy.

"Yep. Barbecue is my favorite cologne."

I serve up the appetizing dinner in my apartment, and Maddy and I share a lovely meal together. We talk about how our work is going, whether we should go for a bike ride, the wonderful weather, and other lightweight topics. Maddy and I don't talk about anything political, religious, or complicated. I don't know if that's because we haven't known each other that long and we don't want to broach uncomfortable subjects yet, or if Maddy just isn't interested in anything that involves a lot of thinking.

After dinner, we settle in on the couch as has become our custom. I start playing a movie on DVD, as is our custom. We snuggle under a throw blanket and watch 15 minutes of the movie, as is our custom. We start to kiss, which leads to petting and peeling off clothes, as is also our custom. Then I suggest that we go into the bedroom, and I get no objection from Maddy.

I know how thin my apartment walls are. I have heard the next-door neighbors during their conjugal "Oh baby! Yes baby!" relations. So while I am having sex with Maddy, I can't help but wonder how much my neighbors are hearing right now. It's only fair that they are "enjoying"

Maddy's screams and squeals just as much as I have "enjoyed" their songs of passion. There has been damn little noise happening on my side of the walls since I moved in here. But tonight, there's a rock concert going on. Any moment I expect to look over my shoulder and see a bunch of long-haired stoners holding up lighters and shouting, "Free Bird!"

After the physical exercise/rock concert portion of the evening's festivities, Maddy and I fall asleep in my bed. It is the first time since my divorce that a woman has slept in my bed. It is a delight to have a warm body next to me in my own bed for the entire night.

In the morning, I make breakfast for Maddy. I make oatmeal from scratch—not that crappy instant stuff. Thus, I earn even more relationship points, which I plan to redeem later for something really, really nice.

Chapter 40: It's Not a Boob Job. It's Breast Augmentation.

Just as Maddy promised on the first night I successfully seduced her, she has gone ahead with her plans to get larger breasts.

All her life, Maddy has been dissatisfied with her breasts. There was nothing wrong with her breasts, really. They sat on her chest right where they were supposed to be, and they gave her a little something to put inside a bra. But Maddy's breasts were always overshadowed by her ample hips. She felt self-conscious because her boobs weren't big enough to balance out her butt.

When Maddy shared with me her plan to get a boob job (which is officially called "breast augmentation") I was very supportive, so to speak. Basically, my response was "You go, girl!" I wasn't about to interfere with her hopes, dreams, and aspirations for a bigger set of ta-tas.

> **BABE MAGNET RULE #37**
> A Babe Magnet is always supportive of a woman's desire to make herself more beautiful. If she says, "I would like to get my breasts done," tell her that you'll drive her home from the clinic. And offer to pay for her new (significantly larger) Victoria's Secret bras.

Maddy says that several of her middle-aged friends have recently gotten their boobs done. (Damn! I mean, they got their *breasts augmented*. I have to get used to the politically correct terminology.) Breast augmentation seems to be a growing trend. Mature women who have the money for elective surgery are buying the breasts they thought they should always have had. That's exactly how Maddy talks about her soon-to-be larger and perkier breasts. She's paying five grand for the boobs she should have been born with.

The day of Maddy's breast augmentation arrives, and I don't even have to take her to the plastic surgeon's office or bring her back home. She's already gotten two of her lady friends to provide the breast possible transportation. I think these two friends have already gotten their breasts augmented, so they can provide all of the support (Ha! There's that word again) and sympathy that Maddy will need.

I don't see Maddy at all on B-Day. She gets dropped off at home and goes straight to bed to sleep. She doesn't answer her phone, so I leave her an upbeat voicemail message. I don't know exactly what to say, because I've never left a message for a woman who just got her boobs surgically enlarged. I ponder telling her that I can't wait to see her new bigger and better boobs, but instead I tell her that I hope she heals fast.

The next morning she picks up her phone, and she sounds awful. "My chest hurts like hell," she says.

"Is there anything I can bring you?"

She has a craving for an ice cream sundae from McDonald's. I guess it makes sense, in a crazy sort of way, that a boob job would make you crave milk products. It's not my job to judge her, it's my job to give her support. (Sorry. I can't help myself.) I vow to be her Wonderbra man, so I buy her an ice cream sundae and a bouquet of cut flowers. I arrive at her doorstep like a shining knight to rescue a damsel in distress who now has larger, surgically enhanced breasts.

I would like to say that Maddy is radiant, and that her newly enlarged breasts fill her bathrobe like two helium balloons. But in truth, when she opens the door she looks like hell. The poor thing had major surgery yesterday, and she is in obvious pain. Instinctively I reach out to give her a hug, and then think better of it. I give her sort of an air hug, in which I grab her shoulders with my hands and pull her ever so slightly towards me, without making any chest-to-chest contact.

It's hard to tell if she is happier with the fresh flowers or the McDonald's chocolate sundae. Either way, my visit is clearly the highlight of her post-operation day. I am very curious to see the new "girls," but they are all taped up and Maddy's not about to let me anywhere near her chest today. The girls are taking a nap, and they can't be disturbed. After all, they are newborns, and they need their rest.

The recovery process takes longer than expected, especially since the post-op exam reveals a problem with her left breast that has to be surgically repaired. I really hope Maddy LOVES her new boobs, because they are really causing her a lot of pain. Maddy sleeps a lot, and when she's awake she's grumpy.

After Maddy has healed for a few more days, I arrive at her house with ingredients to cook her a nice dinner. The menu includes tilapia fillets broiled in butter and garlic, oven fries and salad, with fresh berries and ice cream for dessert. Maddy acts like it's the best dinner she's ever had.

After we eat, we sit on the couch for a while. Then she utters words that are music to my Middle-Aged Babe Magnet ears. "Would you rub some cream on my breasts?"

How could I refuse such a simple request? I got to see the new girls a couple of days ago, but this is the first time they've felt well enough for me to touch them. Using the doctor-approved breast cream, I slather the girls and give each one a careful and thorough massage.

Let me tell you, the new girls are spectacular. I could have massaged them all night. But Maddy just wants them slathered with the buttery cream, not kneaded like lumps of dough. I whisper to them, "I'll be seeing more of you girls later," and then help Maddy cover them in their protective bandages.

Maybe I'll call tomorrow to see if they can come out to play.

I seem to have breasts on the brain. Maddy and her new breasts are still healing after surgery, and I am curious about just how many women are getting their breasts enhanced. So I look it up.

A trade organization called the American Society for Aesthetic Plastic Surgery keeps breast augmentation statistics. According to the ASAPS, 355,671 breast augmentation procedures were performed in 2008. Multiplying the number of augmentation procedures by two reveals a total of 711,342 surgically bigger boobs in 2008 alone.

That's a lot of augmented breasts. That's one augmented breast for each person living in the city of Detroit. (I don't know what the people in Detroit are going to do with one augmented breast each, but statistics are statistics.)

According to the American Society of Plastic Surgeons, the trend toward breast augmentation has been on a steady increase since 1992, when 32,607 breast augmentation surgeries were performed.

It seems that every year, more American women get breast enhancements. That certainly helps explain why the average bra size in the U.S. has increased. Lingerie manufacturer Frederick's of Hollywood reports that in 1996, the average size of bras they sold was 34B. Now the average is 36C. Of course, Frederick's customers may not be a statistically representative sampling of American women. But then again, they could be.

On the blog at accesspro.com I find this:

> • Breast augmentation is likely to be the leader in plastic surgery options for many years to come. It is one plastic surgery that has an immediate, noticeable impact while offering a natural appearance.
>
> • Women have chosen breast augmentation for many reasons, but the most common is simply a way to feel better about the size of their breasts. Studies have shown that very few women opt for their procedure to please a partner, or to attract a partner. Far and away the most common reason is for the purpose of feeling better about their bodies.

That's certainly true for Maddy. She decided to have the procedure done so she would feel better about her body. The fact that I wholeheartedly approve of her larger breasts had nothing to do with her decision. She decided to have her breasts done before she even met me.

But part of me is a little bit skeptical. I think that most of the women who get surgically enhanced breasts know that most men like 'em big. And to those women, I have only one thing to say: Thank you.

Chapter 41: Playing House

Over the next few weeks, Maddy and I settle into a comfortable routine. We see each other three or four times a week, mostly at her house. We talk on the phone during the day and decide if I am coming over for dinner. Sometimes Maddy cooks for me; sometimes I arrive with bags from the grocery store, and cook for her.

I enjoy hanging out with Maddy at her house. We eat, drink wine, and relax on her back porch. Every hour that I spend at Maddy's house is an hour that I don't have to spend in my one-bedroom apartment.

When I met Maddy, her back yard was barren except for a swimming pool-sized oval of lawn surrounded by gravel. It was an underachiever's back yard, virtually an empty canvas upon which a gardener could paint a very nice landscape. Her barren yard was an opportunity that I could not resist. One of the worst things about apartment life for me is not having a yard to work in. I love to grow plants and get my fingers into the soil. So I took it upon myself to transform Maddy's yard into something interesting and colorful.

On the weekends, I have been buying plants and reconfiguring the irrigation system so I can create little groupings of flowering perennials. Maddy doesn't have a clue about what I am doing. "Just go for it," she tells me. So I have added Russian sage plants that will offer bluish lavender flowers, gaillardia for burgundy blooms, salvia for midnight blue flower spikes and Spanish brooms for bright yellow flowers next spring.

Gardening has always been a rejuvenating experience for me. I find great pleasure, even spiritual enlightenment, in coaxing life out of seeds and helping Mother Nature grow flowers and fruits where there was once barren land. Gardening lets me create my own little Eden wherever I am, so I am grateful to Maddy for letting me cultivate a little plot of paradise in her yard.

At my suggestion, Maddy buys a propane grill so we can barbecue on her back patio. I think Maddy always wanted to have a barbecue grill, but she didn't trust herself to assemble it properly. She has the female gene for spatial relationships, which means that it is almost impossible for her to translate a two-dimensional set of printed directions into a three-dimensional barbecue grill. I didn't get it right the first time, but eventually I successfully transformed a box full of seemingly unrelated metal parts made in China into a state-of-the-art cheap propane grill.

When I look around Maddy's yard, I see how I am transforming it to suit my own needs. As much as I like hanging out at Maddy's house, I particularly love being in her backyard. Maddy's suburban lot is narrow, and the houses are very close together. But at least there is *some* airspace between her house and the neighbors. And when I am in her backyard, I have direct access to the weather, the sky, and even a wild bird or two. Living in an apartment at this point in my life has made it very clear to me that I need a little plot of suburban land to feel happy and content.

But the longer I am with Maddy, the more obvious it becomes to me that we are not completely compatible. Although she stimulates my body, she doesn't stimulate my mind. I am fond of her, but I am not in love with her. One afternoon, when I am listening to music and reading a magazine on her back porch, I realize that Maddy's best feature is...her house.

One evening, I stop by Maddy's house to drop off a book that I had borrowed. I hadn't planned on staying, but she offers to fix me something for dinner. I hem and haw. "I don't want you to get sick of me," I say.

Her eyes tell me that isn't a problem. Actually, it is me I am worried about. I don't want to start getting sick of Maddy. This romance has morphed into a quasi-domestic partnership without us ever talking about it. I am afraid that Maddy might be making assumptions that are not based on fact. She could be seeing my work in her yard as evidence that we are beginning to build a life together. If she is assuming that the two of us are going to be together for a long period of time, then I am setting her up for disappointment. I am not ready to make any commitments. I don't even want to think of Maddy and Chad as a couple.

Then the obvious hits me: Maddy is my rebound relationship. Oh my God, I am a living, breathing cliché. There was a void in my life, and I filled it with Maddy and her house. Then the rationalizations begin. I tell myself that it is OK to stay with Maddy for a while. That is, as long as I don't have to make any commitments. And right now she isn't asking me to.

But I notice myself finding fault with her. I notice all of the ways in which she is starting to bug me. So I make a list.

1. Maddy likes to sleep with the ceiling fan above the bed spinning like an airplane propeller. I don't like to sleep in a draft. Sometimes I get up and sleep in the guest bedroom where it's not so drafty.
2. I don't like talking to Maddy on the phone. She doesn't hold up her end of the conversation, and we run out of things to say way too quickly. This is a bad sign.
3. I don't like the sound of Maddy's voice. There is something about it that is unpleasant to my ears. I don't know what it is exactly. Maybe it's the way the pitch of her voice rises when she gets excited. It's a cross between a cartoon character voice and somebody who just inhaled helium.
4. Her collection of toys, on full display in the living room in glass cases, makes me feel like I am in a museum. It's a cool museum, but a museum just the same.
5. Her laugh is starting to bug me. It sounds like a chipmunk laugh.

There's other stuff, but I am starting to sound really crabby. I seem to be talking myself out of being attached to Maddy in any way. Maybe I'm just not ready for a relationship. Perhaps I should have paid attention to:

BABE MAGNET RULE #38
Don't jump into a relationship just because you are lonely and the sex is good.

But then Maddy does something selfless and loving. She gives me a gift—a collector's edition set of bootleg Led Zeppelin concert CDs. It's very thoughtful of her, and it takes me by surprise.

Damn. Now I'm really confused.

Chapter 42: Dancing Queen

It's Friday night, and Maddy wants to go out. "What do you want to do?" I ask.

"Drink and dance," she replies.

She suggests we go to a nightclub called Grand Central Station. It's actually a ginormous place with five different nightclubs inside—Country & Western, Classic Rock, Modern Dance, Karaoke, and a fifth club for people who don't like real music (inside they are blasting out Hip Hop).

Maddy is hot to take me country dancing, so we ease our way into the crowded room full of cowboys and cowgirls. The country-dancing club is the largest of the five rooms, and I am one of the few men who isn't wearing a cowboy hat and boots. Damn! I am dressed for a normal dance club and look like a geek because every other dude looks like Brad Paisley.

Maddy has taken Country & Western dance classes at the local university's Continuing Education program. She has learned the steps to several country dances, and tells me it's easy. "I can show you," she says. "It will be fun."

When the massive sound system blasts a song that she likes, she grabs me by the hand and leads me to the dance floor.

I do not listen to country music, although I am familiar with some of the more popular songs. I know that today's country music isn't just about train wrecks, cheating women who break your heart, and sitting at a bar getting drunk because your old lady ran off with your best friend. Today's country music has gone mainstream, and it deals with topics such as vandalizing your cheating boyfriend's 4x4 pickup truck, reminiscing at a bar over the woman who just left you, and getting shit-faced drunk with your buddies because your girlfriends don't understand how tough it is to be a man. Yep, country music is completely different now.

The only thing I know about country dancing is the Two Step. Not the actual steps—just that it's called the Two Step. Maddy tells me that there are actually four steps.

"Then why do they call it the Two Step?"

"How should I know? Probably because it was invented in Texas by a bunch of drunken cowboys."

We position ourselves at the edge of the crowded dance floor, but immediately we create a traffic jam. The movement on the dance floor is exactly like a NASCAR track. The couples face each other, and the men "drive" the women around the dance floor in counterclockwise ovals. The men get to drive forward, and the women have to drive in reverse. The really good dancers drive really fast. When they have to swerve to avoid Maddy and me, they honk their horns and swear. Maddy and I get lapped 27 times before she can explain the basic steps. We attempt to pull out into traffic, but there is no slow lane on this track, and we are clearly a menace to the other drivers... er, dancers.

I don't know the Two Step, so I shouldn't be too be quick to judge. But based upon the instruction that Maddy gives me, I am not sure she knows the dance very well. At the very least, Maddy is not a very good dance instructor.

After a few minutes of frustration, I pull into the pits and order us a couple of beers. Clearly, I am in over my head tonight. There needs to be a Babe Magnet Rule for a situation like this, so I make one up:

BABE MAGNET RULE #39

Babe Magnets are not afraid to learn something completely new—like dancing. But they are also smart enough to take lessons, so they don't look like total fools.

During the next week, Maddy gets an email confirming her slot in an upcoming series of Country & Western dance classes. She generously gives her spot to me, because she thinks she doesn't need the refresher course as badly as I need to learn the dance steps in the first place. In three weeks, I learn the basic steps of the Two Step, plus a few Country Waltz steps. A week later, I take Maddy back to Grand Central Station.

Maddy is all excited. She has been talking about going dancing with me again ever since I started the classes. She has it in her head that we are going to be a fabulous dancing couple, and that we will go dancing at least once a week for the rest of our lives.

As we merge onto the dance floor, I trade in my cowboy hat for a NASCAR helmet and I start my engine. I start counting the steps out loud for myself and to let Maddy know what beat we'll be starting on: quick, quick, slow, slow. Quick, quick, slow, slow. I lean my torso forward, just like they taught me to do in dancing class, and I start the steps. Quick, quick, slow, slow. Quick, quick, slow, slow. I am doing pretty well. I am hitting my steps right on the beat of the song, and I am walking Maddy around the dance floor. Hey, I'm dancing!

But wait. Something is wrong. The other couples dance past us, and they seem to glide along the floor. They make it look so effortless. Maddy and I are chugging along, and we don't look graceful at all. We look like newborn calves trying to find our legs.

I look down at my feet, and sure enough, I am hitting the beats and moving Maddy around the dance floor. But I look at Maddy's feet, and she is stepping backwards whenever she wants to. She has no clue about stepping to the beat. I have only had three dancing classes and I have the hang of this Two Step. But Maddy, who claims to have been Two Stepping for years, hasn't a clue.

It hits me as we chug along the back straightaway: Maddy is a horrible dancer. Maddy is the worst dancer I have ever danced with. No—Maddy is the worst dancer in the history of the world.

Oh my God! I love to dance—especially when I know what I am doing. But Maddy dances like a deaf woman on drugs. She is oblivious to the music, and oblivious to how bad a dancer she is. I leave the club totally depressed.

This is a problem. I am not kidding—this is a real problem. I refuse to be known as the guy whose woman is the worst dancer in the world.

Chapter 43: Location, Location, Location

Being with Maddy, and especially spending time at Maddy's house, has convinced me that it is time to move out of my one-bedroom bachelor apartment. I am tired of the death metal music blasting from upstairs. I am tired of the lovers' quarrels and loud make-up sex that I can hear through my bedroom wall.

I want to live in a house again. Lord have mercy, I *really* want to live in a house again. (God, I sound like George Bailey in *It's a Wonderful Life.* "Clarence, I want to live again!") But I do want to live—in a house—again. And I don't want to live in Maddy's house. I want to live in my own house. I want to find a place of my own where I can literally feel at home.

So I have started to look at houses. I drive through neighborhoods trying to spot For Sale signs. I stop to take the flyers and look at the pictures of the houses. I imagine myself living in a house with a garden, and maybe even a hot tub. I imagine myself living in a mansion fit for a reality TV show—like *The Bachelor*. While I am at it, I also imagine that I am The Bachelor, and I have 25 beautiful women with perfect teeth and professionally done makeup who all want to go out with me so that they can ultimately earn the honor of my love and my proposal of marriage. And perhaps land on the cover of *People* magazine with a lucrative TV contract.

Then the alarm goes off, and I get up and get ready for work.

In the long days of summer, I find myself cruising through neighborhoods in the late afternoons and early evenings. The Middle-Aged Babe Magnet has turned into a Middle-Aged House Magnet. I call a couple of real estate agents and make appointments to tour houses.

On a Thursday evening after work, I meet Sherrie Perriwinkle, one of the most successful realtors in town. She agrees to meet me at a house that looks interesting—at least from the outside. The house is vacant, and from what I can see, it looks like a fixer-upper. At the very least it needs paint, some routine maintenance, and some serious work in the large backyard. The flyer says it has three bedrooms, two baths, and about 2,000 square feet. But it is sandwiched between two much larger homes with three-car garages, so it might be a good investment.

Sherrie Perriwinkle's face is featured prominently on all of her For Sale signs, and when I meet her in person my first thought is, "You look way better on your signs than you do in real life." Her realtor-sign photos are at least 10 years old, maybe 15. I'm sure she once looked that good and that youthful, but the long hours of driving her Lexus from one house showing to the next have obviously taken their toll. If Sherrie Perri had posted photos that old on her Match.com profile and I was meeting her for a first date, I would be really pissed right now.

But I am meeting Sherrie Perri to check out a house, not to check out her. She turns on the artificial charm and walks me through the house, telling me how wonderful it is and how "it just needs a little work here and there."

The house needs a lot more work than I want to do myself. And there are elements of this house that are just plain ugly and unworkable. The third bedroom is the size of a closet. The kitchen has never been updated, and it would be ugly even if we were still living in *The Brady Bunch* era. I know in a few minutes that this isn't the house I am looking for. But I don't tell Sherrie this in so many words. Instead, I call upon my dating experience.

BABE MAGNET RULE #40

Sometimes social and/or business interactions are a lot like dates. In these cases, be polite, just like you would be on a date. Instead of being brutally honest, be politely honest.

I thank Sherrie and take her card. I tell her that there are many features of the house that I like, such as the backyard, but I just don't think this is the house for me. I am honest, but gentle. But I need not worry about Sherrie Perri's feelings. Realtors, unlike most people on a first date, are used to rejection. Realtors get multiple rejections every day. Sherrie Perri doesn't act the least bit bothered, and she certainly doesn't take it personally. Maybe there's a dating lesson in this, too.

> **BABE MAGNET RULE #41**
> If you go out on a first or second date and you don't "click" with the other person, don't take it personally. It might be that your "recreation area" is too small, or her "basement" is too big. But somebody else is going to think your "recreation area" is perfect. There is a buyer for every house and a perfect mate for every single person.

I do not like Sherrie Perri enough to go on a second real estate "date" with her. But I do agree to go on a first real estate date with Ashley Adams, a friend-of-a-friend of Maddy's.

I meet Ashley at her impressive office, and I like her right away. She is very attractive, with straight brown hair and perfect orthodontist-enhanced teeth. She looks to be in her middle 40s, and her body is fit and slender underneath her tight-fitting yet perfectly appropriate business suit. I am immediately attracted to Ashley, which is a horrible thing because I am romantically involved with her friend.

What's a Babe Magnet in need of a realtor to do? I'll tell you what he does. He stuffs his libido back into his pants and he goes with the Realtor Babe to look at houses. He never lets on that he is attracted to the Realtor Babe who knows his girlfriend. He knows that even thinking about going out on a date with the Realtor Babe is a really bad idea. Nothing good will come of it. Ever. There will be broken hearts and bad feelings and animosity all over town. And on top of that, he won't get himself a house to live in.

During the week I get a call from my ex-wife, Valerie, to discuss Jason's upcoming term at college. In the course of the call, I tell Valerie that I have been looking at houses to buy. I tell her that I haven't seen any houses that I like as well as our old house—which Valerie still lives in with Jason. "If you ever want to sell the house, I would be interested in talking to you about buying it from you," I say.

There is a long pause. Finally, Valerie takes a deep breath and says, "Would you like to come over this weekend and talk about it?"

As it turns out, Valerie is ready to downsize, and she has found a house that she wants to buy. But the only way that can happen is if she sells her house (our old family house) in the next 30 days.

On Saturday, I go over to the house. Zippy the Poodle greets me like I'm a returning war hero. Jason gives me a big hug. Then Valerie and I sit down on the back patio. It feels like *home* for me to be back here.

Valerie has worked out all the numbers, and shows me what she is willing to sell the house for. It is a fair price, and if I buy the house directly from her she won't have to pay realtor commissions. I agree to buy the house, and I promise to call a mortgage banker on Monday.

This is all happening so fast that it doesn't feel quite real. I am moving back to the old family homestead—and I am moving back into my role as a father. Jason will continue to live in the house. Nothing in his bedroom will change at all. But in the master bedroom, his mother will move out and his father will move in.

This is going to be the most comfortable move ever. I will be moving back home. A lot of my stuff is already there, since it didn't fit into my one-bedroom apartment. At the same time, this is going to be an enormous change for me. The Middle-Aged Babe Magnet is going to go back to being a full-time dad—at least until the end of the summer, when Jason goes back to school. And as an added bonus, I even get the dog.

My life is about to take a major change in direction—again.

Chapter 44: Don't Go Breaking My Heart

I am lying in Maddy's bed. It is very early in the morning, and in the darkness I can't see the ceiling fan that is spinning above my head, creating the draft that I detest.

I came over to Maddy's house last night, more out of habit than desire. We ate dinner together (I did the cooking) and then watched TV. We behaved more like an old married couple than lovers. Maddy got tired and went to bed, while I stayed up to watch Letterman's show. By the time I went upstairs, Maddy was already asleep. I slept on one side of the bed while Maddy snoozed on the other.

It's way too early to get up, but I can't fall back to sleep. My brain is already active, thinking about moving into my old house again. I am thinking about what that means to me, my dating life, and my dad life. But, in my masculine mind, I am also pondering the details of the actual move—how I am going to get my stuff from Point A (my apartment) to Point B (my house). How long will it take? It should be a pretty easy process, because there isn't much furniture in my apartment. Plus, my apartment is only a mile away from my new (old) house.

I am looking forward to beginning a new chapter in my life. But lying in Maddy's bed in the pre-dawn darkness, I realize that I do not want Maddy to be part of my life's next chapter. She can be delightful, and she was an important part of my life when I needed a woman to woo and win. But Maddy is my rebound lover, and my rebound is over. Now it's time for me to move on. It sounds cold-blooded, even to me. But I don't want her to be part of my life while I am living with Jason.

Lying in Maddy's bed in the pre-dawn darkness, I face the now-obvious fact that I am going to break up with Maddy.

I am not in love with Maddy. I have never told her that I loved her, because if I had it would not have been the truth. Maddy has never told me that she loves me, but in the past few weeks she has been acting more and more bonded to me. She may be falling in love with me; I don't know for sure. But I do know that her feelings for me run deeper than my feelings for her.

I don't want to break her heart. I really don't. I hate breakups. They suck, whether you are the dumper or the dumpee. Breakups can even be difficult when you are both ready to move on. But it's better to break Maddy's heart now than to break her heart later. The longer our relationship goes on, the worse the breakup is going to be for her.

My mind drifts back to problem solving. I have clothes hanging in Maddy's guest room closet. I am going to have to move them out. I can do that after she leaves for her "girls only" vacation in a couple of days. I will move my clothes and other belongings out of her house when she's away. I will quietly remove the gardening tools that I stored in her garage. I will remove my razor and shaving cream from the bathroom. I will take away all physical items that are mine. But I am not going to cut and run. I am going to sit down with her and look her in the eyes and tell her what is on my heart.

This is one of the most difficult parts of being in a relationship. But just because it's difficult doesn't mean that I am going to run from it.

BABE MAGNET RULE #42

When you break up with someone (and you will have to break up with someone eventually), do it like a man. Tell her face to face if you can, or at the very least on a telephone call. Babe Magnets do not break up via email or text message. Only weenies break up via email, and only assholes break up via text.

I listen to Maddy's relaxed breathing. She is sleeping peacefully. She has no idea that I have just decided to breakup with her.

Maddy has been away on a girls-only vacation for almost a week. She returns in two days. I have rehearsed my breakup speech in my mind, trying to make it sound soft and kind while at the same time sounding decisive and final. It is a delicate path to walk.

Last night I literally tossed and turned. I was lucky if I got a total of two hours of sleep. I agonized over what I was going to say to Maddy. I prepared many possible ways of breaking the news to her, ranging from a soft blow to the relationship equivalent of a nuclear blast.

"We need to talk." (The dreaded pre-breakup line.)

"In fairness to you, I have to let you know how I feel." (A softer version of "We need to talk.")

"I don't want you to think that there's a long-term future for this relationship." (Ouch!)

"I'm just not feeling it." (Ouch light.)

"Maybe we should decide to move on now. Deciding to move on later will only be more painful." (Sounds like a psychologist talking.)

"You deserve someone who loves and cherishes you. Unfortunately, I am not that person." (A kind version of the absolute truth.)

"I need to take some time to figure out what I am looking for." (Wimpy. Come on, Chad, man up.)

"Your butt is too big, and you are the worst dancer EVER." (Mean and totally uncalled for. I slap myself for even thinking this.)

"I need to be free to meet other people and pursue other potential relationships." (Ouch again. She's going to hear this one as, "You aren't good enough for me.")

"I am not in love with you and it's time to move on." (Kaboom!)

The more I think about it, the more convinced I become that I must make a clean break. No wimpiness allowed. I have to be a man and drop the breakup bomb on her—as kindly as possible.

In the morning, I call her cell phone. She doesn't answer, so I leave a soft version of a "we have to talk" message. I don't want to blindside her the moment she steps off the plane tomorrow. I don't want to ruin the last day of her vacation, but I don't want to devastate her when she returns, either.

That plan doesn't work. Maddy hears the tension in my voice and calls me back to find out what I was talking about.

"I didn't want to have this conversation on the phone," I say. But then I tell her what is on my mind and heart. She hangs up so I won't hear her cry.

Oh shit.

I pick Maddy up at the airport the next day. It's not the easy thing to do, but it's the right thing. Her eyes are red from crying. We don't talk much. I don't know what to say that will help her feel better, and I don't want to say anything that will make her feel worse. When we do talk, she asks me "Why?" and "Why now?"

"I thought the longer we were together, the more painful the breakup would be," I explain. "You deserve someone who loves you."

Silence.

"I never expected you to love me," she says. "It's not the same as when you're young. It's not all gooey. It's slower; it's different."

More silence.

I feel like shit. I did not know she was going to take it so hard. I do not tell her, "You're just not the one." Instead, I say, "I'm just not ready."

And just for the record, I want gooey. I want mushy, sloppy, head-over-heels love. I want a Hallmark card relationship with little hearts drawn over the i's in the love notes. I want "I'm thinking of you!" text messages at unexpected times. I want rattle-the-windows and rock-the-world lovemaking sessions that occur spontaneously at all hours of the night and day. And I don't want to settle for anything less.

We arrive at Maddy's house, and I walk her suitcases into the foyer.

"I think I'm going to be sick," she says, and she dashes upstairs. I get myself a glass of water and leave her house key on the kitchen counter. When she comes back downstairs, I give her a goodbye hug.

"I didn't know I was going to get dumped today," she says.

I guess I deserved that.

I drive back to my bachelor apartment, which I still hate. Back when I first met her, Maddy said, "Loneliness sucks," when describing the post-divorce process. She's right, and I have a night of loneliness to look forward to, and many more after tonight.

This is not my favorite part of being single. But tomorrow or the next day or the day after that, I'll dust myself off and get back on the horse and ride.

Chapter 45: A Single Man with Property

I find myself at Barleycorn's (again), having beers and dinner with Karl. I am telling him my breakup story, and he is nodding in agreement. Every middle-aged person has a breakup story or two (sometimes lots of breakup stories), and Karl and I compare notes as I tell him about Maddy.

Karl totally agrees that I did the right thing by proactively breaking up with Maddy. "Hey, if she's not the one, she's not the one," he says, sounding both philosophical and practical. "The longer you wait to break up, the worse it gets."

It's like I am talking to myself. Karl doesn't tell me anything I don't already know, but sometimes life is like a ticket from a parking garage—you just need to get validated.

I tell Karl that I am buying the old house back from Valerie, and he is not nearly as supportive. He thinks buying the old house is a mistake. He thinks I should move forward, not backward.

Karl says that his wife had predicted last year that Valerie would be the first one of us to get remarried. At that time, I would have bet just the opposite. Now it appears that Karl's wife may be right. I think one of the reasons that Valerie was so quick to agree to sell me the house is that she wants to get on with her life. She wants to move into a new space where she can spend time with her new boyfriend, Wimpy McDoofus. She wants a house where my vibes and my memories don't permeate the place.

I met Mr. McDoofus once when I stopped by the old house to visit Jason, and he (Wimpy) seems nice enough. He's a friend of a friend of somebody Valerie met at church. He drives a Honda and he has a white-collar job. He's a caricature of a white, middle class, middle-aged American male. I'm sure he's Republican, pays his income taxes on time, and has never gotten a speeding ticket. He smiled a lot and treaded lightly around me.

I really don't know if he's a Wimpy McDoofus or not, but it's okay for me to not like my ex-wife's new boyfriend. Even though I wish them both well. Really. I just don't want Valerie to be happier than I am—at least for now.

But as I explain to Karl, I need to go back and deal with the elements of the divorce that I avoided. For me, moving back to the old house will give me a taste of my old life while I process my feelings, deal with unresolved emotions, and prepare for a new relationship. Plus, it's the best way I can think of to reclaim my fatherhood responsibilities. With the stroke of a pen and the transfer of thousands of dollars, I will become Jason's primary parent—at least for the rest of the summer, until he goes back to college.

I know that living in the old house will be strange, and in many ways it will be bittersweet. But it has to be better than living alone in an apartment.

I need to be home. I need to feel at home again. I can't find the next love of my life if I am not comfortable with myself, so I am hoping that moving a step backwards will help catapult me forward.

BABE MAGNET RULE #43
A Babe Magnet needs to get his own house in order—literally and metaphorically—before he can attract a worthy Babe.

Almost exactly nineteen years ago, Valerie and I signed papers to buy the house at 1492 Calypso Street. It was pouring rain, and the street outside the title company's office was beginning to flood. Now it's déjà-vu all over again. I sit snugly inside the Homestead Title Co. building as a fierce thunderstorm rages outside. I can hear the rain pounding on the roof, and thunder periodically rocks the building right down to its foundation.

I do not know if the storm is a sign from God that I am doing the absolutely wrong thing, or if He's just messing with me. Or, it could just be a really bizarre coincidence.

Whatever the meaning of the storm, I do not let it stop me from buying the house. I sign papers with a blue-ink pen that legally transfers ownership of 1492 Calypso Street from Valerie Stone, single person, to Chad Stone, single person. As I sign legal form after legal form, I wonder how often a person buys the same house twice. Probably about as often as a person marries the same spouse twice.

I am going to move into the new/old house in one week, right after Valerie moves out. Jason and his furniture will stay in his bedroom, but almost everything else in the house will change. It is a strange situation, but nothing in my life feels quite normal right now.

It is yet another new adventure.

Chapter 46: Middle-Aged Dad

I am excited about moving back home. I am excited to be living with Jason again and seeing him every day.

Jason is now 19, and like most young males he does not reveal his feelings easily or openly. His tendency is to not say anything unless he's asked a direct question. If he is still upset with me for divorcing his mother, he doesn't tell me about it. If he is upset with me for buying the house, he doesn't say anything about that, either. If he would rather not swap custodial parents, he never says a word.

Instead of calling a moving company, I decide that it will be a better father-and-son bonding experience if Jason helps me move furniture from my apartment back to the house. Jason doesn't seem to have a problem with this. If anything, he seems to like the idea of being actively involved in moving my stuff into the house. I take that as his tacit approval. I tell him that I am really excited to be moving back.

"I've missed you, and I'm looking forward to seeing you every day," I say.

"Me, too."

And that's two men, getting all mushy and emotional.

Jason and I make several runs in my full-size pickup truck to move my couch, bed, dining table and chairs, TV, end tables, and other furniture. He helps me pack up my kitchen utensils. The rest of the details, including getting all of my clothes moved in and cleaning my apartment, I can handle on my own during the next week.

The transformation literally happens in one day. Presto! Dad is back! I have bought myself a house, and I have bought myself back into Jason's daily life. At the moment, I think it's a brilliant strategic move. I get most of my old life back, minus the ex-wife. I even get primary custody of Zippy the Poodle, who has lived his entire life in this house.

Sure, this means that I will choose to put my dating life on hold for a while. But the Babes can wait. There will always be Babes out there in Babeland. My son will only be home from college for a short time, and if I don't take advantage of this window in time, it will be gone forever.

BABE MAGNET RULE #44

Sometimes the smartest thing a Babe Magnet can do is to NOT troll for Babes. This is especially true when Babe-related activities would jeopardize your relationship with your kids.

I have a new focus now. I am putting Chad Stone, Middle-Aged Babe Magnet on semi-hiatus. I am still a single, middle-aged man, and I may go out on an occasional date. But for the rest of the summer, my primary title will be Chad Stone, Dad.

Jason and I quickly develop a manly man routine. I get up early during the work week and go to the office, leaving Jason and Zippy at the house. Jason, who has completely adapted to the college lifestyle, gets up at the crack of 12:30 p.m. and begins nonstop eating. Sometimes I come home for lunch to say hello and visit with him.

I know how hard he worked during his first year in college. Then he came home and worked a six-week job as a student teacher during the summer program at his high school alma mater. During my tenure as primary parent in the second half of the summer, I cut him a lot of slack and let him have a vacation as best as I can. I put up with his slobbery and he puts up with my parenting. We eat dinner together whenever our schedules allow—usually several times a week.

I immensely enjoy being the parent-in-residence, and I can tell that Jason enjoys the chance to spend casual time with me. We go see summer blockbuster movies that feature comic superheroes and massive explosions. We jam on our electric instruments (me on guitar and Jason on bass). We hang out on the back patio with Zippy, and grudgingly allow Charlie, the neighborhood cat, to join us.

We have father and son time that unfolds naturally as our lives coexist. Sometimes Jason goes off with friends from high school and leaves me to eat dinner alone. Sometimes I go out for a beer with Karl or Craig or my newest male friend, Mueller. A couple of times I go out on "meet and greet" dates that don't lead anywhere. I let the summer unfold as it may. My summer with Jason is like a lazy river that flows where it wants to go, and it cannot be forced.

The best part of the summer is our trip to New York City during Labor Day week. I decide to start a father-and-son tradition—an annual Big Summer Vacation Trip to Someplace Really Cool. Jason has always enjoyed visiting big cities, so I pick the biggest city in America. We spend a glorious week in The Big Apple, and we both get to do virtually everything we want.

We ride subway cars and visit museums. We eat in fun and bizarre restaurants. We walk through Central Park and visit the Imagine memorial to John Lennon. We see a taping of *Late Night with David Letterman.* (The guests are former President Bill Clinton, who has just written a new book, and Patti Scialfa—Mrs. Bruce Springsteen. We spot Bruce and Patti getting into their limo at the stage door entrance). We see a taping of Conan O'Brien's *Late Late Show*. Jason spends hours in one of the best comic book shops in the country while I take a walking tour of Midtown Manhattan. We hobnob with the professional tennis players who are in town for the U.S. Open. We walk through Little Italy and the Village. We even travel to the top of the Empire State Building at night for a view that's breathtaking no matter how many times you've seen it.

The trip is the perfect exclamation point at the end of a great father-son summer.

My alarm screams at me at 4:20 a.m. That's too damn early to get up for anyone who does not have to milk cows, deliver newspapers, or run the city's snowplow after a winter storm. I run through the shower, and then I walk down the hall to wake Jason up. He is flying back to college this morning, and I know there isn't a Popsicle's chance in hell of him waking up on his own.

Jason's summer at home is over. He stayed up until 3:00 a.m. last night, packing everything he could fit into a large suitcase and an oversized cardboard box. He knows that the airline's weight limit is 50 pounds per item, and he has deftly gotten the suitcase to weigh in at 49 pounds and the box to weigh in at 48.5.

We drive in virtual silence to the airport because Jason is still mostly asleep, and I don't know what to say. He is beside me in the truck, but I am already missing him.

It's still dark, and almost no one is on the road. I pity the people who are driving to work at this ungodly hour of the morning. I am glad that I only see this hour on a rare day when I am heading to the airport. I am sorry that I am going to the airport now, because it means I won't be coming back home with Jason.

We park in the garage and walk to the Delta Airlines counter. I roll the enormous suitcase and Jason carries his enormous cardboard box. With tickets to Boulder, Colorado, safely in Jason's pocket, we walk to the entrance of security. When Jason was in elementary school, not that many years ago, I would have walked him to the gate. In the post 9/11 world, I can't accompany him past the wall of TSA security personnel.

I give Jason a big, manly hug. "I love you," I say, making sure I don't tear up. "Take good care of yourself."

"I love you too, Dad."

And he's gone.

Chapter 47: A Festival of Red Flags

Jason has been back at college for two weeks now, and my house feels like a morgue. Living with my son for two months was wonderful, but living without him, all alone in this big house, is lonely. It's time for me to get my butt out there in the real world again and start having some fun.

I am ready to go out. I am ready to hang out with friends and watch highly paid professional athletes play sporting games. Maybe I can even dust off my Middle-Aged Babe Magnet skills and meet a few women.

I put on my best jeans and my only pair of cowboy boots and go to the Wednesday evening dance classes at Cowboy's nightclub, not far from my house. For eight dollars I can take two dance classes and dance with 20 or 30 different women.

Cowboy's looks exactly like what a nightclub called Cowboy's should look like. The décor, if you can call it décor, is completely rustic wood. The walkway from the parking lot to the club is wood. The swinging entrance doors are solid wood. The large wooden dance floor, which is located in the middle of the club with a wooden stage on one side and seating on the other three sides, is framed off with a wooden guardrail. When you are enjoying a drink while watching the dancers on the dance floor, it almost seems like you are watching a rodeo.

The dance classes are popular because they are inexpensive, and they give beginners a chance to learn a few dance steps in a safe and friendly environment. Tonight there are about 25 men and about 30 women. The men line up on one side of the dance floor and the women line up on the other. The male instructor, Tim, gives the men a beginning lesson on the Two-Step, while the female instructor, Sonja, gives the women their beginning lesson. Then we pair up and try to dance the steps. After a couple minutes, we change partners and continue dancing. Tim the Dance Instructor says that you learn to dance much faster with different partners, so he switches us up regularly.

Thanks to the six-week Country & Western dance class I took a few months ago (back in the Maddy era), tonight's lesson is review for me. I feel good about knowing the basics of the Two Step, and it feels good to be on a dance floor again. From across the room, I recognize one of the women from the Continuing Education classes. I don't remember her name, so when we get paired up to practice the dance steps, I introduce myself and remind her that we were in the same dance classes.

"I remember you," she says, smiling. "My name is Elizabeth."

Elizabeth was the most attractive woman in my age group in the previous Country & Western dance classes. She has short dark hair, big brown eyes, and a smile that could light up Connecticut. For a 50-ish woman she still has a very trim figure. She is dressed in a tight-fitting red sweater and jeans.

We chat amiably while we dance. But too soon we have to move on to the next partner. After the dance class is over, I walk over and ask Elizabeth to dance. She smiles. I take her hand and walk her over to an open spot on the dance floor. For the next three minutes we do a fairly good job of a beginning two-step. Nothing fancy, but we don't trip over each other, and we don't create any traffic jams for the folks who really know how to dance. Unlike Maddy, Elizabeth understands the concept of stepping to the music. She is a delightful dance partner.

Elizabeth has to leave after a couple of songs, so I walk her to her car. All the while, we talk and get to know each other. It's a "meet and greet" date that isn't a date, at least not officially. I admit that I am out of practice, but it *feels* like a date—and it feels great.

We cover many of the "first date meet and greet" topics. Elizabeth acts as though I am the most interesting person in the world. She takes in every word. She nods and smiles and holds eye contact with me. I love it. Elizabeth is making me feel very manly right now. If you're a single woman interested in getting to know a man, this is exactly how you are supposed to behave.

When we arrive beside her car, I get her phone number and suggest that we go out dancing to practice what we've just learned.

"That would be great," she says, never taking her eyes off me.

"I'll call you," I say. "Soon."

Elizabeth is beautiful, articulate, and a good beginning dancer. I will definitely call her. In fact, I will call her tomorrow.

A few days later, I pick up Elizabeth for our first official date. Her house is in the foothills in an upscale neighborhood full of impressive homes with three-car garages. Elizabeth meets me at the door and flashes her delightful smile. She looks great, but not as great as I remember her looking at Cowboy's. In her brightly lit foyer, she looks older and her arms look chunky in her sleeveless blouse. But that's just me being overly critical, and quite frankly, it doesn't matter. I am feeling a good vibe from her, and I am looking forward to dancing with her again.

On the drive to Cowboy's, we share some family history. Elizabeth was raised Catholic, and she still believes. She attends Mass every week. I was raised Protestant. So we share some common beliefs. She is one of 13 kids. That's 12 brothers and sisters with the same mother and father! No blended-family stepkids. Holy Rhythm Method! Can you imagine buying Christmas presents for everyone in that family? You'd have to take out a second mortgage. I have only one brother, so I am used to a small family. Thirteen kids? That's just freakin' weird, and I find it intimidating.

I psyche myself up for an evening of Country & Western dancing. As the man, I have to be the leader on the dance floor. Dancing is one of the few remaining places in the Western world where the man is the undisputed leader. In a pairing of dancers, the man leads and the woman follows. Period, end of discussion. Unfortunately, I don't know many steps and turns. So most of my leading is me driving Elizabeth around the dance floor. And most of our country waltz is me waltzing her around the dance floor without any fancy moves. (I still have to count out the steps: ONE, two three, FOUR, five six).

As we dance, we chat. Elizabeth has been married twice and has kids from both marriages. She got married right after high school when she got pregnant. So she had premarital sex AND she's been divorced twice. In the Catholic Universe, doesn't that mean she's going to hell? Wait a minute ... doesn't that mean she's going to hell THREE TIMES?

There are a few red flags waving at me that are trying to warn me about Elizabeth. Even so, I enjoy dancing with her. We laugh. We touch each other on the arms when talking, the way two people do when they're getting to know each other and they feel the spark of a connection starting.

I take her out for a light after-dancing meal. Elizabeth starts telling me about her new home-based business. It's a multi-level marketing "opportunity" that involves getting people to switch their telephone service. She gets all excited while telling me about it, and I have the depressing thought that the only reason she agreed to go out with me was to try to sell me phone service. I try to ignore the red flag waving at me that says, "Ask Me How I Can Save You Money On Your Phone Service."

We drive back to her house and she invites me in for a glass of wine. Instead of sitting inside (her teenage son is in his bedroom upstairs), we sit out on her back patio. It is a lovely night and the stars are speaking to me. In the darkness, I cannot see the new red flag that appears when she tells me that her ex-husband (who may or may not actually be "ex") is still making her mortgage payment—and all of her other payments.

"It's complicated getting a divorce in the Catholic Church," she says, "especially when you've already had two divorces."

Now there is a festival of red flags in her backyard. It looks like a May Day parade in Moscow, back when everyone in Russia was a Communist.

She has rendered me speechless. I am wondering how I can excuse myself from her backyard and right out of her life. This date has gone from pleasant to downright scary.

Just when I think it can't get any worse, Elizabeth looks me in the eye and says, "So, are you happy with your current phone service?"

BABE MAGNET RULE #45
Run, Chad! Run!

Chapter 48: We Should Be Dancin'

Unfortunately, I didn't go dancing enough in the past few months to reinforce the steps that I learned. Now I've forgotten so much that I have lost confidence in my ability to dance—and that's the kiss of death when, as the man, I have to lead. So, I have signed up to repeat the six-week Country & Western Dance class from the university's Continuing Education Department.

The dance classes are therapy for me on several levels. There's the dancing part, of course. The physical act of moving my body in specific ways is good physical therapy. There is also the social aspect. Humans are inherently social creatures, and it is especially important for men to have regular social contact with other people. Men (myself included), can get used to hanging out in their "man caves" and shutting out the world. Interacting with a large roomful of new people is great social therapy. I get to meet a few new guys, and I get to meet and interact with many new women. That's a healthy activity whether you are a self-proclaimed Babe Magnet or not.

By week three, some of us have gotten friendly enough to go to Cowboy's to practice dancing after class. Our group includes Jackie (an ER nurse), Tiffany (a young lady who works at two retail jobs to be able to afford her first home), Al (a mid 40s guy who owns a fully restored 1961 pickup truck), Heather (a mid 30s office manager for a construction company) and Bob (who is a nice middle-class guy I know nothing about).

After class, we all drive our respective cars to the club. I find the others clustered together at a table near the dance floor. Al pulls up a chair for me and I settle in with my new friends.

I have gotten accustomed to going to clubs alone, because most of my friends are either married or not interested in going out much. So having a group of single friends to hang with is a real luxury. It is wonderful for us beginners to have other beginners to dance with, and it is wonderful to have a place to just sit and talk.

We talk, we dance, we sit, we laugh, and we drink. Basically, we own the place. I notice that our group, constantly ebbing and flowing as dancers come and go, attracts quite a bit of attention. As people pass by, they look over to see who is having so much fun. We say hello, and in a short time we seem to know everyone on our side of the club. Even the other women, who are normally so reticent to engage a strange man in conversation, will talk with us because we are already in the presence of women.

I've seen this happen before. Women trust the opinions of other women. If a man is in the company of a woman, other women are inclined to think he is worthy of their attention. The presence of a woman is an unspoken endorsement that communicates, "This guy is okay."

This is worthy of a Babe Magnet Rule:

BABE MAGNET RULE #46

B.Y.O.B. (Bring Your Own Babes) whenever possible. This is even true in a Babe-rich environment such as a nightclub, because Babes attract other Babes.

When we are not chatting with each other or with our new club friends, we all take turns dancing with each other. That is to say, the men from the class dance with the women from the class. Sometimes one of us will even dance with someone new. But I spend most of the time dancing with Tiffany. She has straight brown hair and the body of a 26-year-old, because that's how old she is. And she is an absolute delight: smart, articulate, and good-natured. She's the youngest of our group, and yet she's perfectly comfortable hanging out with us older folks.

Dancing with Tiffany is fun for me. I am self-aware enough to know that her age has something to do with how she makes me feel. Before, I never really understood why so many older men go out with younger women. Oh, sure, they are beautiful and their skin is flawless. But there is more to life than youth. As I spend time with Tiffany, though, I notice that her youthfulness is rubbing off on me. Simply being in her presence has filled me with some of her youthful energy.

I'm not sure I have ever enjoyed going out to a club more than I have tonight. But, alas, after a full day of work, followed by the 90-minute dancing class and a couple of hours of dancing "in the wild," I am exhausted. Just before 11:00 p.m. I say my goodbyes. Tiffany is ready to leave, too, so I walk her through the dark parking lot to her car. "Thanks for coming out dancing with us," she says. "It's really great that you're willing to do that."

At first I don't quite know what she means. Then I realize she's commenting on my age in a way that is meant to be a compliment. She's saying that it's great that someone AS OLD AS I AM is willing to go out to a dance club with a group of younger people.

Holy Geritol. I didn't feel old all night until right at this moment.

Chapter 49: No, She's NOT My Daughter

Tiffany the Young Babe and I have turned out to be pretty good friends. She is my favorite person at the Country & Western dance class, and she is my favorite dance partner during the class and afterwards when we go to Cowboy's. Once, she even came by my house on the way to dance class (it really was on her way), and I drove us to class, to Cowboy's for dancing, and then back to my house to get her car. When I offered her a glass of wine she accepted, and we sat on my back patio and talked for half an hour.

As Halloween night approaches, there's talk of getting a group of dancing class friends together to go out. But one by one the others drop out, and soon it's just Tiffany and me. I fully expect Tiffany to politely reschedule, but she hasn't yet.

I decide to call her to make sure we're still on. "Do you still want to go to the costume party at Cowboy's?"

"Yes I do," she replies. "Thank you for asking."

So now the casual group outing of dancing friends has turned into a quasi-date alone with a woman who is half my age. I must admit that my male ego is proud, and I am flattered that Tiffany would even consider being seen with me. But my practical side already sees the potential problems. Like this:

"It's so great of you to bring your daughter to this party," says a friendly, well-meaning Babe-alicious woman Tiffany's age.

"She's not my daughter, she's my date."

"Oh MY GOD!! That's just SO creepy!" says the horrified young Babe. She grabs her friend and they sprint out of the club, screaming, "There's a PERVERT in there, RUN!"

Okay, so that's not going to happen. But people might *think* that.

There's also the dilemma that the age difference presents in our common experiences. I was born during the Eisenhower administration. Tiffany was born when Ronald Reagan was president. I like to listen to classic rock. Tiffany wasn't born until after all the really good classic rock had been created. I remember when Michael Jackson (God rest his soul) was black. Tiffany doesn't know that Michael Jackson was in a singing group called the Jackson 5, nor does she understand the hardship of living life before cable TV, cell phones, iPods, microwave ovens, and those little red buttons that pop out to let you know your Thanksgiving turkey is done.

On Halloween night, Tiffany arrives at my front door dressed like the girl from *Flashdance*. She is the perfect 1980s Babe, complete with poofed-out hair, lots of makeup, an off-the-shoulder shirt, and knit leggings. She looks pretty damn hot, actually. I never would have thought to go as an '80s character. But to Tiffany, who isn't old enough to have actually dressed in '80s clothes, looking like *Flashdance* IS a Halloween costume. I, meanwhile, am dressed as a mafia hitman, with a black suit, white tie, and white fedora. Together, we make quite a bizarre couple.

So I, the mafia don, drive the 1980s Babe in my newly purchased, previously owned BMW sedan to a nightclub called Cowboy's. If that's not a bunch of mixed themes, I don't know what is. Once we get to the club, we fit right in. Sure, there are lots of decked-out cowboys and sexy cowgirls, but there is every other costume imaginable, too.

Tiffany and I settle into a tiny table in the corner. We enjoy a couple of drinks, we check out all the other costumes, and we dance. I am having a wonderful time, and so is she. It is easy to forget that there is such a dramatic difference in our ages.

We are ready to leave the club just after midnight, so I drive her back to my house to get her car. We're both tired, but Tiffany doesn't seem quite ready to leave.

"Would you like a glass of wine?" I offer.

She smiles and says yes.

So we sit on my couch, a safe distance apart, sipping wine and talking. A little voice in my Middle-Aged Babe Magnet brain says to me, "Hey, this is the youngest woman you've ever been out with while you've been middle-aged and single. You may never have a chance again to kiss a woman in her 20s. You should go for it."

The voice seems to be coming from my right ear. When I glance in that direction, I see a little Middle-Aged Babe Magnet devil perched on my shoulder, grinning at me.

"You're not going to listen to *him*, are you?" says a voice in my left ear. I look over and see a little Middle-Aged Babe Magnet angel standing on my left shoulder.

"You're a big fat weenie who doesn't have the gonads to move in for a kiss!" says the Middle-Aged Babe Magnet devil.

Now they start arguing amongst themselves.

"She's sitting on the couch drinking wine, isn't she?" asks the little devil.

"Yes she is," says the angel.

"Nobody is forcing her to be here, right?" asks the devil.

"Well, no," says the angel.

"And he has behaved like a perfect gentleman all night, right?" asks the devil.

"Yes, I am proud to say that he has," says the angel.

"And she's still here. She looks quite happy, doesn't she?" asks the devil.

"Yes, she does. She looks almost angelic, if I may say so."

The little devil then sticks his face in my ear and yells at me, "THEN KISS HER, YOU WEENIE!"

Well, she *is* just sitting there, as if she is waiting for something to happen. I guess it wouldn't hurt to see if she's waiting for something *like that* to happen. If she screams or slaps me, I could always blame it on Alzheimer's.

WHAT AM I THINKING? SHE IS HALF MY AGE!

"I love your costume," I say, loudly, so I can drown out the chatter in my head. "You should wear your hair like that all the time." She laughs. "So, tell me something about yourself that I don't already know," I say. "Something important."

Tiffany tells me about the breakup of her marriage. She got married at 21, and it only lasted two years. She's been divorced for three years, and she says it's been a difficult time. She hasn't been in a relationship since—and she hasn't had sex.

No sex in three years? She's only 26. She's in the prime of her sexual life—and she's celibate? She's such a great young woman, so that strikes me as sad.

"I haven't really missed it," she says. "I guess I've been afraid of getting hurt."

I look at her, and the confident 26-year-old has turned into a frightened girl. The fact that she feels comfortable enough to tell me all of this is a tremendous compliment. I am honored by her trust. But I am also intensely aware of my responsibility to her. I am not going to do anything to hurt this woman. My paternal instincts take over, and I want to protect this young lady's fragile heart from any further pain.

I tell her that she will find true love again. I tell her that she doesn't have to be afraid anymore. I tell her to keep her heart open and keep looking.

Then I give her a hug and send her on her way.

Chapter 50: Where Singles Go to Mingle

I have a new affirmation: "I am a Babe Magnet, and I meet beautiful women wherever I go." As I believe it to be true, so it is. To put this new belief to the test, I decide to attend the *City Magazine* Annual Singles Extravaganza.

City Magazine is a young, hip publication that is trying to succeed as the metro area's go-to source for all things trendy and urban. The fact that it's a print publication in an increasingly digital world, and the fact that our fine city is really just an overgrown small town in the middle of nowhere, does not appear to be relevant to *City Magazine*. It seems to be succeeding in its goal to be a cool force in the city. I guess that's more evidence for the power of affirmations.

Anyway, the magazine has been promoting its Annual Singles Extravaganza for weeks. As a subscriber to the magazine, I was sent a free admission ticket (a $10 value!). I couldn't find anyone else who wanted to go to the event with me. "That sounds lame" and "We're too old for that" were some of the responses I received. It's true that the "Top 10 City Singles" who were profiled in the magazine are all younger than me. But I can't be the only middle-aged person who is willing to go to a big singles party, right?

The party is being held at the Hispanic Cultural Center, a new facility that was built with generous donations from major corporations and governmental entities. I can't help but think that a Caucasian Cultural Center would not have benefited from any politically correct funding. I decide to dress up for the event. I wear a sport coat, dress shirt, dress slacks, and leather dress shoes. I am the epitome of a businessman—without the tie.

When I arrive at the venue and troll through the parking lot to find a space, I am glad I dressed up. The parking lot is filled with women in fancy party dresses and men in sport coats. Everyone looks considerably younger than me. The young women are decked out in black dresses with plunging necklines that reveal matching sets of perfect breasts. They (the women, not their breasts) are perched on six-inch stiletto heels that get caught in the uneven spots in the asphalt parking lot. Their salon-styled hair and party makeup must have taken hours to perfect. Their breasts probably took a lot of fluffing up, too.

It takes 20 minutes just to get through the crowds trying to get in. Our photo IDs are checked, and we are given wristbands to prove that we are old enough to drink. When I whip out my wallet to prove I am over 21, the nice young lady laughs and says, "I guess I may as well check it..." That's right, honey. I *am* old enough to drink—with 30 years to spare.

Everything about this event is impressive. A jazz band greets us with music as we enter the main ballroom. Satin bunting is draped everywhere. The tables are covered with white tablecloths and candles. One wall of the large room is set up as a shadow box projection of go-go dancers. Through the frosted glass you can see the silhouettes of bikini-clad Babes doing 1960s style dancing.

Eating and drinking stations are placed strategically around the complex. Crowds of well-dressed singles are already gathered around the refreshment stations, waiting to get Thai chicken on a stick or a sample of the latest flavors of fruity liqueurs. Everyone seems to be in a festive mood.

Even though the place is packed, I can see right away that it's going to be difficult to work this event alone. There are virtually no single singles; everyone is clumped together with their friends. They talk and check out the other attendees from the safety of their own little groups.

No matter. I am going to have a good time tonight. I walk through the crowds, smiling and saying "hi" to people as I go. I chat with dozens of total strangers, but I don't have any meaningful conversations or make any real progress toward my goal of leaving with at least one Babe's phone number.

After we've all had a chance to get liquored up, an overexcited man appears onstage to announce that the Fabulous Charity Auction of Eligible Singles is about to begin! Well, nobody told me I was going to be auctioned off (ha!). The only time I have ever seen an auction of single people is in the Bill Murray film *Groundhog Day*, which was released before most of these party animals were born.

The first person to be auctioned off is a 28-year-old woman who works at an advertising agency. She's a Babe, and she goes for $575 dollars. That's a lot of money to spend on a first date.

The next single up for auction is a 36-year-old man who clearly thinks he is hot stuff. He is short and not very attractive, and when the bids are slow to come he starts working the crowd in that lame way that people do when they think they are hot shit but really aren't. Bad stand-up comedians do the same thing. A "lucky" lady gets a date with him for $179.

The auction gives me a chance to engage women in friendly conversation as we make comments about the auctionees. I have a spirited chat with an attractive short-haired woman who looks about 45. Just when I am getting hopeful that this encounter might turn into something, her boyfriend comes back to whisk her away. Wait a minute, isn't coming to a singles party with your boyfriend illegal?

After they auction off all the young singles, they throw in a token Old Guy. He is five years younger than me. Ouch.

I am thinking about going home to my couch to watch *Saturday Night Live* with my loving and trusty poodle. Instead, I stroll over to a twosome of Babes to strike up a conversation. "Hello, lovely ladies. Are you having a good time tonight?" I say, because all of my good opening lines are at the cleaner's. But I say it with a smile and a twinkle in my eye. Cool and confident.

BABE MAGNET RULE #47

An ordinary opening line delivered with confidence and genuine charm is better than a really great one-liner delivered with creepiness.

It doesn't matter what I say, because both of the women came to the Annual Singles Extravaganza to talk to men, and they are all by themselves. I am a man, so talking to me is better than not talking to me.

Anna Rodriguez introduces herself first. She has black hair and Hispanic features, which makes sense for someone named Rodriguez. She is all of five foot two, but her little body is absolutely perfect. She's probably in her mid to late 40s, and her olive-colored skin is gorgeous. She's cool, and she doesn't smile unless she really means it.

Her friend is also named Anna, which is great because now I can talk to two women and only have to remember one name. Anna Number Two has Caucasian features, with reddish-brown hair and freckles. She's friendly, but she almost immediately starts talking about her boyfriend. Instant red flag here—my bet is that she and her boyfriend are about to break up even though it isn't her idea. At least she had the decency to tell me right away. I focus my charm and attention on Anna R.

Anna R. is impressed that I had the confidence to walk up to the two Annas and initiate a conversation, and she tells me so. (See, I told you the importance of confidence.) As far as I can tell, I had her at "Hello."

We talk for 15 minutes, sharing what I now refer to as "the highlights of our dating resumes" in a question-and-answer format. (What brings you here? Are you really single and unattached? Have you been married and/or divorced? What kind of work do you do? What part of town do you live in? How do you like this party? Etc.) We don't run out of things to chat about, and I get her to smile often enough to stroke my ego. I ask for her phone number, and she writes it on the back of one of my business cards. I have a pocketful of cards for this very reason. I give her a fresh one to keep, and I promise to call her.

Success! I have my Babe phone number. Now I can stroll around for a few minutes to see if I can get a backup number. A short blonde woman, also about five foot two, laughs when I ask her if she comes here often. It's such a stupid line that it works. Her name is Tracy, and she works for the public school system. We end up having a very friendly conversation, which culminates in me getting her phone number.

There is a bounce in my step as I walk to my car. Mission accomplished.

Chapter 51: Battle of the Five Foot Twos

My natural high from meeting Anna R. and Tracy at the singles party lasts for more than a week. I am in the enviable position of having two nice dating prospects. Based upon the fact that I am convinced that each one is suitable girlfriend material, I feel as though my dating luck has finally changed for the better.

I feel like a bona fide Babe Magnet.

I talk to Anna and Tracy on the phone a couple of times, but arranging dates turns out to be more difficult than I expected. Middle-aged American adults have work and multiple other responsibilities, and we tend to fill up our schedules with additional projects and activities. We don't have any "free" time. It's as if we are afraid of spending any time not doing something—anything. We have forgotten how to be *human beings.* We have become *human doings.*

Both Anna and Tracy chose to go to the *City Magazine* Annual Singles Extravaganza, but they didn't plan for the dates that might follow. That's worth remembering as:

> **BABE MAGNET RULE #48**
> It's difficult to attract a Babe into your life if your life is already full. If you want to attract a date, make room in your schedule. If you want to attract a lover, make room in your bed. If you want to attract a live-in significant other, make room in your closet.

Almost two weeks pass before I meet Anna for our first official date.

Anna lives on the far side of town, so being a gentleman, I schedule a lunch date reasonably close to where she lives. I arrive promptly and wait for her. And wait some more. Finally, she calls.

"I'm at the Jupiter Moon, where are you?" she asks, unapologetically.

"I'm here. Where are you?"

It turns out that she went to the wrong Jupiter Moon restaurant. I wait some more, flipping through the free weekly newspaper in search of ideas for future dates. Anna arrives almost 45 minutes late, and I forgive her only because her tardiness gives me something to good-naturedly tease her about.

Anna seems quite sure of herself. She works as the office manager for an architectural design firm, and she dresses well and cares about her physical appearance. The good news is, she looks great. The possible downside is that she might be a high maintenance woman who needs a lot of prep time to get ready to venture out into public. That could be a problem, because I gave up on high-maintenance women many years ago.

We talk about work, and we talk about dating. Anna has never tried online dating. In fact, she seems fundamentally opposed to it. Plus, in her words, she has "never needed it." Anna was married for many years, and has two daughters in their early 20s. One is married and lives in Arizona; the other is a senior at the local university. After Anna got divorced, she was in an eight-year relationship that ended before they got married. Most recently, she was engaged to be married to another man, but they broke up before the wedding. Anna tells me all of this with an emotionless, matter-of-fact delivery that makes it sound like she is talking about someone else.

Our lunch goes well, and I automatically pick up the check because of:

BABE MAGNET RULE #49

The man always pays for the first date. And the second and third. Probably the fourth and the fifth, too. In fact, you can pretty much expect to pay for everything until you and your Babe are in a committed relationship. A Babe needs to feel adored and cherished, and paying for dates is one sure-fire way to communicate that to her.

I like Anna, even though she is a little reserved. I really have to be "on" with her, because she doesn't project a lot of natural energy. That could be because we're still getting to know each other. We'll see.

Tracy is so busy that she is almost never available to do anything else. We finally meet for a casual lunch, and we both have a good time. It turns out that Tracy's passion is tennis. She is in at least two different tennis leagues, and she plays in tournaments all the time. I played tennis for a while, but that was 10 years ago. I can't muster much enthusiasm for a sport that I am not involved in. But if I continue to date Tracy, I foresee some tennis in my future. Perhaps lots of tennis.

I like Tracy. There are no fireworks or sparks of instant passion or anything I can breathlessly report to *People* magazine or TMZ.com. But Tracy and I get along well enough for me to ask her out on a second date.

Tracy seems more down-to-earth than Anna. She projects a natural beauty that doesn't rely on makeup or perfect salon-styled hair. I like her practical, uncomplicated vibe, and I am looking forward to seeing her again. But when the specified time for our second date arrives, she isn't there. I wait for 15 minutes and then call her cell phone.

"Didn't you get my email?" she asks.

Nope. I haven't checked my email since yesterday. My bad.

"I had to cancel, something came up," she says. "I'm really sorry."

I am, too. But at least when you've got two active Babe prospects, it's not an ego-crushing experience when one of them cancels a date.

Meanwhile, I take Anna to see a movie for our second date. The film is called *Across the Universe*, and it features a soundtrack full of Beatles songs. Anna is very gracious and pretends to like the show. Out in the parking lot after the movie, Anna and I share our first kiss. Or, rather, Anna is gracious enough to allow her lips to touch mine for a nanosecond.

As all Babes and Babe Magnets know, not all kisses are created equal. There are tentative kisses exchanged between two people who don't know each other yet. There are air kisses, which are the currency at cocktail parties and fundraisers. There are friendly kisses exchanged by longtime spouses. And then there are passionate, full-body-contact kisses that emit pheromone fumes powerful enough to strip the paint off walls.

The tiny first kiss between Anna and me is not what I was hoping for. It is a "runt of the litter" kiss. It is a kiss that says, "I didn't want to give you a real kiss, but I felt obligated."

I look at Anna's face, which is totally devoid of passion. "That's the kind of kiss you give your grandpa," I say.

She smiles wanly. But that is the only kiss I get.

After she stands me up and/or cancels on short notice (depending upon how you look at it), Tracy and I reschedule our date. She mentions on the phone that she is playing tennis four times this week. Perhaps that's why she's single: she's dating a tennis racquet. Anyway, we are finally able to agree on a date, time, and place.

But two days before our scheduled date, Craig makes me an offer I can't refuse.

"Hey, buddy, I have an extra ticket to the basketball game on Friday. Would you like to join Brad and me? We could do barbecue and brews before the game."

So I call Tracy to cancel and get her voice mail. She doesn't call me back. She probably thinks I am doing this on purpose because she cancelled on me. But I really don't care what she thinks. Tracy doesn't have room for me in her life, which is okay because I am no longer feeling warm and fuzzy about her. I never call her again.

For my third date with Anna, I treat her to a fabulous dinner at a new restaurant called Brazilian Grille. We meet at the restaurant because she declines my offer to pick her up. She's moving slowly, and apparently she isn't comfortable with having me over to her house quite yet.

Anna admits that earlier in the day, her 21-year-old daughter asked her if she likes the man she's going out with tonight. Anna's response was, "I don't know."

That's not a very positive endorsement on date number three. Out in the parking lot, Anna gives me another grandpa kiss.

On our fourth date, I do the same thing that Anna did on our first date. I take a wrong turn on the way to the restaurant and get lost. Anna forgives my tardiness—but her graciousness seems forced. She is clearly is a woman who likes to get her own way, and she isn't happy about being inconvenienced.

It isn't until our fifth date—a little more than a month after we met at the singles party—that Anna begins to warm up to me. I cook a light dinner for her at my house, and then we attempt to watch a movie on DVD. Anna falls asleep for a while. When she wakes up, we sit on the couch and talk.

After a few minutes, I get a new vibe from Anna. It takes me a while to recognize it, but when I do, the signals are unmistakable. Anna is waiting for me to kiss her. The veil that has been guarding her eyes has been lifted, and she is gazing at me, waiting for me to make the move.

I lean in to kiss her, and for the first time she kisses me back. Her lips separate, and our tongues dance for the first time. It is delightful and sensuous. It is a breakthrough—the first time that Anna has kissed me and really meant it.

I am a man, of course, so I say to myself, "Wow! Anna is finally showing me some passion. We are making out. Maybe I can get her naked." I reach under the back of her blouse, and with one hand I deftly unclasp her bra.

It's as if I have just set off a burglar alarm at a jewelry store. She sits up straight, gives me a look that could melt wax, and quickly reaches back to re-clasp her bra. Ladies and gentlemen, we have reached the end of the evening's festivities.

Still, a breakthrough is a breakthrough. Well, sort of.

Chapter 52: Still Waiting for the Big One

I am going to come right out say this: Men like to have sex. Yes, it's true. Men like to have sex as part of a responsible, loving, and mutually enjoyable relationship. Men don't like to be teased, and they don't like to be strung along, thinking they are going to get laid when they're not.

Studies have shown that, when it comes to sex and sex drives, men and women are fundamentally different. According to WebMD.com, "men's sex drives are not only stronger than women's, but much more straightforward. The sources of women's libidos, by contrast, are much more difficult to pin down."

Amen, brother.

Men think about sex *a lot* more than women. Edward O. Laumann, author of *The Social Organization of Sexuality: Sexual Practices in the United States*, says most adult men under 60 think about sex at least once a day. I believe he vastly underestimates the male libido. I'll bet the average man aged 50 to 60 thinks a sexually related thought about 10 times a day. The average man in his 30s or 40s probably thinks about sex 100 times a day. And the average man 18 to 29, his veins surging with testosterone, thinks about sex 14,000 times a day. Young men's brains are so preoccupied by sex that it's a wonder they can remember their own names or what to order at Starbucks.

By contrast, many women only think about sex once or twice a year, fleetingly, on the birthdays of their children. And it's a bittersweet thought.

While I am ranting, let me give you another news flash. When it comes to *why* they have sex, men and women are also fundamentally different. The best way I ever heard it explained was this: Men want to have sex so they can fall in love; women want to fall in love so they can have sex.

Here's another complication: men are naturally impatient. They want results NOW. By contrast, women are so patient that they will watch entire episodes of *The View*. Knowing this, it's nothing short of a miracle for a man and a woman to meet, get to know and like each other, begin a relationship, do some more relationship stuff, and ultimately have wild, passionate sex. Thankfully, miracles happen every day.

What got me started on this topic is—you guessed it—Anna. The "breakthrough" at the end of our fifth date, when she kissed me like she meant it, didn't last long.

On date number six, we meet for dinner at a restaurant and have a very enjoyable time. As we sit in the bar, I notice that for the first time we are touching each other periodically. You know, giving each other little touches on the forearm and occasionally on the thigh to emphasize a point or share a funny moment. That's a sure sign of attraction. I get a nice after-dinner kiss in the parking lot. But even though it is still early, Anna will not let me come over to her place for a nightcap.

For date number seven, I cook a fancy dinner for Anna at my house. We watch a movie. We kiss and talk on the couch. We kiss some more. No body parts are groped, and no clothing is removed.

The very next night is date number eight, and Anna is finally convinced that I am not a perverted stalker. She invites me to her house for dinner. We finish the DVD movie that we didn't quite get through the previous night. Anna falls asleep on the couch, so I watch part of a college football game. When she wakes up, Anna, claiming to be tired from the previous night of no sex, kicks me out at 10:30 p.m. On the drive home, I have a strange déjà vu feeling of being in high school again.

Worse still, Anna has cancelled a couple of dates—once because she had a headache. Hell, I'm not even sleeping with her and she is already using that excuse. One evening she tells me that she is a very visual person, and she can't see herself with me yet. With a comment like that, I can't get real optimistic about this relationship.

This pattern of high school, PG-rated dates continues pretty much the same for a few more weeks. We are slowly building a stronger emotional bond, and that feels nice. I know that emotional bonding is important to women, and I embrace that to the best of my male ability. Anna and I talk about past relationships and why they ended. I tell her about my divorce. During our most recent date (#12), she tells me about her last fiancé, and how she refused to make love to him until they were actually married.

That gets my attention.

Anna has no deeply held religious beliefs that preclude premarital sex. She just wanted to wait. As it turns out, Anna and her fiancé broke up before they got married, so she never did sleep with him. And to hear Anna tell the story, it was no big loss. It almost sounds like Anna enjoyed the control she had over her fiancé.

Can anyone spell R-E-D F-L-A-G?

I now have been seeing Anna for nearly three months. I have been very, very patient. My friends have started to call me Job. (That's ridiculous. Job had to deal with a lot of horrible stuff like plagues, famine, flatulence, baldness, and the loss of his 401K—but at least he was getting laid once in a while.) I may not be a real-life Job, but I am not sure how much more of this slow-motion relationship I can take.

"I have been dating you exclusively for almost three months," I tell Anna. "So, when do you think you will be ready to get more physically intimate?"

She smiles, but she doesn't answer the question.

Hmmmm. I flash forward to the wonderful moment when I behold Anna's naked body for the first time. Lo, I have waited patiently. I have truly earned the name Job "The Former Babe Magnet" Stone. And now, my patience will finally be rewarded. On this glorious night—the five year anniversary of our wedding date—I will finally "know" my beautiful wife in the Biblical sense.

Anna likes to have a man around, but it has to be on her terms. She is as stubborn as a rock, and by now I know that all of my Babe Magnet skills have absolutely no effect on her. She will not change her mind until she is damn good and ready to do so.

"I'm not sure how much longer I can wait," I say, honestly.

"In that case, you might just have to move on," she says, with no emotion whatsoever.

Anna tells me that she thought she'd always be with her last love—her eight-year man. He left her without fully explaining why. That might be the real problem here. I think she's still in love with him. Maybe she's punishing me for what he did to her.

By now I have invested a lot of dating time, emotion, and money in Anna. And it seems like I have gotten a rotten return on my investment. Yes, I know that dating isn't the same as a business relationship. Nevertheless, I feel that I have made a bad investment at the First National Bank of Babes.

BABE MAGNET RULE #50

Dates are like $100 bills. It's not smart to throw good ones after bad.

So I have to ask myself—is Anna worth the wait? Is she worth the money I have spent on her? As I think about this during the next week, I realize that there are many things about Anna that I am not fond of. She's got an arrogant streak, and she is probably narcissistic, too. There's also this nagging feeling that she reminds me of what I like least about my mother. After Mom divorced Dad, she only went out on a couple of dates. Basically, she thought that men were too much of a bother, and she prized her independence. The word "compromise" was no longer in her vocabulary. And everyone knows that a romantic relationship isn't possible without compromise.

I decide to go out with Anna one more time to see how I feel about her. I take her to see B.B. King in concert. Mr. King, now in his 80s, still knows how to play his guitar, lovingly named Lucille, and he still knows how to put on a great show. During one song, he playfully sings about women giving their men "some sugar." He stops the song and tells every woman in the audience to give her man some sugar right now. After a few nervous giggles, the auditorium is filled with women kissing their men. B.B. eggs everyone on. "Come on, ladies! Show your man what he means to you."

Now there's some serious making out going on. I turn to Anna, expecting a passionate kiss, and she gives me…a grandpa kiss.

And that's when I know I'm done with Anna.

I share my Anna story at the men's group that meets biweekly at the Unity church. We formed the group a few months ago after a very successful weekend retreat that involved lots of awesome male bonding and beating of drums around a campfire. (I am not kidding about this. Women might get together to discuss all kinds of personal experiences and share their feelings about *everything*, but men get together and beat drums so they *don't* have to talk to each other.)

But then a strange thing happened at the men's group meetings. We started to talk, and we started to talk about meaningful things. We started to share our feelings. We started to let our macho facades drop, and we revealed inner insecurities and vulnerabilities. We talked about our relationships. We talked about joy and pain and emotions. We even said that we loved each other—in an acceptable male sort of a way.

I told my buddy Karl about the men's group to see if he might be interested in joining, and he said, "It sounds like you guys sit around and talk about your vaginas." Karl respectfully declined my invitation to join the group.

So during the past few weeks, I have shared some Anna stories at the men's group. When I tell them about the "grandpa kiss" at the B.B. King concert and that I have decided to stop seeing Anna, they unanimously agree that I have made the right decision.

"She's not worthy of you," says Mueller, who, ironically, makes his living as a divorce therapist. "You need a woman who is emotionally there for you."

Leon, the athletic trainer, agrees. "She was jerking you around. It was time for you to move on. I am proud of you." He gives me a manly man hug.

Bruce, the openly gay member of the group, teases me by saying, "I told you women aren't worth the trouble. Especially *that* one."

The support of fellow men is great. I love them for it. Having a tribe of men to confide in makes it easier to deal with the hurdles that men sometimes have to jump over in this journey called life.

But the fact is, now I have to start the dating process all over again. Damn. After all that dating, I am back to square one.

Chapter 53: A Bird in the Hand and a Babe in the Bush

I am sitting in the passenger seat of a Subaru Outback as it rolls down a suburban road. In the driver's seat is Mildred Hendrix, a friend from the local garden club. It is dark outside, and slushy rain falls against the windshield as Mildred drives us to a holiday party at the Desert Flower restaurant.

A week ago, I ran into Mildred at a party. She asked me if I was dating anyone, and I said no. Then she sheepishly asked if I would accompany her to a work-related party, "just as friends." Most of the attendees at the invitation-only party would be couples, and Mildred didn't want to go alone.

I agreed to go for four reasons:

1. I did not have plans that night.
2. It sounded like it might be fun.
3. The Desert Flower is one of my favorite restaurants.
4. I was happy to help Mildred out.

The Desert Flower is a magnificent property located at the edge of hundreds of acres of open space. It was once a homestead, long before anyone else had settled in the area. Over the years the facility grew and expanded. Today it is a one-of-a-kind restaurant and banquet center that is a favorite local venue for weddings and fancy parties.

Mildred and I arrive at the restaurant and are escorted to the special events area, which is resplendent in Christmas décor. Right away, Mildred does a wonderful job of introducing me to the people she knows. This is the annual holiday party of Robin Henderson Homes, and Mildred was invited because her company is the primary interior decorator for the company's model homes.

My Babe Magnet training comes in handy. I am friendly and charming as I chat with the people to whom Mildred introduces me. I make entertaining small talk about work, Christmastime, kids, and whatever subjects come up in the conversation.

"Have you gotten all of your holiday shopping done?" I ask a nice couple in their 30s. This gets a big laugh because it's the first week in December.

"Does Santa still come to your house?" I ask a couple in their 60s. "No? How about Hanukah Harry?"

I am the perfect guest and the perfect non-date date. I can tell by the look on Mildred's face that I am doing her proud. There's no date pressure on me; I'm here simply to enjoy a pleasant evening. It doesn't feel like Mildred and I are on a date at all. It feels more like we are an old married couple.

After dinner, we move en masse to the adjoining room, which is set up for casino night. We each have $500 in play money chips with which to gamble. The big winner gets to choose a fabulous prize from the table where Carol Merrill is standing.

I park myself at a blackjack table and start chatting up the dealer. Mildred takes the seat beside me, and we commence some heavy duty, high-roller, comp-me-a-suite-for-the-weekend Las Vegas gambling—except for the fact that we're using play money. My cards start out cold, but gradually my luck changes. Mildred starts winning, too. We are chatting with each other and joking with the dealer and the other players, and pretty soon we attract a crowd because we are having more fun than anyone at the party.

I notice one of the employees of the restaurant coming and going behind the door where the bar is set up. I notice her because she is beautiful, and she has an "I'm in charge" aura of authority. She is dressed in a red cashmere sweater and nicely tailored charcoal black slacks. She's about five foot nine, with a slim, athletic body. I would guess that she is about 40, and her dark red hair is short in a stylish but businesslike cut.

Every time she walks into the room, my eyes just lock onto her. After a few times, she starts to notice me noticing her. I give her a small but friendly smile. She is in and out of the room, talking to the bartender and answering other employees' questions. Now I catch her checking me out when she comes back into the room. And that makes me watch her even more. So without a single word spoken between us, there is this charge of energy passing between us. And all of this is happening as I sit next to my "date" for the evening as we play blackjack.

I have never been in this situation before. Is this what it's like to be a Babe Magnet? Do women just pick up your vibe from across the room? I know that it would be tacky for me to try to pick up the Restaurant Babe while I am already on a date—even if it's a totally platonic date. But I don't want to let an opportunity to meet a beautiful woman pass me by. (Based on her naked ring finger, I think she's single, too.) What should I do?

As the party is winding down, Mildred excuses herself to go to the restroom. I see the Restaurant Babe at the other end of the room, saying goodbye to some of the other guests. So I walk over, introduce myself and thank her for a great party. I do not get her phone number, and I do not ask her out. But I do find out that her name is Rachel and that she's the catering manager. I now have enough information to follow up—if I choose to do so.

As Mildred drops me off at my house, she suggests that I call her if I ever "want to go to a movie with a friend." That's a nice offer, but I don't expect to take her up on it. Right now, I would much rather have a girlfriend than a friend.

I wake up the next morning thinking about Rachel the Restaurant Babe. If there's any hope of her remembering me, I have to call her today. Now, in the light of day, I know that I might have exaggerated the "connection" we were sharing last night. Maybe I imagined the whole thing. But the only way to know for sure is to call her.

I phone the restaurant in the mid-afternoon and ask for Rachel, the Catering Manager. I am put on hold, the annoying kind that tells you every 20 seconds how important your call is and plays really bad Muzak in between the announcements. My heart is racing like a teenager's making his first call to a girl. I've made these calls dozens of times, so why do I still get nervous? Fear of rejection, probably. No matter how experienced and accomplished a man becomes, he still hates to be rejected by a woman—even a woman he doesn't know. I was less nervous when I shook the hand of the President of the United States.

A minute in real time passes, but in "waiting for a woman to pick up the phone so you can ask her out" time, that's 4.7 hours. I finally hear Rachel's voice. "Hello?"

"Hi, Rachel. My name is Chad Stone. We met last night at the Robin Henderson Homes party. Remember? We talked at the end of the event and I complimented you on that great red sweater you were wearing."

Rachel is silent for five seconds. (That's 23 minutes in "first call to a woman to ask her out" time.) The memory file is accessed in her brain.

"Oh, hi!" she chirps. "Yes, I enjoyed talking to you."

Her voice is music. I briefly explain that I was at the party with a platonic friend, so it didn't seem right to ask for her card.

"I almost gave you one of my cards last night," she says, "but I talk to so many people at the ends of events, and I wasn't really sure."

No problem, Rachel. I was deliberately holding back. But I am SO GLAD that you remember me. I am on a roll, so I waste no further time. "So, what's your schedule like in the next week?" I ask. "Can I take you out for coffee or lunch or..."

She's crazy busy. In the restaurant and catering business, the holiday season before Christmas is the busiest time of the year. She can meet me for drinks after work on Wednesday. That means I will miss the dance classes at Cowboy's, but that's an excellent trade-off. If we don't get together on Wednesday, we'll have to wait another week until she can squeeze me into her schedule.

BABE MAGNET RULE #51

When scheduling a date with a Babe—especially a first or second date with a Babe of high potential—be as flexible as possible. If you don't have time for her now, she knows you won't have time for her later.

"I would love to get together with you on Wednesday," I say.

We exchange cell phone numbers, and choose a location for our date. I hang up the phone and do a little celebration dance like I just scored a touchdown.

I got me a first date with a new Babe!

Chapter 54: First Date Jitters

I have a mild case of First Date Jitters, but that's probably because I haven't been out on a first date in quite a while. I think the jitters are a reminder that I am truly excited about going out with Rachel.

I arrive at the restaurant just as my cell phone rings. It's Rachel, calling to let me know that a fire alarm went off at her restaurant, and it took a while to get it turned off. I know the feeling. I feel like a fire alarm is going off inside of me right now. What's up with that? I am a Middle-Aged Babe Magnet, not some wimpy high school kid who is lucky to get a date with the geeky girl that nobody understands. I have been in this situation dozens of times before. I am the King of Cool, the Swami of Smoothness, the Duke of Dating. I know how to turn on the charm, and I know how to create a great first date. Why am I getting more and more nervous now that Rachel is about to arrive?

Rachel and I have talked so little that this feels like a blind date—except of course that I have seen her and know first-hand that she is stunningly beautiful. But as far as knowing her personality, I really am going in "blind." In a weird way, I find that very exciting.

I settle into a table at the front of the bar where I have a clear view of the front door. There is an NBA game on TV, but I am too nervous and excited by Rachel's impending arrival to pay attention to the game.

Rachel arrives 10 minutes late, looking fabulous. Before she even sees me, she immediately starts chatting with the waitress who was standing just inside the door. It turns out that Rachel worked here before she got the catering manager job at the Desert Flower. I suddenly realize that Rachel suggested this restaurant for our meet and greet date to give herself the home field advantage.

With her dark red hair and her radiant smile, Rachel looks just as stunning as I remembered her from our first meeting. She seems a tad nervous as we say hello with a brief, noncommittal hug. We decide to split a bottle of Robert Mondavi Cabernet, and we start talking.

We share our relationship resumes. She was married for 12 years, but got divorced when she realized that "good enough wasn't good enough." She knew she didn't want to spend the rest of her life in a marriage that was no longer working for her. She has no kids, but she does have three very large dogs—Great Danes. She lives in a house on an acre of land, which gives her enormous dogs room to run around. Her dogs are her family, and she proudly shows me the photos of them stored on her phone.

Rachel works crazy hours six days a week for much of the year. Her only day off is Monday. "My job doesn't give me many chances to date," she says, wistfully.

I gaze into her green eyes and think, *That's okay, honey. I can work with that.*

Rachel's work schedule is actually a "good news/bad news" proposition. The bad news is this: if I end up seeing her regularly, we'll never be able to go out on Friday or Saturday nights. The good news is: it doesn't sound like I have any competition in the dating department. That would explain why a Babe like Rachel was so quick to say "Yes!" when I asked her out. If she had a normal work schedule, someone would have already snapped her up by now.

We finish our first glasses of wine and I pour us more. Rachel is not a big fan of traditional medicine, and she goes to a homeopathic doctor. Me, too! She is tired of the old school religious doctrine, and finds New Thought intriguing. Me, too! She loves red wine, almost to the point of being a connoisseur. Me, too! She wants to marry me and live happily ever after. (No, that was just me.)

We talk for two and a half hours. I am so focused on Rachel that I don't even notice we are the only two people left in the bar. I finally become aware of my surroundings when the restaurant staff starts putting the bar chairs up on the tables so they can sweep the floor.

I ask Rachel when she can fit me into her busy schedule. She says Monday. I tell her I will call with some date ideas.

We hug each other when we say goodbye. This time it's a warm, full-body hug, and I can feel her tall, athletic body next to mine. I could get used to this feeling. We chat for another few minutes. After another goodbye, she hugs me again. I do not want to let her go, but if I hold onto her any longer she will think I am a pervert.

I know it's only been one date, but I *really* like this woman.

I find myself thinking about Rachel a lot in the next two days. I think she might be just as excited about me as I am about her. We have been exchanging emails several times a day. She sent me a photo of herself and her dogs. Once again, I am struck by her natural beauty. Then she sends me a photo of her Christmas tree, which looks like a shot from *Martha Stewart Living*. In response, I send her a photo of a "Christmas tree" made out of wine bottles that someone forwarded to me.

BABE MAGNET RULE #52

If you can't impress the Babes with your classiness and sophistication, at least make them laugh.

We set the agenda for our next date. We're going to meet for a casual dinner, and then we're going to see the Festival of Lights at the zoo. When we go back to get her car at the restaurant, we'll stop in for dessert if we're in the mood. Basically, the Festival of Lights was Rachel's idea. I know that the man is supposed to plan the date, but I was having a brain freeze. I was going to suggest going bowling, but her idea sounds so much more romantic.

I can't wait to see Rachel again. I am excited about her in that very-beginning-state-of-a-fantastic-relationship way when everything is new and fun. I know that it is way too early to feel this way, but I already do.

I never felt this way about Anna. She never gave me the thrill of electricity running up and down my spine. Anna was always so aloof, controlled, and reserved. Rachel has a playful goofiness that is endearing.

Already she is showing me little gestures of affection—in the form of the photos and silly jokes that she has emailed to me. That's something I never got from Anna. Ever.

What a difference between two women. I find it very easy to like Rachel—especially when I compare her to Anna.

Chapter 55: It Smells (Almost) Like a New Romance

I arrive for our second date bearing a potted miniature rose plant for Rachel. Her face brightens when she sees it. (Score some points for me.) Then she tells me she has trouble keeping houseplants alive. (Take away some of the points that I just scored.) So I challenge her to see how long she can keep the cute little rose bush alive.

"I will be coming over to your house periodically to check on the health of this little plant, so give her lots of love and attention," I tease.

Rachel and I order dinner and the conversation flows. It is so easy to talk to her. Rachel is open and unpretentious. Sitting across the booth from her, I have ample opportunity to drink in her loveliness. She is wearing little or no makeup, a yellow sweater, and just-tight-enough jeans. Her red hair is the perfect complement to her nicely freckled face. I am not sure if it's the light in this restaurant, but her hair looks much redder this evening. It's redder and shinier. You could even say it glows.

We get into my BMW sedan for the short drive to the zoo. I have never been to the Festival of Lights display because, frankly, it always sounded kind of cheesy. I pictured an overly cute display of Christmas lights designed to appeal to old ladies and young children. Tonight, though, I am quite willing to give it a try.

When I pay the hefty entrance fee and we walk inside, I am blown away. There are hummingbirds in lights, jumping frogs in lights, cacti in lights, zoo animals in lights, honeybees in lights, and an old pickup truck (a real one) decorated in lights. I am thoroughly impressed by the variety and creativity of the displays. The place is packed, and there are loads of families with kids and old ladies ooohing and ahhhing about the lights. But

I am with Rachel, so I don't care how many kids and old ladies surround us. I hardly notice them at all.

I am walking around with Rachel, doing my very best to be charming. I am using all of my Babe Magnet conversational skills. I want to gently take her hand and walk around the park like lovers. But we are not quite there yet, and I don't want to move too fast. I want to move forward, but I don't want to scare her away. After all, this is only our second date.

Rachel is fun to be with, and she has a youthful spark that I find very appealing. She also has a delightfully goofy laugh that I didn't know about until tonight. Perhaps it is the irresistible power of my wit and charm, but as I crack jokes and make humorous comments, I hear her endearing goofy laugh again and again.

She tells me her birthday is August 29th, which makes her a Virgo. She admits to being organized, methodical, and punctual. I tell her my birthday is September 27th, making me a Libra. I admit to being creative, romantic, and balanced.

BABE MAGNET RULE #53

Given the choice of talking about politics or astrological signs on a first or second date, go with the astrological signs.

Back at Jupiter Moon for dessert, Rachel convinces me to get a glass of red wine with a piece of exotic dark chocolate and butterscotch cake that we can share. Sounds like a weird combination to me.

"Red wine and dark chocolate go great together," she assures me.

I don't believe her until I take a bite of chocolate and a sip of the wine. Oh my God. My tongue is having an orgasm. I love red wine. I love chocolate. But I have never had both in my mouth at the same time. Rachel has awakened my taste buds to a new combination that I will never forget.

When I walk Rachel out to her car, I see that she drives a red Miata convertible. It's perfect for her. She claims to drive the speed limit, but I am not sure how you can never exceed the speed limit in a car like that. There's no way that I could drive a sports car and never speed, which is precisely why I have never owned a sports car.

I give Rachel a goodbye kiss. It's our first kiss, and it's too chaste for the way I am feeling about her. But that's all right. She'll warm up. The women worth having are the ones who hold back at first. At least that's what I am learning as a Middle-Aged Babe Magnet in the 21st century. Some things about dating haven't changed much at all.

Rachel has another crazy busy week at the restaurant (no surprise there), so her next open slot is for a 5 p.m. drink before an existing dinner commitment. My only serious doubt about Rachel is whether she has room for me in her life. The way I feel about her right now, I'm not sure if I can wait six days between dates. But, of course, I will.

I am waiting in the bar when a stunningly beautiful redhead walks in. She flashes me a big smile, and then she gives me a friendly hug.

"Hey gorgeous, want to buy me a drink?"

She laughs. "Sure, I'm in the restaurant business, I've got lots of money." It's the first time I have heard a touch of sarcasm in her voice, and I do not like it. Perhaps I have struck a nerve.

We order glasses of red wine. This is our third date, and they have all involved red wine. We talk for an hour. Then, right before she has to leave, she locks eyes with me and asks, "How old are you?"

Well, I'm not going to lie about my age. I am proud to be a 50-something man with lots of life experience and the wisdom that results from it. I am proud of every wrinkle on my face and every hair that has fallen out of my head. I am proud to be in my middle years, in the prime of my prosperity. I am happy with my middle-aged body and my Baby Boomer heritage. "How old do you think I am?" I reply, flashing a sly smile.

"Fifty."

"You're very close."

"Forty-nine?"

"I'm actually 53." She doesn't react, which I take as a good sign.

"How old do you think I am?" she asks.

Oh no! Not that question! That's one of the most dangerous questions that a woman can ask a man. The only two worse questions are

"Do these pants make my butt look big?" and "Would you mind if we stayed home tonight and just talked?"

How old do I think she is? I'd say early 40s. But I don't want to say 44 if she's 42. You never want to guess too high on a woman's age. You always want to be under the actual number.

BABE MAGNET RULE #54

When a woman asks how old you think she is, underestimate. Better yet, say "I don't know, honey, but you sure look great."

I decide to be safely vague. "I'd say you were in your early forties."

"Forty-one."

Well, there you have it. At this point we are both doing the math. I am 12 years older than she is. But she told me she once dated a man who was 58, so I don't think my 53 years are going to scare her away. At least I hope not.

We say a pleasant goodbye. I'm not sure when I will see Rachel again. She's got plans for Christmas Day, then she works the after-Christmas rush at the restaurant. I'm out of town over the New Year's weekend to see my dad, and then Rachel's off on a skiing trip. I have a business trip scheduled for mid-January, and then Rachel leaves for a vacation. Life—not to mention the schedules of two adults with busy careers—is not making it easy to see each other.

"Please let me know if you can work me into your schedule," I tell her while we hug in the parking lot. "I would really like to see you."

She smiles noncommittally and drives her sports car into the sunset.

Chapter 56: One That Got Away

Sometimes you can predict the future. Sometimes you know things before they happen. Sometimes you get a feeling about something, and you push it out of your mind because it's not what you wanted.

I had a premonition about Rachel. I sent her an email to see when we could get together. I got no reply, so today I sent her another email. Still no reply. Why won't she answer me? I hear a little voice, a nagging little voice, warning me not to get my hopes up. But it's too late for that. I already have my hopes up. I really like Rachel, and I want to see her again.

The little voice is still warning me. Sometimes I really hate that little voice. Especially when it's right.

I check emails one more time before I go to bed. There's a message from Rachel. I open it. The little voice tells me, "Sorry, Dude." I take a deep breath and begin to read.

Rachel sent me a Dear Chad letter.

She dumped me.

Shit.

She says her sixth sense tells her we aren't a good match. We're both busy and it wouldn't make sense for us to invest time in a relationship that wouldn't work.

Well, shit.

I must admit that for the last few days I've had a sense that this was coming. I didn't want it to be true, but I already knew. So I've been sending Rachel psychic messages such as, "Rachel, give us a chance" and "Rachel, don't give up on me."

But it didn't work. She gave up on us.

I call Rachel's cell number. It rings and rings. I imagine Rachel looking at the phone number of the incoming call and deciding not to answer it because it is me.

I leave a pleasant but direct message. "Hi Rachel, it's Chad. I just read your last email and it's not what I wanted to hear. Hey, I'm not going to try to talk you into anything that doesn't feel right to you, but please call me when you get this message."

It's not manly to sound desperate, so I desperately try to not sound desperate. A man shouldn't come begging to a woman. One of the things that women find most appealing about men is their strength. And you can't beg from a position of strength. But dammit, how could Rachel take the chickenhearted way out and dump me via email? What if I never get a chance to talk to her again?

I reread Rachel's email. It hasn't changed a bit. Every word is exactly the same. It still sucks. Screw her—and the three Great Danes she calls her "kids." Why would I want to be with a woman who refers to her dogs as her kids? I SPECIFICALLY told my buddy Karl that I would NEVER go out with a woman who treated her pets like human children. Treating pets like kids is crazy behavior. I don't know why women can't see that when it's SO DAMN CLEAR to men.

I expected more from Rachel. I expected her to have the guts to talk to me. I was *excited* about this woman. She had a childlike spark of fun and adventure. I was already envisioning us together as a couple. I was visualizing the beginning of a wonderful relationship. I was so sure about her. I was so sure about *us*.

And now this. I am crushed. It sucks to get dumped—even when it happens very early in a relationship. It sucks to be the person who is doing the dumping, too (which is probably why Rachel dumped me via email). But at least if you're the dumper you're in control. It's your idea; you decided to end it.

Poets have known for thousands of years that love hurts. Romantic rejection is a painful experience, which is why we talk about "breakups" and "broken hearts." You say "my heart is broken" because that's what the pain feels like.

Science has proven that the brain doesn't really distinguish between the physical pain of injury and the intense emotional pain of romantic rejection. In your mind, both physical and emotional experiences can trigger responses in the neural pathways that generate pain.

In a recent study, scientists recruited volunteers who had just been abruptly rejected by their lovers. The researchers showed them pictures of their ex-partners, and their brains lit up the same pain circuits that are activated by a heat sensor when skin gets hot enough to burn. In other words, the brains of the jilted lovers actually generated physical pain when they were thinking about their exes. Emotional pain really is the equivalent of getting burned.

There is a classic rock song by Nazareth called *Love Hurts* that was clearly written by a man in the midst of a heartbreak. A line in the song goes, "love is like a flame, it burns you when it's hot," which turns out to be literally true.

I remind myself that I only went out with Rachel three times. I try to take solace in the knowledge that getting dumped very early in a relationship is far better than getting dumped after you have bonded and fallen in love and bought real estate and made babies. I have to put things into perspective, after all.

I know I am going to feel like shit tonight. But tomorrow I will feel a little better, and the next day I will feel better still. I will remember Rachel for a while as the fish that got away. But soon, I will cast my line into the dating waters and I will get a nibble. Then I will get a fish on the line and the process will begin anew.

Or, to use another metaphor:

> **BABE MAGNET RULE #55**
> Dating doesn't always go in a straight line. When your dating life zigs and zags like the Dow Jones Industrial Average, go with the ups and downs and keep believing that you will find the love of your life.

Chapter 57: Lessons from a Series of Meet and Greets

So here I am on Match.com again, using the search function as entertainment. Instead of reading a book or watching TV, I am reading profiles and viewing pictures of single women.

As I peruse the list of profiles that come up when I search for women aged 44-49 with no kids, who don't smoke and who make $50,000 or more per year, I realize that what I'm doing right now would make a great reality TV show. We'll call it Match.com TV. (Somebody get the CEO of Match.com on the phone right away!) The premise is simple and easy to grasp, which is essential for a TV show. A single man (me) finds 10 women on Match.com that he wants to date. A TV camera crew follows me on each of the 10 first dates, recording the Meet and Greet process and revealing how well I get along with each woman. I talk to the camera after each date, commenting on how well the date went and whether I want to ask the woman out again. Then I go on second dates with five or six of them, and the shows reveal subsequent dates until I end up dating one woman who seems like a long-term relationship candidate. The camera crew checks in periodically to see if we are a dating success story.

During the season, the Match.com TV series would invariably include some horrible dates, during which there's just no chemistry and the conversation is strained. The worse the date, the better. Everyone likes to watch a date become a train wreck. Conversely, if it's a great date, then that's also good TV, because viewers will get inspired. If a dating couple finds love and marriage, then all of the women viewers will shed tears of joy as they see themselves walking down the aisle with their own online prize. Possible TV show sponsors include Match.com, *Brides* magazine, Zale's jewelry stores, Weight Watchers, Secret Deodorant, Hilton Resorts, 1-800-Flowers, and Trojan condoms.

It's perfect! I decide to approach my next few Match.com Meet and Greet dates as research for the Match.com TV show pilot.

Fade in. We see two people, a man and a woman, sitting across from each other at a coffeehouse....

Lacey Conklin

After the obligatory exchange of emails and a couple of phone calls, I schedule a Meet and Greet with Lacey. This is truly going to be a blind date, because Lacey has not posted photos online. She claims to be inept at using digital cameras.

Judging by the sound of her voice and the conversations during our phone calls, I've predicted that Lacey is not a major Babe. There was no confidence in her voice, and I did not get any Babe vibes from her. We meet for coffee at Jupiter Moon, and immediately I give her a 4 on the 10-point Babe scale. She looks out of shape, which I find ironic because she's a nurse. Shouldn't everyone in the medical profession follow their own advice and take good care of their bodies? Exercise! Eat right! Get plenty of sleep! Don't drink too much! Isn't that what doctors and nurses are always saying? If they are so smart, why don't they take their own advice?

Anyway, Lacey is a sweetheart in her own way. But bless her heart, I am simply not attracted to her. There is no point in seeing her again.

> **BABE MAGNET RULE #56**
> Beware of blind dates, especially if physical appearance is important to you. Get a photo before your first date to avoid wasting time—yours and your date's.

Courtney Smith

We begin with the familiar pattern: I send an email, she responds, more emails are exchanged, I suggest we talk on the phone, she gives me her number, and I call. When I meet Courtney for lunch, she turns out to be tall (she listed her height as 5'10") but more matronly than I had expected. Babe rating: 5.

Poor Courtney acts like she hasn't been on a date in 20 years, which is probably true. Halfway through our lunch, she admits that I am her first

Match.com date, which explains why this successful professional woman is acting vulnerable and unsure of herself. She doesn't know what to talk about, so she spends way too much time telling me about her 21-year-old son, who still lives with her.

I don't want to slam the door in her face, but I don't want her to get her hopes up about me, either. During lunch I decide that I probably won't call her again.

After our date, she sends me a cute, hopeful email. Well, hell. I feel like I HAVE to respond, now. I don't want to seem like a complete jerk, so I reply with a friendly but non-committal phone call. I tell her that I am really busy at work this next week (which is true), so I can't say for certain when we can get together again.

Then I enact The Chickenshit Principle, otherwise known as...

> **BABE MAGNET RULE #57**
>
> If a man doesn't make any post-date contact, the woman will probably never call him. So ending a potential relationship the Chickenshit way (especially after one or two dates) is as simple as never contacting her again.

Patty Wiles

After I send Patty an email, she writes back telling me that my profile is wonderful. She says I had her at "Enrico's" (referring to my mention of a favorite local restaurant). Unlike many other Match.com women, she is quick to agree to talk to me on the phone.

She tells me all about her career in human resources consulting. When I start to tell her a short version of my work history, she already knows most of it. "I Googled you," she admits. With my name, city, and type of occupation, she was able to locate my company website, which includes a bio and photo of me.

"When I started Internet dating, I took a one-day seminar on how to make sure that what people are telling you is the truth," she explains.

Good for you, Patty. I'll have to Google you, too.

On paper, or rather on Match.com, Patty and I are a perfect match. She's 46 years old, has two teenaged boys, has her own business, and sounds athletic (tennis, golf, and mountain biking). I have high hopes for our Meet and Greet.

In person, Patty is cute, with short blonde hair and a nice but flat-chested body. She gives off very little warmth, and I find it difficult to get her to crack a smile. I take pride in my ability to charm women and make them laugh. But Patty is a tough audience, and she makes me work too hard.

Patty is focused to the point of being intimidating. She plays tennis, even though "plays" is the wrong word. She wants to achieve a 3.5 ranking in tennis, so she practices a lot. She wants success in her business life. She is very involved in her kids' lives. She is busy. I don't think there is room for a man in her life.

After 45 minutes, she seems finished with our date. "Are you going to get a take-home box for that?" she asks, pointing to my chocolate éclair, of which I only ate half.

I give Patty a brotherly hug in the parking lot. I don't plan to call her again.

BABE MAGNET RULE #58

If there are absolutely no sparks during the first date, don't bother to ask for a second date—unless you want a brother-sister relationship.

Liesel Schumacher

Liesel's online profile reveals that she's 42, blonde, and attractive. She was born in Austria, lived for a while in Paris, and then moved to New York. In my first email to her, I have to deliberately try not to gush. I can't believe this woman is single.

Liesel sends me her phone number almost immediately, and on a rainy Friday evening I decide to call her. She has a delightful accent, which I find very sexy. We talk about her job with an independent record company that started in Europe and moved to the States. She has also done some professional makeup work for a small-budget movie. Oh, and she started taking ballroom dancing lessons for fun.

Holy Exotic Babe! I have trouble coming up with things to talk about that don't sound lame. Her life sounds so much more interesting than mine. I realize, while I am talking to Liesel, that my life is WAY too boring. I have to get out more and do more.

When we meet, our faces both light up. Liesel has a Euro earth-mother vibe, and a childlike energy that is very contagious. She's wearing her blonde hair in Heidi pigtails, and her Bohemian dress looks handmade. There's a small gap between her two front teeth that is very endearing. I am instantly smitten.

Our Meet and Greet lasts for two hours over dinner. Our conversation flows easily over the widest possible variety of topics. Liesel is a free spirit, and follows her whims and dreams across many professions and many countries. The longer we talk, the more boring, predictable, and conservative I feel. If we get together, one or both of us will have to do some major lifestyle readjusting.

I simply must ask Liesel out on another date. And I do. But during our second date I already know that my safe, secure, dependable life is way too dull for Liesel. She's going to make someone a delightful girlfriend or wife. But as wonderful and sexy and appealing as she is, I'm not the right man for her.

BABE MAGNET RULE #59

Trust your instincts. If your gut tells you she's not the one, then she's not the one.

Colleen Peterson

I arrive early for my first date with Colleen, and take a booth in the front of the restaurant that gives me a clear view of the door. I want to see Colleen when she arrives.

Then I wait. And wait. And wait. Maybe she's stuck in traffic.

My phone rings. It's Colleen. "Chad, are you coming?" She arrived at the restaurant before I did to get some work done, and she's sitting at a table in the back.

I slide into her booth just as she is turning off her laptop. So much for my home field advantage.

Colleen is five foot two, eyes of blue, with bright white perfect teeth. She is dressed in a stylish black leather jacket with a blue patterned blouse and a single string of white pearls. She is just as cute as her Match.com photo.

We talk for two hours, and not once do we encounter the SILENCE OF A DEAD DATE (when the conversation grinds to a halt and neither of you has anything left to say). We share the same taste in movies. Like me, she enjoys comedies and dramas, but she hates horror films. She has two kids, the youngest of whom is 21. She is an interior decorator who stages houses for sale, and she also teaches Zumba fitness classes. She is cute, spunky, and fun.

At one point, I gaze into her very blue eyes and, like an idiot, say, "Are those your eyes?" Fortunately, she knows what I mean.

"My eyes are the color of yours," she replies. "Sometimes I'll wear green contacts. I used to change the color of my eyes to match my outfit."

Hey, me too! (Can you imagine a man saying that to a woman on a first date? She'd run away like someone fleeing from a burning dynamite factory.)

As is now my custom, I share some of my middle-aged dating stories and Colleen shares some of hers. That's always a topic that generates interest among actively dating singles.

"I have found that the harder I look, the harder it is for me to find somebody," Colleen says.

Maybe that's been my problem. I've been trying too hard. Maybe I should take a deep breath and let the elusive butterfly of love land on me, instead of racing to capture it and wrestle it to the ground. Maybe I have been scaring it away.

By the end of our first date, I feel the gentle touch of Butterfly Colleen landing upon my outstretched hand.

BABE MAGNET RULE #60

Don't try so hard to impress a Babe with witty banter and death-defying stunts of bravery. The best dates are the ones that are effortless.

Chapter 58: Fast-Forward Dating

Colleen hasn't returned my calls. I'm not sure what is going on with her. Our Meet and Greet date went so well, and she told me that she would like to see me again.

When I started dating, I thought women would appreciate meeting a man who was ready to get involved in a relationship. I thought I would stand out from all of the aloof, relationship-phobic men that you always hear about.

Apparently I was wrong. Perhaps I need to play a little harder to get. I need to dangle the bait, then act like I don't care if the woman is interested or not. To continue with the fishing metaphor, I'm trying to reel them in too soon. The women are still nibbling on the bait when I give my line a tug, the hook flies right out of their mouths, and they swim away.

Maybe it's time for me to admit that I really suck at fishing. Or that I really suck at dating. Or both.

On an otherwise normal day, I find a handwritten note in my mailbox from Hanna Hanson, who used to live next door. Hanna and her husband, Ray, both very nice people, were our "stealth" neighbors for years. They were practically invisible; both of them worked a lot and they didn't have any kids or dogs. If "quiet" is your idea of great neighbors, then Hanna and Ray were the greatest neighbors in the history of the world.

After I moved out of the house and divorced Valerie, Hanna moved out and divorced Ray. When I re-purchased my old house from Valerie and moved back in, suddenly Ray and I, two middle-aged divorced guys, were living next door to each other—alone in these huge suburban houses. Now Ray is my *bachelor* stealth neighbor.

Hanna's note says she noticed that I was active on Match.com. She's on Cupid.com, "just checking out the possibilities—not seeing anyone yet." She wants to know if I'd be interested in an upcoming "speed dating" event. She and her friend are going. Hanna says her friend is six feet tall, looks like a model, and has a hard time finding men who are tall enough for her. "Aren't you six feet tall?" she asks.

Why, yes I am. And I'd love to date a six-foot-tall Babe who looks like a model. But I've learned that women always overestimate the attractiveness of their friends. "Six feet tall and looks like a model" probably means she's about five foot nine and is slightly more attractive than Hanna.

I go to the website that Hanna provided to read the information about the speed dating event. Cupid.com calls it a Pre-Dating Event, which sounds a little classier. It's for singles ages 41-52, so I'll have to fib about my age—but only by one year.

The speed dating event is scheduled for the same night as my next men's group meeting. Should I go to meet Babes or go hang out with the guys? Hmmmm. Babes or guys? It's not a tough choice.

> **BABE MAGNET RULE #61**
> When faced with a decision between Babes and the guys, opt for the Babes. Beg forgiveness from the guys and make it up to them. They will understand.

According to the fountain of all online information, Wikipedia:

> Speed dating is a formalized matchmaking process or dating system whose purpose is to encourage people to meet a large number of new people. Its origins are credited to Rabbi Yaacov Deyo of Aish HaTorah, originally as a way to help Jewish singles meet and marry. "SpeedDating", as a single word, is a registered trademark of Aish HaTorah. "Speed dating", as two separate words, is often used as a generic term for similar events.

> The first speed dating event took place at Peet's Café in Beverly Hills in late 1998. Soon afterward, several commercial services began offering secular round-robin dating events across the United States. By 2000, speed dating had really taken off, perhaps boosted by its portrayal in shows such as *Sex and the City* as something that glamorous people did. Supporters argue that speed dating saves time, as most people quickly decide if they are romantically compatible...

I find it hysterical that the speed dating concept was invented by a rabbi. That sounds like the basis for a *Seinfeld* episode (had the series not gone off the air in May of 1998). In the *Seinfeld* episode, the rabbi would have invented SpeedDating™ to meet chicks, and when Elaine came to the event with Jerry, George, and Kramer, the rabbi would have become smitten with Elaine.

Clearly, rabbis have *way* more fun than priests. There is no way a priest would invent something like speed dating. And leave it to a rabbi to register the SpeedDating™ trademark.

I register online for the Cupid.com speed dating event. If I can meet 10 to 12 women in the same amount of time it takes for one Meet and Greet date at a coffeehouse, then it's a great investment in time and money. Let's speed up the dating process and get me a girlfriend!

Ah, but the universe is teasing me. As soon as I send in my reservation for speed dating, Colleen finally returns my calls. Her voice is perky, and her tone is friendly. I had basically given up on Colleen, so I was surprised to hear from her. "I've been so busy," she says. "I have staged three houses in the past three weekends. But it was worth it, because two of them sold."

Colleen is a little dynamo. She never stops moving, and the conversation flows effortlessly because she always has more things to talk about. I don't waste any of this little dynamo's time. "Would you like to see a movie this weekend?"

She says yes.

The next day, when I go in to see Dr. Sanchez, my homeopathic physician, and tell him my current dating status, he smiles knowingly. Dr. Sanchez is a few years younger than me, but he always gives me wise, fatherly advice. An appointment with Dr. Sanchez is part medical exam and part psychological pep talk. If you have ever gone to a homeopathic doctor, you know that a homeopathic visit involves talking about your life and your preferences in ways that are strikingly different from a visit with a "traditional" medical doctor.

So I tell Dr. Sanchez about my dating life. I tell him about how I am using online dating sites for entertainment. I tell him that I'm getting really good at first dates. "It's getting second or third dates that seems to be a problem right now."

Dr. Sanchez gives me a knowing smile and offers this advice: "Relax. Don't try so hard. Don't go on so many dates. Stay home more. Find yourself again. When you regain your own equilibrium, you'll be able to find the right person to be with. You can't find her now because you're not yourself."

Well, hell. I wish he'd told me that before I paid $50 for the speed dating event.

Colleen calls in sick for our date, and I don't think she is doing that "calling in sick to work" thing where you make your voice sound really tired and hoarse so the person on the other end will know how horrible you feel and there's just NO WAY you can come in today. Colleen sounds sick, and I'm pretty sure it's for real. Either that, or she's an incredible actress and she should book herself a flight to Hollywood.

"I am so sorry," she croaks. "Can we reschedule?"

I say sure.

Then, a week later, I get the same phone call from Colleen. She sounds all croaky, like a frog that got run over by a car. "I wasn't able to take any time off this week, so I need the weekend to just take it easy. Can we go see a movie next week instead?"

A week later it's déjà vu all over again. Colleen cancels our date for the third week in a row. Sure, she still sounds sick. But enough is enough.

I like Colleen a lot, based upon meeting her once and talking to her on the phone a few times. But the stars seem to be against us. I am not going to call Colleen again, because I am invoking:

> **BABE MAGNET RULE #62**
> In baseball and in dating, three strikes and you're out.

I am done chasing women who don't want to be caught. It's a waste of my time when there are thousands of women within a 10-mile radius who are actively looking for male companionship that will lead to a long-term relationship. In fact, I feel strongly enough about this to make it a Babe Magnet Rule.

> **BABE MAGNET RULE #63**
> Don't bother chasing women who don't want to be caught.

So I take the rest of the weekend off. I engage in no Babe-related activities whatsoever. No dates, no phone calls. I don't even turn on my computer and troll for chicks online. Cold turkey, baby. Doctor's orders!

After a weekend off, I am all rested for my speed dating event.

Chapter 59: Bring on the Babes

I meet Mueller to have a beer and talk about guy stuff. Mueller is one of those sensitive, semi-metrosexual guys who loves to talk about his feelings. But God bless him, he can also talk about manly man subjects such as baseball and women.

Mueller is fascinated by the speed dating concept, so I tell him how it works. There are 12 women and 12 men. The women sit at small tables placed around a large room. There is a large number written on a card at every table.

The women "own" the tables. The men travel from table to table to meet each woman in turn. Each mini-date lasts for six minutes. At the end of that time, the moderator rings a bell and all of the men move to the next table in line.

"Six minutes? What if you run out of things to talk about?" asks Mueller.

"Are you kidding me? This is the perfect format for me! I can talk to a rock for six minutes."

Best of all is the perfect efficiency of the process. I get to meet 12 women in one evening! Based upon all the first dates that I've already had, I am confident that I can learn enough about each woman in six minutes to know whether I want to go out with her. Hell, I've been on dates where I knew after two minutes that there wasn't going to be a second date. The rest of the hour I spent with those women was me just being polite.

I tell Mueller that out of 12 women, I'd like to meet two who want to see me again. Of course, they'd also have to be women that *I* want to see again. Mueller says, given that scenario, he'd be delighted to leave with one woman of dating potential. "You're an eternal optimist," he tells me. Maybe. But I'm not going to a speed dating event to NOT meet nice women. I am a Babe Magnet, and I expect to find Babes!

On the evening of the speed dating extravaganza, I stand before my closet and examine my clothes. I'm sure the women have spent the whole week choosing the perfect outfits for this evening. They have probably consulted with their friends, and perhaps even had their friends come over so they could carefully try on several combinations of apparel in order to create the perfect outfit. But 30 minutes before the event is the first time I have thought to myself, "Hey, I'm going to have to wear clothes to the speed dating thing tonight."

So what kind of look am I going for? Casual but respectable? Bad-boy jeans and a tight t-shirt? Sunday-go-to-meeting dressed up, complete with a tie? None of those sound right. I'm going to be the oldest person in the room, so the bad boy look is out. So is anything that looks too casual. I don't want it to appear that I'm wearing clothes that I could have worn to a sports bar. The super dressed-up look is wrong, too, because I don't want to look like I'm trying too hard or like I work in a mortuary. I opt for safe, middle-of-the-road (but prosperous) business casual. Nice slacks, a nice button-down shirt, dress loafers, and a sport coat with no tie. I look at myself in the mirror and smile. I am the epitome of a Middle-Aged Babe Magnet.

As I drive to the speed dating extravaganza, I start to formulate a plan for how I want to approach each mini-date. Theoretically, a six-minute date gives each of the two participants only three minutes to talk about themselves. So what should you cover? You have to talk a little about what kind of work you do. You have to talk a little about your relationship history. And you have to mention whether or not you have kids and some of the things you like to do for fun. If both people cover all of these topics, it will take at least six minutes. So I expect these mini-dates to fly by very quickly.

I arrive at the banquet room of the restaurant for the Big Event and quickly scan the room to see how everyone is dressed. I have selected the perfect outfit. Most of the men have gone for the sport coat-and-no-tie look, so I am in the comfortable majority. A couple of the sport coat guys look like they haven't gotten this dressed up in years, and they're having trouble pulling off the look. Not me, because I am in my element. This is the look I have been sporting at business conferences and trade shows for 20 years. My clothes make me look more prosperous than many of the other guys, which is fine by me. Most women would rather date a man who can bring some bread to the table. The guys who opted for a more casual look tonight look like the youngest in the group. They remind me of kids at a party for grownups.

The women are gorgeous. Most of them are in stylish dresses that show off their curves. Those with cleavage are displaying it proudly and effectively. Their faces are tastefully made-up and rouged, and their lashes have been fluffed up with mascara. They even smell nice, with a dozen delightful feminine scents wafting through the room.

It's a smorgasbord of women, and I am ready for the feast.

I see Hanna standing with a very tall brunette. Hanna's friend looks to be about six feet tall, with long, model-like legs and straight model-like hair (circa 1975) and a very photogenic face. Hanna wasn't exaggerating about the attractiveness of her friend.

I walk over to say hello to Hanna, and, right on cue, Hanna introduces me to Amanda. She smiles coyly. It is clear that Hanna has already told her about me. Hanna's endorsement has given me the inside track with Amanda. It's going to be difficult for the other men in the room to compete with *Chad Stone, Middle-Aged Babe Magnet, officially recommended by Hanna Hanson*. Already, I am feeling really good about this evening.

As I look around the room, I spot another woman I know. She and I met each other on Match.com and went out once, but then I never called her again. Oh, crap—what was her name? I quickly access the files in my brain in a desperate attempt to find it. Patty Wiles! She's the human resources person who is wound a little too tightly for me.

Now, how do I handle this? What would a Middle-Aged Babe Magnet do? He'd walk right over to Patty and say hello like they were old friends. That's exactly what I do.

Patty recognizes me right away and smiles. We exchange pleasantries, and both reveal that "this is the first time I have ever done anything like this!" It's like we're admitting to watching reality TV. Sure, millions of people watch it every week, *but I don't have time for that nonsense.* I wonder if anyone ever admits to doing speed dating more than once.

Patty introduces me to her friend, Raeline. Patty tells me that instead of 12 men and 12 women, there are actually 13 men and 13 women participating tonight. So already I know four of the 13 women, and I feel like I own the place.

The moderator of the event corrals us together and goes over the rules and procedures of the event. We all get name badges with our first names and our assigned numbers. I am Man #8. We also get note sheets with a list running from 1 to 13 so we can write each woman's name and a few notes about her. Next to that are two choices to circle: Let's Talk or No Thanks.

If we should run out of things to say to each other during our mini-dates, there is a helpful list of opening questions that we can use to stimulate the conversation. I am confident that I won't need this list.

The moderator walks the women into the event room so they can get settled at their tables. That leaves the men to wait impatiently just outside the door. The testosterone level in the men's waiting area is so high that if somebody lights a match, the whole room is going to blow.

The moderator fetches the men, and we sit at our designated spots across from our first "dates" of the evening. The 13 women are nervous, and they smile self-consciously. The 13 men are all drooling like Pavlov's dogs.

As Man #8, I sit across a small table from Woman #8. We smile at each other, not sure if we can talk before the bell rings to officially begin the Cupid.com Pre-Dating Extravaganza.

"Are we all ready to begin?" asks the cheerful moderator.

Then she rings the bell.

Chapter 60: Ding! And They're Off!

Suddenly, all 26 of us single people are engulfed in a tsunami of hormones as we launch into first dates. These are, quite literally, first dates on speed, so the talking begins immediately, filling the room with a decibel level normally heard only at rock concerts and middle school cafeterias.

For the next hour and a half, we are men and women on a mission to date. In numerical order, here's how my 13 dates go:

1. **Mary.** She's pleasantly attractive without being a Total Babe. Mary is a massage therapist and alternative healer. In six minutes, I don't have enough time to find out just what kind of alternative healer she is. For all I know, that's what she tells people so she doesn't have to admit that she's underemployed. In her previous life she had a corporate job. Ding! goes the bell. On my little scoring sheet I circle "No Thanks" and move to the next table.

2. **Canasta.** We start by talking about work. She works for the Social Security Administration. Doing what, exactly, I don't know, and I don't really care. I change the subject, and tell her about going snowshoeing at night under a full moon. She's done that, too! What are the odds of that? Canasta seems nice, but she's not a Babe and I don't feel any sparks. I circle "No Thanks."

3. **Hanna.** My former next-door neighbor. If it weren't for Hanna, I wouldn't be at this bacchanal of dating excess tonight. So I owe her one. I am having fun, because I have excellent verbal skills and I clean up well. Hanna is a sweetheart, but there is no way I would date her. (Her ex-husband is my next-door neighbor,

so if she were to come over to see me it would be VERY WEIRD.) But I circle "Let's Talk" on my score sheet as a way to say thanks to Hanna.

4. **Amanda.** Hanna's friend *is* a Babe. She could have been a professional model back in the day. Now, in her mid-forties, she still has a tall lanky body and a sparkle in her brown eyes. She'd be perfect as the middle-aged but still-cute woman in a pharmaceutical ad. "I didn't think I would ever get relief from (name of illness), but that was before my doctor told me about *Flomagranstropamene*." Amanda has been single for a long time, and she has a 16-year-old daughter. We click right away. Our six-minute date goes by in a flash. I really like Amanda, so it's a no-brainer to circle "Let's Talk."

5. **Katrina.** Another massage therapist, which sounds like a strange coincidence until Katrina tells me that she and Mary came to tonight's event together. Katrina's got short brown hair that's cut in a cute but not Total Babe way. It's a professional working woman's haircut. It turns out that she also does some office work. She has two kids, both in their early 20s. There is something about her that I find comfortably intriguing, and six minutes goes by in a flash. "Let's Talk."

6. **Sabina.** Special Education teacher and administrator. I end up going off on a rant about how society doesn't value teachers. "When I'm President, I'm going to make sure the shortstop for the Yankees doesn't make more than a teacher," I say. I spend so much time talking that I learn little about Sabina. It's not my finest six-minute date, which is entirely my fault. But I circle "No Thanks" anyway.

7. **Dori.** Moderately attractive and moderately interesting. Dori works for the highway department in some sort of public outreach position. Maybe that means she writes news releases telling why it takes 11 guys on a roadwork crew to stand around watching the one guy who is actually working. Her family moved here from New York. No apparent reason to see her again. "No Thanks."

8. **Clarissa.** Something magical happens when I sit down across from Clarissa. We gaze into each other's eyes and connect instantly. She travels out of town a lot for her job. Clarissa has straight blonde hair and blazing white teeth. She has one son. When the bell rings I ignore it. I am not finished talking to this woman yet. Clarissa seems to be bitten by the same "I really like this new person" bug as me. The guy behind me is pissed because I won't move on. Reluctantly, I relinquish the chair. I will definitely be seeing Clarissa again. "Let's Talk."

9. **Winter.** Another single mom, but Winter has never been married. That's basically the end of the date for me. I don't like it when unmarried women have kids. Call me old-fashioned in this regard. I am. What's the problem with these women? Can't they make a commitment? What kind of message does that send to the kids? "He was good enough to have sex with, but he wasn't husband material." The last four minutes of this date are a waste of time. I would have rather have spent another four minutes with Clarissa. "No Thanks."

10. **Patty.** My Match.com friend and I have a very pleasant conversation. Patty is nice enough, but there was no spark between us when we went out on a real first date, and there's no spark between us during our six-minute speed date. Patty doesn't know how to have fun, and I'm not looking for a business partner. We both pretend that we're going to go out for coffee after tonight. I'll probably give her a "Let's Talk" but not really mean it.

11. **Raeline.** Patty's friend and I actually have a few things in common. She, like me, moved to Springfield from California for "quality of life" reasons. She's a consultant. (Code word for underemployed.) She's nice, but she has a cartoon voice. She sounds like Mel Blanc doing a character on an old Looney Tunes cartoon. Six minutes of talking to her is all I can stand. I can't imagine having a relationship with Raeline and having to listen to her on the phone. I would constantly be laughing at her because of the way she sounds. What if she said, "My cat got hit by a Ben

and Jerry's truck today and died at the vet," and I laughed because of her helium voice? "No Thanks."

12. **Joyce.** Of all of the women here tonight, Joyce is the perfect match for me on paper. She's a horticulturist; she grows plants for a living. I'm a suburban gardener at heart. You'd think we would have lots to talk about. And you'd be wrong. I don't like her AT ALL. Joyce is sarcastic, cynical and very difficult to talk to. She doesn't smile—as if she has a limited supply and she's afraid she will run out. I look at my watch after three minutes and think, "How much longer is this going to go on?" The longest six minute date of my life. "NO THANKS."

13. **Raine.** As I arrive at Raine's table, I'm thinking she's probably the youngest person in the room. So here's the oldest man in the room talking to the youngest woman. Raine is friendly and vaguely cute. She comes across as a genuinely nice person. But she has the semi-clueless demeanor that sometimes results from never leaving the town where you grew up. The only thing that seems to excite her is Bon Jovi. Yep, the band. She and her friends plan their vacations so they can watch Jon Bon Jovi strut his stuff in as many cities as possible. "No Thanks."

Thirteen rapid-fire dates impress upon me the importance of meeting a person face to face. Online dating is a tremendous time saver (and quite entertaining), but the magic of chemistry between two people happens in person.

BABE MAGNET RULE #64

The chemistry of attraction happens in person, and it usually happens quickly. When it does, pay attention to it.

After the event, we're all so charged up with adrenaline that no one wants to leave. Most of us re-congregate in the restaurant bar for a post-predating beverage or two. I join Hanna and Amanda and buy them drinks. I ask them how many men they think they are going to vote for. "One or two" is the response. Since Amanda is on my "Let's Talk" list, I focus most of my attention on her. She seems a little guarded, but I also catch her giving me "the look" when she thinks my attention is elsewhere. You know, the look a person gives to another person when the hormones are starting to flow and the beginning of an attraction is starting to form.

On the way out I chat with Patty. She also thinks she will vote for two men. If I were to hazard a guess, I would say that women are much more selective than men at a speed dating event. Even when 12 or 13 men are served up on a platter, most women aren't going to find more than one or two they would like to see again. I think a lot of men, on the other hand, treat a speed dating event as an all-you-can-eat buffet and go out with as many women as they possibly can.

When I get home, I decide to immediately go to the official event page on Cupid.com to cast my votes. I end up voting for five of the 13 women. Two of the votes are "friend" votes for Hanna and Patty. But I have three solid dating opportunities: Amanda, Katrina, and Clarissa. I hope that at least one of them also votes for me.

The next morning I am still on the high from the previous night's speed dating event. I got an emotional lift and a self-esteem boost from going on 13 dates in one evening. Cupid.com should ask me to write a testimonial statement, because right now I think speed dating is the coolest thing that ever happened to dating since...sex.

And it gets better. Of the three women I voted for that I really want to go out with, ALL THREE of them say they'll go out with me. Great Bounty of Babes! Three for three! I am batting 1.000!

Better still: I am getting inside information from Hanna about how to approach her friend Amanda. Hanna tells me to take it slow. "Amanda spooks easily," says Hanna. "Treat her like a jittery horse that needs to reassured before you put a saddle on her." Giddy-up!

Hanna says I need to approach Amanda right away "while she's still interested." With the confidence brought on by inside information, I schedule a lunch date with Amanda for tomorrow.

Chapter 61: Amanda, Clarissa, and Katrina

I am excited that Cupid.com's Big Three, the Trio of Speed Dating Babes, the Triumvirate of Tantalizing Tigresses, have all agreed to go out with me on official dates. Each one of them seems to be as excited as I am. I have spent a grand total of six minutes with each woman (plus a few additional minutes with Amanda). So in many ways, these will be first dates. But these wonderful women have all been pre-screened by yours truly.

Plus, all three of these women have already pre-screened *me*. They have all determined that Chad Stone is USDA Prime Male. Not that I am getting all big-headed about it or anything... But woo-hooo! Let the festivities begin!

Amanda

I arrive at the restaurant just as Amanda is getting out of her car. First I see the long, lanky legs appear from her Honda CRV. Then I get a flash of her long brown hair flipping up as she stands. She sees me watching her and smiles self-consciously. I walk toward her, and it seems like we switch to slow motion because it takes a long time to reach her. We give each other a quick hug that has no sexual undertones.

Our lunch lasts for an hour and a half, and between the chewing and the talking our mouths never stop. Amanda is a wonderful woman—smart, personable, kind, curious. She has a great sense of humor, and she asks thoughtful questions that prod me to reveal myself. She wants to know everything about me, so I tell her about my family history and my "moving to Springfield" story. She is particularly interested in my relationship with my son, Jason. Without telling me so, she wants to know what kind of father I am.

It's hard to believe this woman put her dating life on hold for so long. She's been divorced for almost 10 years, and now that her daughter is 17 Amanda is just now comfortable with the concept of dating again. I cannot imagine the devotion it must take to focus on being a parent and completely abandon all thoughts of finding a romantic partner. Even if you aren't interested in marriage, does that mean you must turn off your passions like you would turn off a water faucet? My heart would have to be broken beyond repair for me to contemplate a life without love—without even the hope of romance.

After telling her a recent story about Jason, the way Amanda looks at me changes. She lets her guard down. Her eyes open up, and I am suddenly able to look into her soul. I don't know if she knows what is happening, but I see it clearly in her eyes.

Shortly after our lunch, Amanda sends me a very nice "thank you" email. She's a classy lady, and I am looking forward to getting to know her better.

Clarissa

How long has it been since I had a Saturday night date? It's been so long that I don't remember. That's why I wanted my first real date with Clarissa to be an old-fashioned Saturday night dinner date.

I have selected my favorite Italian restaurant, with white linen tablecloths and waiters who wear black ties. The food is fabulous, the wine list is impressive, and the ambiance is old-school romantic.

BABE MAGNET RULE #65

Quirky and creative dates are wonderful, but don't underestimate the tried-and-true value of an expensive dinner at a classy restaurant on Saturday night.

Clarissa seems to be following the unofficial dating guidelines for single women in an age of stalkers, weirdos, terrorists, and fear-based media. (Guideline Number 6: Don't let a strange man know where you live.) I offer to pick Clarissa up, but she says she'll meet me at the restaurant.

Clarissa is wearing a bright red jacket over a simple but classy off-white top. She's probably about five foot eight in her bare feet, but tonight she's wearing boots with three-inch-tall stiletto heels, which puts her almost eye-to-eye with me as we greet each other in the restaurant's reception area.

My heart is fluttering as I give her a friendly hug. I have only spent six minutes with her at the speed dating event. But during those six minutes, I felt an energy connection with Clarissa that I didn't feel with any of the other women.

I want to see if I feel that spark tonight.

We are seated at the perfect table in a dark, romantic corner of the restaurant's main dining area. We start the festivities with a nice bottle of merlot. The fire between us has cooled a bit in the past week since we saw each other, but Clarissa and I pick up our conversation right where we left off. The wine flows and so does our dialog, seamlessly moving from one topic to the next. Throughout three hours of wine, appetizers, salad, dinner, and dessert, we never run out of things to talk about. She is as adept at the fine art of conversation as I am.

She tells me about her 9-year-old son. For some reason—wishful thinking, perhaps—I thought he was older. Nine-year-olds need babysitters, and that's a complication in a courtship. But Clarissa downplays this by telling me her mother and her ex-husband both live in town and provide child care whenever Clarissa needs it, either for work or for play.

After I have given her a rather thorough synopsis of my professional career, I hand her one of my business cards. She focuses intently on my phone number, which ends with 6222. "This number has followed me around all my life," she says, with a touch of amazement in her voice.

"What number?"

"Two-two-two."

"Really? What does it mean?"

"I'm not sure exactly, but it appears whenever there's a change in my life."

Cue the *Twilight Zone* music.

I walk Clarissa to her car, a little SUV so new it still has a temporary license plate. I tell her I had a great time and ask if I can see her again. She says she'd like to go out with me again, too. "There's an energy about you that I like," she says.

We hug tentatively. Then I watch the taillights of her new car fade into the distance.

Katrina

It's Sunday afternoon at 3:00 p.m., and I am almost on time for my first date with Katrina. In the restaurant parking lot, a white Honda brakes, then backs up to take the only spot left in the lot. I grumble and have to park a block away.

Katrina is waiting for me at the front of the restaurant, reading the postings on the eclectic bulletin board. Flyers and cards for alternative healthcare for dogs, yoga for singles, a rafting trip to Mexico, a house for sale by owner for $499,000, and a band looking for a female lead singer vie for her attention.

My very first thought when I see her is, "She looks older than I remember her." She is 51 years old. Then I remember I'm 53, so I have no reason to be picky.

Because this is my third post-speed dating date, I am relaxed and comfortable. I have already had two great first dates with Amanda and Clarissa, so this is really just a bonus date. But, of course, Katrina doesn't know that.

Katrina is a massage therapist, but she also does medical transcribing for doctors. She has two kids—25 and 21—and she also has a 4-year-old grandson. I tell her she looks way too young and way too beautiful to be a grandmother. She loves hearing that, and gives me a big smile.

Katrina has already told me that she loves the key lime pie here, yet she orders only iced tea. I can't get her to eat anything, despite the fact that I haven't eaten yet and I order a full lunch.

Katrina launches into the saddest online dating story I have ever heard. Ten years ago she was on a singles website and she started corresponding with a man from Wyoming. Then they started talking on the phone. They talked to each other nearly every day. "He was everything I was looking for in a man," she says.

Their phone conversations continued, and after a couple of months Katrina completely fell for this guy. Finally, they made arrangements to meet. A few days before he was to fly into town, Katrina got a phone call from his brother. Her lover-to-be had been killed in an accident. Katrina was heartbroken, and she started grieving for her loss.

Three days later, her phone rang and it was her supposed-to-be-dead lover-to-be. He hadn't died in an accident. There was no accident. That was a lie. And virtually everything else he told her was a lie, too. He was married. The photos he sent to her via email were from many years ago. He said he was sorry.

Katrina was devastated. The man that she thought she loved was a lying, stinking butthead. That was almost 10 years ago, and Katrina is just now able to date again. Ten years! If that asshole were here, I'd beat him with a rubber hose for pulling that kind of crap. Hey, men, check out this Babe Magnet Rule and take it to heart:

> **BABE MAGNET RULE #66**
> Don't be a lying, stinking asshole. Don't hide behind the anonymity of an online dating profile and tell lies to trusting, unsuspecting women. Lying, stinking asshole men give all the rest of us decent guys a bad reputation. (If there is a Hell, then men who lie about themselves on dating sites will be cleaning toilets in the diarrhea ward of Hell for all of eternity.)

Let me tell you, a story like Katrina's can take all the fun out of a date. I try to change the subject to something current, something more fun. We talk about our speed dating experiences from last week. Katrina decided to participate only after her friends, Mary and Canasta, talked her into it. And then, one of the men that Mary and Canasta both picked from the speed dating event started telling them completely different stories about himself. They confronted him, and he got all huffy and pulled his profile from Cupid.com.

Jesus H. Christ. What is this world coming to when men are so fast and loose with what they tell women? It's no wonder that so many women have given up on men altogether. If I were a woman and went through what Katrina has already been through, you can bet I'd seriously consider becoming either celibate or lesbian.

I walk Katrina out to her car. Yep, it's the little white Honda that took the last spot in the lot when I arrived. I think the universe is trying to tell me something here.

I won't be seeing Katrina again.

Chapter 62: Here Today, Gone Tomorrow

I take the week off from dating, and the following Saturday I spend at the Real Love Men's Workshop at the Unity Church. It is emotionally challenging, but very uplifting. There are 20 men sitting around talking about their feelings—and their relationships with women, their kids, and even their parents. It is not a typical gathering of men, and I doubt if there are any Rush Limbaugh fans here. The three gay guys talk openly about their "significant other" relationships, and I find it fascinating that they have many of the same issues that heterosexual couples face.

I guess romantic relationships, whether straight or gay, are inherently complicated and challenging. Maybe that's what makes them so satisfying when they work.

After the workshop, I have plenty of time to get ready for my dinner date with Amanda. I have selected a hipster restaurant near the university that serves gourmet pizza and salads, and also has a good beer and wine menu. It's casual and upscale at the same time (kind of like me!).

Amanda arrives looking like a New York City fashion model in a black leather jacket and black jeans. She flashes me a big smile and gives me a friendly hug. As we stand in line to place our order, we are exactly the same height, blue eyes to blue eyes. I am not used to being with a woman who is as tall as I am, and I find it a little unnerving. We order a fancy pizza to split and individual salads.

"I need a glass of wine tonight," says Amanda. "A 53-year-old friend of mine died of cancer this week."

Well, crap. I order a bottle of Chianti. If Amanda is going to talk about her dead friend, I'm going to need some wine, too.

In spite of Amanda's sadness, we have a pleasant date. I tell her all about the Real Love Men's Workshop, and she seems very interested. I tell her about the concept of Real Love versus Conditional Love, and how most of the love we have received during our lives is conditional. Our parents withheld their love when we misbehaved or underperformed. So what we experienced and what we learned was that love was generally withheld whenever the other person thought we weren't "good enough."

That leads to a lengthy discussion about how much easier it is for women to love and support each other. Men tend to talk about sports, the weather, and business. We don't talk about emotions because emotions make us uncomfortable. Women are naturally better at sharing their feelings, which results in closer emotional bonds with friends and family members.

"I think that's why the death of a close friend is so much more traumatic for a woman than a man," I say. "That's why the Real Love Men's Workshop was such a departure for most of the men who attended, and that made it all the more powerful."

That's pretty heavy stuff for a second date, and if I had been playing the odds I should have lightened up the conversation. Hanna had told me to go slowly with Amanda. "Keep it light, don't scare her away." But Amanda and I talk for nearly two hours over a leisurely dinner, and it seems to be going fabulously well. I love the way Amanda is gazing into my eyes as I talk, and how she gives me her undivided attention. I don't know if it's my brilliant conversation, or if she's paying attention to every detail because she's trying to decide if she wants to invest her emotions in a relationship with me. Either way, she is fully present, and she processes every word I say.

With the death of her friend heavy on her soul, Amanda wants to talk about deep, emotional topics. We talk about love, life, and death. The Babe Magnet Rulebook is not happy with me as I venture bravely into these topics with a woman I barely know:

BABE MAGNET RULE #67

Tread lightly and carefully through the mine field of deep, emotional topics during early dates. This is not safe territory

> for men. Women are experienced at discussing the big emotional issues, but you are not. If you're not extremely careful, you could accidentally step on a land mine and destroy any possibility of a follow-up date.

As far as I can tell by the clues I get from Amanda's face and body language, I successfully navigate the land mines. I even get extra points for venturing into dangerous territory without getting my leg blown off.

After dinner we walk down Central Avenue looking into shop windows. It seems very natural and very comfortable—as if we are already a couple. In front of a shoe store, I make her pick the shoes that she likes best. She chooses the shiny gold boots with the impossibly high heels.

"You think those heels are tall enough for me?" she asks. I know that she is self-conscious about her height, so I take her willingness to joke about it as a good sign.

As we say good night at her car, she gives me a hug before I have a chance to move in for a kiss. I am surprised that she is not feeling more passionate, but it is the only part of the date that disappoints me.

The big disappointment hits me like a ton of Hallmark Cards from CyberHell two days later. I get an email from Amanda with "Hey" as the subject line. "Hey" could mean anything, including "Hey I had a great time" or "Hey I have decided that you are the Antichrist."

I click open the message and read:

> Hey Chad,
> Thanks again for dinner on Sat. I had a nice time.
> After reflecting over these past couple of weeks I am feeling that this is probably not the relationship for me. You are an amazing, funny, attractive and extremely kind gentleman who I find so easy to talk to. I am just not feeling the connection that I think I should be feeling with you for this to keep going. I don't want to lead you on because I think you are a wonderful guy. In the past, I have tried to talk myself into feeling a certain way about someone and it ended up that we both got hurt. I am trying to learn from my past

> mistakes. Thank you for enriching my life. I feel very privileged to have met you.
> Take care,
> Amanda

WTF? Where did that come from? I thought Amanda and I were starting to bond. I was enjoying her company, and I thought the feeling was mutual. And now she sends me a Hey Chad letter.

Didn't I *specifically* ask her at the speed dating event if she was ready for a relationship? Hanna warned me about her, but Hanna also assured me that Amanda was now ready for a man in her life. Well, Amanda, if you keep running away from suitable candidates like me, you will live a lonely life, comforted only by your menagerie of animal shelter rescues and your stack of *Spinster* magazines.

In my logical mind, I know that we only went out on 2.5 dates. But I still feel hurt. Rejection after 2.5 dates is still rejection.

I had high hopes for Amanda, but she has dumped me with an email. It used to be that only men would pull a stunt like that. Welcome to post-feminist America, where women can be assholes just like men.

I hit the reply button and I send an email to Amanda.

> Amanda:
> Really?????? You're bailing on me already? I thought we were enjoying each other's company. We've only been on two dates. What kind of connection were you expecting after two dates?
> I think you're a wonderful woman and I hope you figure out what you're looking for. Call me if you change your mind.
> Chad (the "amazing, funny, attractive and extremely kind gentleman" that you just dumped)

There is no way I am going to change her mind. Two seconds afterwards, I regret sending the email. Crap. What was I thinking? I know better than that.

BABE MAGNET RULE #68

Sending a reply to a “break-up” email is a waste of time. Don’t do it. Have a little self respect. It’s okay to write a reply if it makes you feel better. BUT DO NOT SEND IT.

Chapter 63: Another One Bites the Dust

Two days later I meet Clarissa for dinner at India Temple restaurant. She arrives late, with an apology on her lips. If she had let me pick her up, we would have both been here on time. But she's not ready to tell me where she lives. Maybe she's ashamed of her house. Maybe she's a terrible housekeeper and she doesn't want me to see how messy her place is. Maybe Clarissa is trying to protect her son from being exposed to her dating life.

We settle into a nice table for two and gingerly review the menu. Clarissa doesn't know much about Indian food, and she looks to me for guidance. I suggest a couple of dishes that I like, and she adds a nice selection of curried chicken.

Dinner is delicious, and we both dig in with healthy appetites. "The food here is fluorescent," she says, and it clearly delights her. The strange colors, intoxicating scents, and exotic flavors make the meal special, which is exactly what I was hoping for. By the end of dinner, we have consumed most of a bottle of white wine. Our conversation flows as easily as the wine, but we don't talk about anything of consequence. Perhaps I am still a little stung by the seriousness of my last date with Amanda, and the less-than-satisfying aftermath.

Clarissa seems a bit reserved for a second date. I think something might be bothering her, but I don't know her well enough to know for sure. Out by Clarissa's car, I give her a quick kiss. She turns away before it can become passionate.

The next day she calls me on the phone to thank me for the nice dinner, which I think is a very classy move. We chat for a few minutes, and I can tell by the tone of her voice that there is something that Clarissa wants to tell me. She finally gets to it. "There is something that I haven't been completely honest with you about."

Okay. I wait for the other shoe to drop.

"The reason I can always get my mother to babysit for me is because she lives with me and my son."

I am not sure how to respond, because this situation has never come up before in my dating experience. It sounds like a Good News/Bad News proposition. The Good News is, Clarissa has a built-in babysitter. The Bad News is, Clarissa isn't just a two-generation package deal, she's a *three-generation* package deal.

My mind jumps forward. When a woman has a child (or multiple children), there comes a time when "dates" between the mother of the children and the Babe Magnet sometimes include the kids. Instead of going to see a sexy R-rated movie, the whole family goes to see the latest Pixar animated extravaganza. So, when there's a grandmother involved, does she sometimes come along, too? Does that mean that I get to take the whole family to see Wayne Newton in concert?

On a 10-point Babe Rating scale, Clarissa has just dropped two points. But wait, there's more.

I also find out that the father of Clarissa's son isn't her ex-husband. The father was the significant other in a previous relationship, and Clarissa never married him. (Have I told you how much I hate the whole unmarried parent thing?)

But wait, there's *still* more.

Her son's father lives 200 miles away, and on his weekend visits with his son, sometimes he spends the entire weekend at Clarissa's house rather than driving back and forth all of those miles.

So now the package deal includes three generations, plus the never-married father of Clarissa's child.

"Is there a large number of cats that you also need to tell me about?" I ask. I say this as a joke—sort of.

"What?"

"Has anyone in the family been convicted of a felony?" I ask.

"Huh?"

"Have you or any previous lovers, wed or unwed, ever served time in prison?"

She is not amused. But that's okay, because I am not amused by the additional information she has given me about her complicated living situation.

I am not looking for ways to complicate my life. At this point, I am looking for true love. Pure, and hopefully, simple. There, I've said it. I don't want to be a Babe Magnet any longer than is necessary to find true love.

> **BABE MAGNET RULE #69**
> Seek simplicity in a potential romantic partner. If you find out that a woman has a complicated past or current living situation, move on. This goes triple if you are looking for a long-term relationship.

With all due respect to Clarissa, I gently break the news to her that I won't be calling her again. She is not happy about it, but if she has listened to what she just told me, she can't be surprised.

Chapter 64: When One Babe Shuts a Door, Another Opens a Window

Until two days ago, I had written Colleen off. She cancelled Friday afternoon movie dates three weeks in a row, claiming to be sick. I told her to call me back when she wanted to reschedule, and she never did.

So I am surprised to get a text message from Colleen late on a Friday afternoon, asking me if I am going to go to the dancing lessons at Grand Central Station. Rather than answer with a text, I pick up the phone and call her.

Colleen is chatty and friendly, and we talk for more than 20 minutes. I tell her about my recent Men's Group workshop, and she seems intrigued. "It sounds more like an event that would appeal to women," she says.

"I think that was the point," I explain. "It was designed to get men to discuss things that we don't normally talk about."

On our one (and thus far only) date, I thoroughly enjoyed Colleen's company. She was clearly holding back, because she told me upfront she wasn't going to rush into a relationship, but she was still bubbly and fun. Even when she called to cancel dates, we ended up having great phone conversations. But once the speed dating whirlwind took over my life, I stopped thinking about Colleen.

And yet, the life of an unattached Middle-Aged Babe Magnet can change faster than you can receive a Hey Chad email. One week you go out on 15 dates (if you count 6-minute speed dates as actual dates). A couple of weeks later, your calendar is completely empty and you are back to rearranging your sock drawer on Saturday night.

I ask Colleen if she'd like to have dinner with me on Tuesday, and she says yes. So there you go, Sports Fans: I am back in the game.

* * * *

Now that we have a date scheduled, Colleen must be thinking of me. The next morning she sends me a text message to let me know that it is freezing cold outside. I take it as a compliment.

Later in the day, Colleen calls me to see if I am willing to alter our date.

"You're not calling to cancel, are you?" I ask. She better not be. If she is calling to cancel, I am never going to talk to her again. I will call up Verizon Wireless and have her calls and text messages blocked. They will go into a vault and never be heard by a human being. Ever.

"No, no, no," she says, sheepishly. "I got free tickets, and I want to know if you'd like to go to the basketball game instead of going out to dinner."

Hmmmm. Instead of me taking her out to dinner, at great personal expense to myself, she wants to take me to the last basketball game of the season at the local university, whose team is headed to the NCAA Tournament. I have to think about this for 0.0016 seconds before I make up my mind.

"Absolutely," I say, smiling to myself. I might end up liking this woman.

So I meet Colleen at the Walgreen's parking lot because that's the most centrally located spot we could think of. Colleen lives on the other side of town, and neither of us wants to drive to the other's house. She sees me standing by my car in the parking lot and parks nearby. "You ready to go?" she asks. No "hello," no "it's nice to see you again." No attempt at an awkward hug.

I put a CD in the car stereo to serve as background music in case there are any uncomfortable silences in our conversation. But during the 20-minute drive to the stadium, we engage in a chatfest that covers topics that range from the secondary infection that forced Colleen to cancel three dates to the best rock concerts we have ever attended. It feels like we already know each other very well.

We are running late, and the game has already started. The road leading to the stadium is choked with cars, and the parking lots closest to the stadium are already full.

"Turn here," says Colleen. "I'll show you my secret parking spot."

But her "secret" spot clearly isn't, because it is filled with cars. So is her other "secret" spot. We end up parking so far away we're in a different zip code. Then we walk. And walk. And walk. Colleen is only five foot two, and her boots get her up to about five-five. She is clearly not enjoying the fast-paced walking on her little legs.

"I taught three fitness classes, so I already got enough exercise today," she says.

She jokes and gripes good-naturedly as we walk. Her straight brown hair bounces off her shoulders with each step she takes. When she smiles, Colleen's face glows in the dark. Even when she's being grumpy, she is still cute.

Once at the stadium, we stand in a long line to buy food. Both of us are famished, and dinner is going to be whatever crappy food we can get from the concession stand. I buy hot dogs, peanuts, and Cokes. At least we're going to be watching a Division One college basketball game as we eat our crummy dinners.

The game is close, and the crowd is so loud that it's hard to talk. So Colleen and I simply watch the game. It is a wonderful date for a man: sports and no talking.

On the drive back home, Colleen does all of the talking that she had stored up from the game. To be completely fair and honest, I thoroughly enjoy listening to her. She is fun; she is spunky. By God, I already know that she is opinionated and sometimes bossy. But she is opinionated and bossy in a friendly way.

I pull up beside her car in the Walgreen's parking lot. We talk for a few more minutes, and I find out her birthday is next week. "Then I must take you out for a proper birthday dinner," I say, magnanimously. She smiles and accepts.

Before she gets out of my car, I lean over to kiss her. She leans in and we kiss briefly, but I lose my nerve mid-kiss and pull back. Just as I am pulling back, I realize that she is still hanging in for more.

Oh no! I blew our first kiss. I pulled back too soon! Aaaarrrrggghhh! You never get a second chance for a first kiss. Fifty years from now, when we are both so old we hardly remember our own names, I will still remember screwing up our first kiss. “I could have really made out with her that first time, if I hadn’t been so chicken.”

My only consolation is that I know there is going to be a second kiss. And a third, and…

Chapter 65: R U there yet?

During my last date with Colleen, I told her a little bit about my short relationship with Anna. I told her that I liked Anna quite a bit in the beginning, but the more I went out with her, the more there was about her that I didn't like.

I told Colleen that Anna said she would never call me to initiate a date, because that was my job. I don't have a problem with that, and I happen to agree that it's the man's job to call a woman to initiate a date—especially during the early phases of a courtship. Even though it's not politically correct to say so, men are hard-wired to be the hunters in the dating process, and women are hard-wired to be the hunted. Even in the post-post modern 21st century, where women are proud to earn 77 cents for every dollar a man earns in the workplace, men like the hunt of dating.

Women, when they are being honest, will tell you that they love to be approached by a man. A woman loves it when a man demonstrates his masculine energy by choosing her and taking the risk of asking her out. There are primal forces at work that defy logic, and that's what makes them so powerful.

But Anna took that "I'll never call you" policy to the extreme. She literally never called me. Not once did she send me a friendly, unprompted text message. I understand why she never called me to say, "Hey, you wanna go out tomorrow night?" But not contacting me EVER to say "hello" struck me as being one degree short of frigid.

Apparently, Colleen took this story to heart. She has emailed and/or texted me every day since our last date. They are cute little messages, asking me where I am and if I'm having fun. Basically, they tell me that she is thinking of me.

On the day of our next date, Colleen is clearly bored at work so she passes the time by sending me text messages. By the end of the day she has sent me 10. And that doesn't include the "R U there yet?" message she sends me when I am driving to the restaurant for our date. Hey, it's great that she is excited about me, but I hope I don't receive 10 text messages from her every day.

Colleen gives me a big smile and a full body hug when I arrive at the restaurant. I think Colleen has decided that she likes me.

We settle in for dinner. The food is delicious. The wine is intoxicating. The conversation is invigorating. Dessert is scrumptious. Colleen is delightful. Life on Planet Earth is perfect.

How great is dinner? We spend FOREVER in the restaurant. By the time we leave, the waiter, who looked to be about 25 years old when we arrived, is showing us photos of his grandkids. Neither Colleen nor I want to leave, for fear that the magic spell cast over our table will be broken and we'll have to venture out into a world filled with crime, fast food, wars in foreign lands, cars made in Korea, and Glenn Beck.

When we simply can't stay in the restaurant any longer without buying an ownership stake in the business, I walk Colleen to her car and kiss her. I give her a bouquet of sweet kisses, but not passionate. I chastely keep my tongue in my own mouth.

I ask her if she'd like to see me again. She laughs out loud because the answer is so obvious. "Of course I would."

As I am pulling my car into my driveway, my phone beeps with a text message.

Thx for a nice evening. I enjoyed ur company.

I did, too, Colleen. I did, too.

A week goes by between dates with Colleen. In the meantime, we talk or message each other every day. Interestingly, it is Colleen who is initiating most of the contact, most of the dialogue. If anything, I am the one who is holding back.

During this dating break, I have time to check in with my man friends. Craig's marriage is starting to unravel. He's trying to hold things together, but his wife is beginning to show signs of extreme stress. Her mother died unexpectedly, and to help with the grief she has been taking prescription medications. She is just not acting right. Now she is accusing Craig of having affairs, even though Craig assures me that he has been completely faithful. When she found his "little black book" from a few years back, she went postal.

"How dare you go out with her!" she screamed.

"That was before I even MET you," he retorted.

The rest of their conversation was punctuated by his angry wife throwing breakable items from the kitchen cabinets.

Mueller is also having marital difficulties. He and his wife are clearly moving in the direction of divorce. Mueller has moved out, and she is already talking about how to divide up their possessions.

Thankfully, Karl and Cassandra are still happily married. They are even talking about a major remodel of their house. However, Karl tells me in strict confidence that he isn't having much sex these days. Things in that department have slowed to an end-of-the-month clearance sale.

Hmmmm. Do I really want to have a relationship if that's what I have to look forward to? Do I really want to get aboard the Love Train once again if the odds say the ride will make stops at Conflict Junction, Argument Township, Sexless Hills, or even Divorce City?

The most-often quoted statistic about marriage in America is that one of every two marriages now ends in divorce. But even more shocking are the statistics for second and third marriages. According to Jennifer Baker of the Forest Institute of Professional Psychology in Springfield, Missouri, 67% of second marriages and 74% of third marriages end in divorce.

Do I really want to venture into love—and eventually, marriage—if the path is so fraught with pain and failure?

You bet I do. As Han Solo (played by Harrison Ford in *The Empire Strikes Back*) says, "Never tell me the odds." Like Mr. Solo, I choose to remain an optimist no matter what kind of evidence there is to the contrary.

> **BABE MAGNET RULE #70**
> Don't let the odds get you down. Just because every couple you know is breaking up doesn't mean that you can't meet someone, fall in love, and live happily ever after.

I know love is out there. In my heart, I know that it is possible to fall in love again—no matter who you are, what your relationship history is, or how old you are. There is plenty of love to go around if you just open yourself up to it.

Chapter 66: Moving Closer Toward the "R" Word

I arrive early for my dinner date with Colleen. I have chosen a fancy restaurant so that Colleen will get the message that I am making an effort to impress her. I am wearing a sport coat and nice slacks to reinforce the message.

Colleen arrives with a beautiful smile on her face and a sparkle in her bright blue eyes. She looks gorgeous, in an elegant black-and-white dress that reveals plenty of her ample cleavage. She is wearing more makeup than usual, and she has chosen a deep red lipstick that gives her a sexy, retro appearance.

We order wine to drink while we examine the menu. Our dinner selections fall along strict gender lines—a salad for her and spaghetti and meatballs for me. Our easy-flowing conversation picks up right where we left off a week ago.

What I love about being with Colleen is that it doesn't feel like work. We effortlessly jump from one topic to the next, and it's fun and exciting as we get to know each other, share our hopes and dreams, and sometimes reveal glimpses of our souls.

There is something quite intoxicating about getting to know a new romantic partner. At its best, a date is an adventure into an unknown place. What is inside this woman's head? What makes her tick? What makes her laugh? As I sit with Colleen, it feels as though I am watching a rose bud start to open. Little by little, she is revealing her petals, and the flower is becoming more and more beautiful.

After dinner we see a foreign film I have selected called *Under the Same Moon*. It's a great little movie about a nine-year-old boy in Mexico who pines for his mother after she has "crossed over" to the U.S. to work in Los Angeles. When his grandmother dies, he decides to travel alone to L.A. to find his mother.

The movie is delightfully charming, and both Colleen and I love it. I am a sucker for a movie with a heart, and the fact that Colleen also loves the movie bonds me closer to her. When we arrive back at Colleen's car, it is still fairly early and neither one of us wants this lovely evening to end. We go across the street for tapas and drinks.

Colleen wants to know more about me. She asks me how long I was married, and how long I have been divorced. She asks me about my ex-wife. I tell her that Valerie is a wonderful woman in many ways.

"If she was so wonderful, why did you divorce her?" she asks. Colleen is not one to beat around the bush. I know she wouldn't be asking me these questions if she wasn't interested in me. So I must be honest, and at the same time I must tread carefully.

BABE MAGNET RULE #71

Watch for cues that a woman is starting to get interested. Smiles, prolonged direct eye contact, a tilt of the neck and playing with her hair are signs of her sexual attraction to you. When she starts asking probing questions to get inside your brain, she wants to know if you are worthy of a relationship.

Why did I divorce Valerie? It's not the first time I have been asked that question. My mother wanted to know. My brother wanted to know. My friends wanted to know. My counselor wanted to know. It's not an easy answer, because my marriage was acceptable for a long time. When does "good enough" become unacceptable?

"I guess I was tired of carrying her baggage," I tell Colleen. "I got tired of her panic attacks. I got tired of her pessimism. Her first reaction to everything is negative. It's 'Oh My God, Oh My God!' I couldn't deal with the emotional roller coaster ride any longer." I pause to gather my thoughts. "I know that when I enter another relationship, I'll have to deal with someone else's baggage. But at least it will be different baggage."

Later, Colleen asks me why I don't get back together with my ex-wife.

"I have no desire to do that," I say. "That would be going backwards. I want to move forward. There are new adventures in my future."

That makes her smile.

The date ends with passionate kissing. Real, spare-no-tongue passionate kisses. It is clear by the way she is kissing me that I said something during the date that Colleen wanted to hear. Maybe it was simply my willingness to be open and honest about my marriage. Now Colleen's body is pressed against mine and we are heating up the night.

After we can kiss no more without melting into a puddle of unresolved sexual passion, I open Colleen's car door and say goodnight. Alas, her car won't start, and I don't have jumper cables. She calls her daughter for a ride home.

As they drive off together, I feel like a failure. I wasn't able to rescue the damsel in distress—and isn't that what men are for? Isn't that one of the main reasons that women want to have men in their lives? Aren't we supposed to be there to jump-start cars, unclog toilets, kill spiders, and unscrew impossibly tight jar lids?

I failed in my first opportunity to be a manly man for Colleen. I can't tell my beer-drinking, football-watching friends about this. They will hoot me out of the sports bar. Even my metrosexual men's group friends are going to click their tongues in disapproval.

A dead car battery is a bad way to end an otherwise wonderful date. But I am impressed with Colleen's reaction. "It's no big deal," she texts me after she gets safely home.

I like the way this woman thinks. And I sure do like the way she kisses.

After our date, I start having sexual fantasies about Colleen. I think about her many times a day. We talk on the phone every day, and we text each other multiple times a day. Even though we haven't consummated our relationship, there is definitely a relationship that needs consummating.

But it's going to have to wait, at least for a week.

Jason comes back from college for a week off, and I put my dating life on hold—except for the phone calls and the texts. Jason is making the delicate transition from teenager to manhood, and I want to spend as much time with him as possible. He needs a father in his life to reassure him that everything is right in his world.

It is a blast from the past for Jason to be occupying his bedroom again. It has been empty for so many weeks while he has been away at school. Even though he is doing quite well as a semi-adult when he is at college, he seems to revert back to his high school days when he gets back to the old homestead. It bugs me that he sleeps until after noon. But Zippy the Poodle doesn't mind. Zippy is delighted to have Jason back, and the dog sleeps happily on his bed.

I don't share my dating life with Jason. It is entirely inappropriate for me to subject him to his father's Middle-Aged Babe Magnet persona. He is still adapting to his parents' divorce, and I know that it is strange for him to come home and have everything seem normal except for one huge thing—his mother doesn't live here anymore.

Chapter 67: Cue the "Rocky" Music

After Jason returns to college, Colleen and I resume our slow and steady pattern of dating. I take Colleen to a play starring three young male actors who do comedy mash-ups of William Shakespeare plays. The show is absolutely hysterical, and Colleen and I both howl with laughter. Colleen has an infectious laugh and she's not shy about using it.

Our next date is a midday hike in the foothills near my house. Colleen agrees to meet me at my house, so I spend the entire morning straightening up and cleaning. This is the first time I have had a female visitor here in MONTHS, and I want to make sure Colleen has a good first impression of my home.

In advance of Colleen's arrival, I move piles of papers and magazines. I put things away that have been sitting on tables and chairs for weeks. I vacuum the entire house so there are those little vacuum cleaner lines in the carpet.

BABE MAGNET RULE #72
It is always worth cleaning the house to impress a Babe.

Colleen seems suitably impressed. She doesn't come right out and say it, but I know that my house passes inspection. She says that because I am an avid gardener, she thought my house décor would be of the frilly, country, homey-dippy variety. She is surprised to see Danish Modern furniture and contemporary artwork.

We get out to the hiking trail, and Colleen is a little dynamo. She is too short to have what I would call a fitness instructor's body, but on the hike I have trouble keeping up with her. For a while we walk hand-in-hand down the trail, and although this is a new expression of affection between us, it feels as comfortable as a favorite T-shirt.

When Colleen comes over to the house a few days later, it's for one of my trademarked "man prepares food to impress woman" dinners. I am not sure why this is such a big deal to women, but apparently, when women get together and compare notes about men, they absolutely LOVE IT when a man makes the effort to prepare food for the woman he is trying to impress. (See Babe Magnet Rule #36.) Colleen and I have decided on a dinner salad, which clearly reveals Colleen's input because I don't usually have salads for dinner. But I am going to "man it up" with some grilled salmon and a side of fresh bread to keep it from being so metrosexual.

I find that I am nervously excited as I prepare for the date. Why would an experienced Middle-Aged Babe Magnet get pre-date jitters? Could it be that I've finally found a woman who interests me? Could it be that I am having my longest romantic drought since I became single? Could it be that I'm not sure if I remember how this whole sex thing works anymore?

Not likely.

Dinner is fabulous, and we settle onto the couch after dinner. The wine has transported us to Mellowtown. I pop a DVD into the player and we start watching a romantic comedy.

Five minutes into the movie I start thinking: Do I want to wait until this entire movie is over before I make my move? What if Colleen is asleep by then? Why not make my move right now?

I lean over toward Colleen and give her a friendly kiss. The kiss becomes more passionate. Colleen adds some passion, and then I add some more.

We leave a trail of clothing leading to the bedroom. By the time we make it into my bed, we are both naked, and one of us is so swollen with passion that he can hardly walk. We spend the entire night together in various states of bliss. It is a wonderful ending to a delightful series of getting-to-know-each-other dates. And it feels like the beginning of a wonderful relationship.

* * * * *

I didn't realize how much I had missed passion in my life these past months until Colleen came along. Now that passion has been reintroduced into my life, I am basking in its glow. The next time I see her, Colleen is glowing, too.

We meet for a Friday lunch date. Colleen is already done with her work week, so after lunch we go back to my house. Again, we pretend we are going to watch a DVD, but within minutes we are flinging off clothes and completely ignoring the movie.

The next morning, Mueller and I decide to play nine holes of golf. We do a reasonable imitation of golfers who know what they are doing, and we have fun doing it. Mueller asks me if there are any new developments on the dating front.

"Huge developments," I say. "I am finally having sex again, after a hiatus of 13 years. At least it *felt* like 13 years."

Mueller laughs, and then he gives me a manly congratulatory slap on the back.

I give him a CNN Headline News description of Colleen. Interior decorator who also teaches fitness classes. Lives on the other side of town with her 21-year-old daughter. Has an infectious laugh and a positive outlook that makes her a joy to be around. Passionate. A tad bossy. Five foot two with a well-endowed chest and great big beautiful blue eyes.

A smile begins to spread across Mueller's face. "Nice," is all he says.

"It looks like I have a girlfriend," I say. It is the first time I refer to Colleen as the "G" word.

"How does that feel?" asks Mueller, instantly reverting back to a metrosexual.

I take a practice swing with my five iron and ponder the question. "It feels good. It feels really good."

After Mueller and I have navigated our way around the golf course, I call Colleen to see how her day is going. She's been driving around all over town looking for a Western style couch and leather pillows, so she's not in the mood to drive across town to come to my house. I offer to take her to dinner on her side of town.

I am thinking the program for the evening is "dinner and sex," but it doesn't turn out that way. After a pleasant Mexican food dinner in an almost-empty restaurant, Colleen refuses to take me back home to her apartment. I plead; I cajole; I use every bit of charm in my arsenal of sure-fire Babe Magnet seduction moves. But I cannot get her to change her mind. "My place is small, it's a mess, and I don't know if my daughter is going to be there."

Aha, so this is really about her daughter. I understand it, because I wasn't ready to introduce Jason to Colleen when he was in town. Dating after divorce is so much more complicated when there are kids involved—even when the kids are young adults.

After a few more minutes of talking, she tells me the unvarnished truth. "I don't know if you are going to dump me in two or three weeks, and I would rather not introduce my daughter to someone who is not going to be around."

Wow. I am still disappointed that she does not want me to come over, but now I completely understand why. The best I can do is to get her to agree to come over to my house for dinner on Thursday. The date ends with us making out in the parking lot like a couple of teenagers.

I wake up in the morning and check my email. There is a friendly message from Colleen, who shares with me the title of a spiritual self-help book that Oprah loves. Colleen highly recommends the book, because "it has made me more aware of the peace that is possible, and can happen if I would only allow it." She continues: "I also wanted to thank you for coming into my life as one happy person to another. It is wonderful to share laughter when we are together. Very nice! Have a wonderful day!"

I read her email again and again. Each time it makes me smile. I knew Colleen was fun, but I am still learning about her depth and her serious side. I am looking forward to spending time with her and getting to know her better.

By the end of the next day, Colleen has completely filled up my text message inbox. The last 44 text messages have all been from her. We now have two dates scheduled for this week—Thursday and Saturday.

I can't wait.

I should be feeling fantastic right now. During the past two months my life has truly been blessed. A wonderful woman has become part of my life. We have shared laughs, meals and assorted good times. We have enjoyed simply hanging out with each other, and we have celebrated the peaks of passion. Colleen is fun, sexy, and wonderful company.

So why am I so melancholy tonight?

Is it because the chase is more exciting than the prize? Is it because sex is really not the answer? Is it because, deep in my heart, I already suspect that Colleen is not the ultimate destination, that she's a resting place along the journey?

I like Colleen a lot. I enjoy being with her, and I think about her when we are apart. I love her infectious laugh. I love her energy and her joy. She is always looking for what is right with the world, and she doesn't care to dwell on what is wrong.

But there are things about our relationship that are less than perfect. I was looking for a taller woman. (Am I really that shallow? Apparently, yes.) I was looking for a woman who was more financially prosperous. I was looking for physical and emotional chemistry. I was looking for a woman who would melt into a pool of hot juices at my very touch. While Colleen is a wonderful and generous lover, I cannot routinely satisfy her. I want to please the woman I am with, and my fragile male ego gets deflated every time I fail to bring Colleen to the mountaintop. (Am I really that ego-driven that I feel less of a man if I can't please my woman? Again, apparently yes.)

Colleen called me to apologize for not climaxing when we made love last night. She apologized to me! How weird is that?

Perhaps I should count myself lucky to have found a woman who is so concerned about how I feel—even when what I feel is a melancholy sadness over not being able to sexually please her.

She said she was sorry; she was tired and stressed. I told her not to worry about it. Worrying about it only makes it worse. So I will relax about it, too. I will relax and not worry and not obsess that my male ego is getting a bruising.

I thought I was well on my way to being a Middle-Aged Babe Magnet Zen Master. But now I realize I still have a long way to go.

Chapter 68: Girlfriend

I am using a new word that hasn't been in my vocabulary for quite a while: Girlfriend. I like the sound of it. I like the idea of having a girlfriend once again, and I love thinking of Colleen as my girlfriend.

It's funny how much difference there is between a "girlfriend" and a "girl friend." As we commonly use the term, a girlfriend is a romantic partner. A girlfriend is the one special female who, by mutual consent in a modern relationship, shares your bed and occupies a special place in the rest of your life, too. However, a "girl friend" (two words) is a friend of the opposite gender, a friend who happens to be a female.

When I was in middle school (which was so long ago that they called it junior high), it was common to formally negotiate a boyfriend-girlfriend relationship. This often involved a serious discussion about "going steady," which meant that the boy and the girl would promise to date only each other. Sometimes, the boy would give the girl a St. Christopher pendant that she would wear around her neck. The girl would then have proof to show her girl friends that she was indeed going steady and had a boyfriend. The two kids in the "steady" relationship could then go about their lives as if nothing had changed. Once in a while they would eat lunch together, but that was about it.

Decades later, it makes me laugh that we don't have better words for "boyfriend" and "girlfriend." After the age of 40, should you really refer to a woman as your girlfriend? Ladyfriend is more accurate. But if I were to introduce Colleen as my ladyfriend, I am not sure that the term would carry the same implied understanding of "yes, this is the woman with whom I am having a sexual relationship." In fact, tabloid newspapers often refer to a woman as a man's "lady friend" when they are not exactly sure if the two adults in question are having a romantic relationship.

The French gave us the perfect word for the next step along the relationship path: fiancée. I have heard some people refer to their romantic sweeties as "partners," but that's such a cold word. A partner can also be the other guy at your law firm. And the word "partner" is commonly used in homosexual relationships. If Colleen had a unisex name (Pat, Terry, Randy, etc.) then some people might think I was gay if I talked about my partner, Terry.

The French really need to invent a word for a girlfriend/boyfriend of advanced years.

Colleen and I haven't talked about being each other's girlfriend or boyfriend. No St. Christopher's medal has been given. (In fact, St. Christopher was demoted in 1969 when his business manager failed to pay the Pope the required Saint Dues. Now he is commonly referred to as The Really Good Guy formerly known as Saint Christopher.)

In the past few months, my relationship with Colleen has evolved. When I no longer had to seduce Colleen toward the end of every evening, I knew we had gone beyond simply dating. Now, Colleen sometimes just walks herself to my bedroom, strips naked, and jumps into my bed. The sex is assumed.

When I meet Karl at Barleycorn's for a beer, he asks me how my dating life is going. "It's great," I say. "I am seeing Colleen exclusively. We are in a monogamous relationship, and I am really enjoying it."

Karl drinks to my health. The cute 23-year-old barmaid comes by to see if we need another beer. I flirt with her a little, just for fun. So does Karl.

"I thought you had a girlfriend," admonishes Karl.

"I thought you had a wife," I retort.

BABE MAGNET RULE #73

A little harmless flirting with a waitress can be fun, and it's a great way to keep your conversational skills honed. But if there is a steady Babe in your life, make sure you remember

> this: There's a big difference between harmless flirting and trying to pick up a woman. Don't cross the line.

While I am chatting with Karl, Colleen texts me to let me know she is going home to change clothes before our date.

"I have time for another beer," I say to Karl.

Having a girlfriend takes some of the pressure off the rigid schedule of dating. Besides, last week I made it official. I gave her a key to my house, which is the grown-up version of the St. Christopher medallion.

Chapter 69: Meeting (and Dealing with) the Kids

Colleen and I have settled into a comfortable relationship routine. In the typical week we spend Wednesdays and Saturdays together. She drives to my house and parks in my driveway. (She used to park in front of my house, but one evening Ray next door was driving his sports car a little too fast toward his driveway, and he almost took Colleen's car door clean off. It scared the crap out of both of them. Since then, Ray has apologized to me 15 times for "almost killing your girlfriend" and Colleen refuses to park on the street.)

Colleen rolls her overnight bag from her car to my front door, and then she puts it on her side of my bed. It's as though she is checking into a hotel where she has stayed a hundred times before.

I love the familiarity of having a girlfriend. I love the overnight stays and waking up in the middle of the night with a woman in my bed. It is so much better than the life of celibacy that quickly vanished with the arrival of Colleen in my life.

I love having an automatic date on Saturday night. I enjoy the regular companionship that Colleen provides. I love the phone calls and the text messages that we exchange on a daily basis. Sometimes the sheer volume of text messages gets a little ridiculous, though. But I suppose having a small "pet peeve" is part of the joy of having a girlfriend.

The Colleen and Chad Weekly Routine has caused me to be a much more consistent housekeeper. I do my weekly housecleaning before Colleen arrives to spend the night, scurrying around so that my home looks neat and tidy before she arrives. Our relationship is new enough that I find myself still trying to impress her, and I am not ready for Colleen to see the disorganized, messy side of me yet.

Colleen always comes over to my house to spend the night because of her daughter, Amber. I have met Amber a few times, and she has the personality of a rock. (Okay, that's a little harsh. A rock is a completely inanimate object, without any life at all. Amber has the personality of a *tree*.) At 21, she is a legal adult, but she acts like a spoiled teenager. She is aloof to the point of not even acknowledging my presence. When I arrive to pick up Colleen, Amber glances at me quickly, sighs, and leaves the room.

Amber is one of those teenagers/young adults who feels that the world owes her something. She is entitled to whatever she wants. She has a part-time job in a restaurant, and she uses the money she earns for her own personal enjoyment. Colleen is paying for her tuition and books at the local community college, and Amber lives rent-free with Colleen. So basically, Amber is getting a free ride—without having to do any chores or take on any family responsibilities.

I have not had a meaningful conversation with Amber. Even though I try to be friendly, she simply won't talk to me. Maybe it's because I am a man who is dating her mother. Colleen has been single for a long time, and I suspect that Amber has met a lot of men who have dated her mother over the years. Because Amber's parents divorced when she was young, she did not grow up with a father figure in her life. Maybe that's what she wants most of all, and maybe that's why she's so bitter.

It's possible that Amber will slowly warm up to me. I will treat her with kindness, and she will eventually learn that I am a wonderful human being. Over time, we could begin to actually like each other, especially as she sees how well I treat her mother. It's possible that Amber just needs a loving and dependable male role model in her life, and that I can be that man.

Of course, it's also possible that Amber is never going to like me. I could be a combination of Gandhi and Santa Claus, showering her with love and gifts, and she would still hate me because I am with her mother, and yet I am not her father.

This is a common challenge. Millions of mid-life daters bring children from previous marriages into their new relationships. Honestly, Amber is a huge red flag for me and my relationship with Colleen. Right now, I can't imagine welcoming Amber into my life in any permanent way. I don't want to buy her birthday presents, and I don't want to spend Thanksgivings and Christmases with her moping around.

BABE MAGNET RULE #74
Consider the children. A relationship with a Babe with children will always include her children. So if you don't like her kids (or they don't care for you), the relationship with the Babe probably isn't going to be permanent.

I talked with a woman friend named Julia about this. I have known Julia professionally for several years. She is a freelance writer, and sometimes our paths cross at conferences.

Julia is newly single, and she has two kids—ages 17 and 12. In just a few months of dating, she has discovered how profound a challenge it is to date with her 17-year-old daughter and her 12-year-old son living in her house.

"There is no way I am going to expose my son to a casual date," Julia tells me. "I am not even going to introduce my daughter to anyone until I am sure that there is a long-term relationship potential."

It makes sense to keep kids away from your casual dates. Getting to know someone new is difficult enough on a one-on-one basis. Bringing your children into the mix too early can muddle things up.

But when is the right time to introduce your kids to your new love interest? That's a judgment call that every new couple has to make. Last week Jason arrived back home from college for the summer, so I think it's time for him to meet Colleen. I have told Jason about Colleen, so he knows we are dating. But I haven't introduced the two of them to each other. Until now.

Colleen talked me into going to a Pilates class with her this evening. I didn't really want to go, because my impression is that Pilates should really be called Exercising for Chicks. Pilates is all about vegan women in tights lying on the floor doing endless abdominal exercises and physical routines to tone the muscles that keep women from becoming incontinent. It is not the kind of exercising that a manly man does.

A manly man goes to the gym so he can lift large quantities of iron weights. Lifting weights builds large biceps, big shoulders, six-pack abs, and rock-hard pectorals. Babes dig men with muscles. I have never heard a Babe say, "Your well-toned anti-incontinent muscles really turn me on!"

Colleen arrives at the house wearing her workout clothes—blue shorts and a tight white V-neck T-shirt. I introduce her to Jason, and they are very nice and personable to each other—just as I knew they would be. Jason is both friendly and respectful toward Colleen. He does me proud.

"I am taking your father to a Pilates class," announces Colleen.

It turns out that Jason is more familiar with Pilates than I am.

"I've done 'the hundreds,'" he replies. I have no idea what he is talking about.

When Colleen and I arrive for the Pilates class, the large exercise room is already packed. Counting me and Colleen, there are 38 women and two men.

See, I told you it was for chicks.

We find the last possible open spots for our mats, and then we commence to getting our butts kicked. Actually, the class kicks me in the abs. It is no wonder that men are outnumbered 38 to 2. The male body was not meant to do Pilates exercises. We were not meant to lie on our backs and alternately lift our arms and opposite legs. We weren't meant to stick our legs up at a 90-degree angle and breathe like women in labor. We weren't meant to do 30 different kinds of sit-ups and leg lifts and tailbone tilts.

Men were meant to lift heavy things and grunt. I don't care if this exercise regimen was invented by a man (Joseph Pilates, 1883-1967). Mr. Pilates obviously invented these exercises so he could meet Babes when he wasn't lifting heavy things and grunting.

After 60 minutes of Pilates, I am nearly dead. My abdominal muscles are exhausted and I can hardly walk.

"I really want to take the next class on Friday," Colleen says brightly.

"I'm going to need six months and a lot of heavy lifting to recover from this," I reply.

Chapter 70: The Sleepover Thing

One of the reasons modern adult dating can so confusing is that the so-called experts disagree on so many aspects of dating. For example, a story posted on Yahoo.com called "Should you let your new boyfriend meet your children?" says that you should date each other exclusively for six months before introducing your significant other to your kids. "This type of commitment shows you both are serious about each other and, as a result, are stable."

Hello? What planet are you living on? If I dated a woman for six months and had not met her kids yet (if they live in the same city as I do), I would assume that they are unruly little monsters who are locked up somewhere by court order.

And then there's the whole dating sleepover thing. Again, the "expert" advice about this monumental step is as varied and plentiful as Hollywood divorces.

The advice ranges from the heartfelt (just be honest and straightforward in a way that is age-appropriate for your children) to the practical (soundproof your bedroom with extra pillows under the door and behind your headboard) to the questionable (make the first sleepover a slumber party with the kids so that everyone will have lots of fun!).

I think the key to dealing with something this important—and inevitable—is to know your kids. The "proper" way to deal with sleepovers has a lot to do with your parenting style, the age and emotional maturity of your kids, and how open and honest you are with them.

Up until now, it has been easy for me to keep Jason from knowing about the sexual part of my dating life. But now that Jason is once again living with me for the summer and Colleen has become part of my weekly social life, it's time to cross the Dad's Girlfriend is Sleeping Over bridge.

BABE MAGNET RULE #75

If you and your Babe are going to have sex, your kids are going to find out about it. Assuming they are old enough to understand what is happening, it is far better to talk to them about it up front than for them to discover it embarrassingly on their own.

So, in as nonchalant a way as I can, I talk to Jason. I tell him that Colleen and I are going to a movie tonight, and afterward she will be returning home with me. She might spend the night. And she won't be sleeping in the guest room.

"Are you going to have a problem with that?" I ask.

Jason looks at me like I am a ridiculous old fool. "No, why would it be a problem?"

"Well, we're going into new territory here, and I didn't want to upset you or embarrass you."

Again, I get the "ridiculous old fool" look. "Dad, I know that you aren't going to be living the life of a monk," says Jason.

"No, of course not...."

"I've just spent two years living away from home at college, so I know that men and women spend the night with each other."

"I just wanted to be sure that...."

"It's okay, Dad. I'm 21. I can handle it."

Bless his young adult heart. That went better than I expected. Although I do feel a bit like a ridiculous old fool.

So Colleen arrives for our date and I give her the good news. She admits that she is a little nervous about her first sleepover with Jason in the house, but we both agree that it is the next logical step in our relationship. "I think our kids have already figured out that we are having sex," I tell her.

After the movie we drive back to my house, and I offer Colleen some tea and dessert. Jason passes through the kitchen, grabbing a snack on the way out to a friend's house. The three of us visit for a while, and then Jason politely says good night. "Don't wait up for me," he says with a sly smile. "I'm going to be out late."

With that, Jason is out the door. Colleen and I have the house to ourselves for the rest of the night, and we don't even have to worry about making too much noise.

So another milestone in my post-divorce, middle-aged dating life is reached. As the summer progresses, Jason seems comfortable with the presence of Colleen in my life, and he seems genuinely glad to see her when their paths cross.

Colleen is also her friendly self when interacting with Jason, and he responds well to her humor and her level of comfort. The simple fact that she is at ease with him and enjoys talking to him makes Jason more relaxed, too.

One evening when I have invited Colleen over for a home-cooked meal, I invite Jason to dine with us. I expect him to politely decline, and I am surprised and delighted when he says, "That would be great!" with uncharacteristic enthusiasm.

As I sit at the table and listen to the two of them converse about the latest blockbuster movie, I have a Proud Papa moment. Here's my son and my girlfriend, getting along just fine. I have raised a fine young man, one who can handle the unexpected bumps in life's road (such as having dinner with his father's girlfriend) and rise to the occasion.

It warms my heart.

Chapter 71: On Vacation

I am sitting in the large lobby area of Dallas/Fort Worth Airport. For the past few days I have been in nearby Fort Worth at a conference. Since the conference was scheduled to end on a Friday afternoon, I suggested to Colleen that she fly into Dallas and meet me for a weekend getaway. She said yes before the words were out of my mouth.

As I wait in the airport just outside of the security barrier, I watch the people who are arriving and those who are meeting them. There are married couples who greet each other warmly but not passionately. There are lovers who race together as if they are in a TV commercial for K-Y Jelly. And there are parents picking up their teenaged kids who aren't sure if they are supposed to hug or kiss, so they just awkwardly say hello.

It's fun to be waiting at the airport for my girlfriend. It's fun to see her walk through the greeting area, looking over the crowd for my familiar face. It's fun to watch her eyes find me and see the smile that spontaneously sweeps across her face. I give her a hug and a kiss, and then I dutifully take her suitcase as we begin the long walk to the car.

Because of the distance and the traffic from the airport to the hotel, Colleen and I have plenty of time to talk as we drive. I can tell she is excited to be with me on our first vacation weekend together.

We check into the hotel and go up to the room. Colleen is in her no-nonsense mode, when she gets a tad bossy and demanding. She wants to know what the agenda is going to be. "What do you want from this weekend?" she asks.

I know exactly what I want from this weekend, but I can't tell her about it. This weekend is a test. We're going to see what it's like to spend three straight days together. We're going to see just how compatible we are.

My friend, Matt, once told me he uses his Girlfriend Vacations as opportunities to move his relationships to the next level. If he is interested in a woman, he asks her to accompany him on an out-of-town trip to a place that sounds fun and exotic. Then he does everything he can to bond with her.

Spending every moment together for several days is a crash course in getting to know someone. After a few days, your defenses break down. Through familiarity or simple exhaustion, you begin to show elements of your true personality that you can keep completely hidden during three-hour dates. Matt was positively glowing when he took one girlfriend to Sonoma County with him for four days of wining and dining (literally). He said the trip to California bonded him with his girlfriend in ways that would have taken months of normal dating.

But Matt's approach has also backfired. He once made the mistake of taking a girlfriend to the south of France for two weeks. Before they left there were signs that maybe their relationship wasn't built to last. But he ignored the signs because he wanted to go drink French wine, eat French cheese and bread, and have French sex with his American girlfriend. The first five days of their vacation were great, and the next three days were fine but not spectacular. But on day nine, his girlfriend had a meltdown. Matt saw all of her faults and flaws—all at once.

The Good News: Matt broke up with her because it was clear that she wasn't The One. The Bad News: the last part of his vacation in France with his soon-to-be ex-girlfriend was tense, tense, tense.

BABE MAGNET RULE #76

A vacation getaway can be a fabulous way to get to know your lover—for better or for worse. Spending days together without a break will let you see "the real" person, warts and all.

Matt inspired me to go on a short vacation with Colleen (rather than an extended one). I don't really want Colleen to snap and become a wild banshee, revealing every quirk, imperfection, and serious flaw. But at the same time, it would be all right if that happened—because then my nagging suspicions would be confirmed, and I would know for sure that she isn't The One.

Colleen and I have settled into a comfortable relationship. Comparing her to an old shoe doesn't sound very flattering—but you know how great it feels to slip on your favorite pair of running shoes, the ones that have been so completely shaped by your feet that it almost doesn't feel like you're wearing shoes at all? Sometimes being with Colleen feels a lot like that.

We hang out together. We know each other. We like each other. I have deep feelings of affection for her, and when we are together I feel connected. I care about her, and I care about how she feels.

And yet, neither of us has ever said "I love you" to the other. Neither of us has ever asked, "Do you love me?" Neither of us has ever talked about moving in together or making a long-term commitment. Perhaps neither of us wants to face the possible truth that we aren't *really* right for each other—at least not in the "'til death do us part" sort of way. After all, Colleen has never invited me to meet her parents, even though they live in town. And I have not completely integrated her into my social life. We have both been holding back. Is that because, deep down, we both already know? Is it because an enjoyable, but ultimately shallow, relationship is better than no relationship at all?

I think we are both afraid to talk about the future. And yet, that little voice of conscience in my head tells me that we should. That little voice tells me not to get too secure in this relationship, and not to let Colleen think that she should start buying *Brides* magazine. The more I think about it, the more I am convinced that I need to man-up and have a heart-to-heart talk with Colleen. Perhaps that will happen this weekend.

We start our weekend with cocktails and dinner at a very nice restaurant. It is the first fancy dinner date we have had in quite a while, and Colleen enjoys every moment and every bite. It's nice to see her so happy.

Afterward, we walk to a bar called Sing Sing, where two singers (playing their respective pianos) run through an endless list of classic rock and sing-along songs. Colleen and I get a table near the stage, and the buxom young waitress starts bringing us drinks. Clearly, alcohol consumption is encouraged here. Some of the patrons seem intent on getting shit-faced, especially the bachelorette party of young women two tables away.

Sing Sing turns out to be bawdier and rowdier than I had expected. When the piano duo sings, "You picked a fine time to leave me, Lucille," the audience is encouraged to shout, "You bitch, you slut, you whore!" This isn't the kind of place to which I would bring my mom or my young adult son.

The crowd gets drunker as the evening gets later. Colleen seems to be channeling her inner 20-year-old, and she is getting hammered. She isn't just in vacation mode, she's in Spring Break in Ft. Lauderdale vacation mode. I am probably the oldest and least drunk person in the room. Quite frankly, the longer I stay the more appalled I am—at Colleen and everybody else. I feel like the only responsible adult in the bar. If the drunken bachelorette party girls start taking off their tops, I am afraid that Colleen will join them. I finally coax Colleen to leave before she can make a major spectacle of herself.

The next day we visit the Dallas Arboretum and Botanical Gardens. Colleen has a major hangover, but she is trying not to let it show. It's brutally hot outside, and the heat adds to Colleen's grumpiness. Nevertheless, the gardens are beautiful, and I enjoy strolling through the grounds. Colleen is not having a good time, though, so we cut the tour short and go back to the hotel room for a nap.

In the evening, I manage to get tickets to a Texas Rangers game. Colleen turns into a loud, vocal, rabid Major League Baseball fan for the evening. She doesn't understand the game as well as I do, but she certainly enjoys it. But I have to admit that Colleen's behavior is starting to bug me.

The next afternoon, we go to an upscale neighborhood to window shop and hang out. We find a sunny outdoor table at a chic café, and we order iced tea and dessert. The warm sun is lulling me into a sleepy contentment, and without thinking about it, I start sharing the story of how I fell in love for the first time.

I was a fairly late bloomer, and I didn't fall madly in love with a woman until I was 21. I fell hard, and it affected me both emotionally and physically. I lost my appetite, I couldn't sleep, and I could think about nothing except my new love.

Unfortunately, my first romance was not destined to last. I had fallen in love with a woman who had commitment issues and didn't fully trust men. As quickly as my love affair had started, she dropped me for another hapless man. I was devastated, and I lost my appetite again.

Without thinking, I tell this story to Colleen. I tell her that a loss of appetite has been a recurring pattern in my life during every new love and every subsequent broken heart. And then I mention that, fortunately, my appetite since I met her has been just fine. Colleen is dead silent as she processes what I have just told her.

"So this isn't love?" she asks.

"No. This isn't love. At least not yet."

Oh shit. It's too late for me to retract my words. If I could back up the tape and rewind what I just said, I would do so. I would use softer words. But in a moment of unguarded honesty, I have revealed the truth about our relationship. As fond as I am of Colleen, I am not in love with her.

If I were to be completely honest, I would also admit that I don't *want* to fall in love with Colleen. After spending the past two and a half days with her, I realize she's not The One. She's not the one who makes my heart sing. She's not the one who ignites the elusive "chemistry" that makes it impossible to live without someone. I know she's not the one that I want to spend the rest of my life with in a loving, committed relationship.

I watch the expression on Colleen's face change, but she doesn't say anything. She doesn't have to.

Chapter 72: If You Could Read My Mind

Shortly after Colleen and I return to our normal lives in Springfield, Colleen changes her work schedule so that it is no longer possible for her to spend Wednesday nights at my house. We still communicate daily, but we only see each other on the weekends.

Then Colleen starts to cancel dates. Her excuses sound perfectly reasonable. "I can't make it this Saturday; I need to spend some time with Amber." Two weeks later it's, "Sunday is not going to work out after all. My sister wants to celebrate her birthday." The one that really hurts is when she cancels a small, intimate celebration we had planned for *my* birthday.

It isn't until I see the pattern in her behavior that I know what's going on. I have been running on Relationship Auto Pilot. I have been willing to put up with a mediocre relationship because it was better than no relationship at all. I have been content with "good enough" instead of moving on to find a woman who can be my soul mate.

One evening, when she calls to cancel yet again, I finally snap.

"This isn't working for me to have a girlfriend who isn't available," I say.

"Oh really? I thought that's what you wanted."

Suddenly it is crystal clear. I realize that Colleen and I have come to the end of our time together. I also realize that she has been pushing me—cancelling plans and simply being too busy with other things and other people—until she finally gets me to react. Well, I am reacting now. And I know that it is time for me to move on.

I know I can have the "break up" talk with Colleen right now, but I don't want to do it on the phone. I want to be able to look into her beautiful blue eyes and say what I need to say. “Are you going to be on this side of town anytime today?” I ask. “We need to talk.” (Yes, I actually used the dreaded pre-breakup words.)

Colleen says she can swing by my house after her late afternoon class in a few hours. I thank her and hang up.

I know what is going to happen. I am going to break up with Colleen. It is time. I know it and she knows it. So I begin to mentally prepare for it.

Breaking up is one of my least favorite things in the world. I hate the confrontation, and I hate the crushed spirits and the bruised emotions. The only breakups in my life have involved sadness, anger, and arguments. These are not comfortable emotions for me. I am a man, and I freely admit to being emotionally stunted and unwilling to discuss my feelings. I would rather have a lively discussion about the improbability of the St. Louis Cardinals winning the World Series in 2006 than talk about how it feels when the woman I am dating stands me up for the opportunity to see a really crappy movie with her sister.

So I begin to work myself up to a sufficient level of righteous indignation. “How dare she do this to me! I’m mad as hell, and I’m not going to take it anymore!”

By the time Colleen knocks on my door, I have an impressive list in my head that details just how bad and wrong she is.

Then a funny thing happens. Colleen arrives bearing a symbolic olive branch, and there is no reason for me to be angry.

We sit on my couch and talk. I tell her that I care deeply for her. I tell her that I have enjoyed (nearly) every moment I have spent with her. I thank her for her positive attitude, her spontaneity and her ability to enjoy the moment. I also tell her that it upset me whenever she cancelled our plans. The more I talk, the more I realize that my feelings for Colleen have crept closer and closer to love without me even knowing it.

I wipe a tear from my eye. A real, honest-to-God tear.

“So, what do you want to do?” she asks.

“The kindest thing I can do is to let you go,” I say. “You deserve someone who loves you dearly and wants to spend the rest of his life with you. That’s just not me.”

Colleen smiles sadly and gives me a hug. "I'm sorry for cancelling on you all those times," she says.

She returns the key to my house and we say our goodbyes, promising to remain friends. From my front door, I watch her drive away. When she is gone, I realize that Colleen has just given me a tremendous gift. She showed me that a break-up doesn't have to be angry or hurtful. Nobody has to be the bad guy, and no one has to be wrong. Sometimes two people who are not destined to be together can simply agree to venture onward on their separate paths.

Thank you, Colleen.

BABE MAGNET RULE #77
When you need to learn a lesson of the heart, listen to a Babe.

Chapter 73: Back in the Saddle Again

Now that I have broken up with Colleen, I miss her terribly. She has been an important part of my life, and suddenly not seeing her, not talking to her, and not getting 10 text messages a day from her has left a huge hole in my life. I miss her even more because our break-up talk was such a loving and enlightening experience. She taught me how to part ways and still remain cordial friends.

On the golf course with Mueller, I tell him the Colleen and Chad Break-Up Story, and he seems genuinely impressed. "I wish breaking up with my soon-to-be ex-wife was that easy," he says.

"It's not that it was easy. But it *was* different. We behaved like grown-ups who wanted the best for each other, only the best wasn't each other. Does that make sense?"

"It makes perfect sense," says Mueller. "So, now what are you going to do?"

"I'm going to take a little time off, and then I'm going to get right back in the saddle."

"The Middle-Aged Babe Magnet will ride again!"

"Yes, but this time it's going to be different," I say with confidence.

"How so?"

"This time I am not going to settle for anything less than 'The One.'"

"Good luck with that, Chad."

After playing golf, Mueller takes me out for a beer. A baseball game is on the big-screen monitor, and the bar is starting to fill up. Mueller points out a pair of attractive women sitting by themselves. "Maybe Chad Stone, Middle-Aged Babe Magnet, should go over there and talk to them."

I smile. Mueller means well, but right now I would much rather sit with him and drink beer. The Babes can wait.

I spend the next few weeks embracing my singlehood. I take weekly guitar classes and start learning some new songs. I ride my bike through the foothills, and I work out at the health club. I have beers with Karl, Craig, and Mueller while we watch sporting events on large-screen TVs. I throw myself back into my work. I read a couple of trashy paperback novels and one poorly written book about how to find the love of your life.

Now I am ready to get back into the cyber saddle. I am wearing a pair of gym shorts and little else as I stare into the vastness of my flat-panel computer screen. I am wrestling with the words that can best describe just how wonderful I am. Yes, ladies, I could be the man of your dreams. But only one of you will win the prize of Chad Stone, the World's Most Eligible Middle-Aged Divorced Man.

This, sports fans, is no time to be humble.

Yes, I have boldly ventured back into the online dating universe and joined Match.com again. The first time I joined I met Maddy. The second time I met Colleen. I am hoping that the third time is the charm. This time I am going to win the dating lottery. This time I am going to meet the elusive and legendary Ms. Right.

I am ready to reach for the heavens and pluck a star out of the night sky.

This time around I am going to write a profile that describes the real me, the inner me, the enlightened me.

In the box under "About my life and what I'm looking for" I start typing:

> I'm an optimist—I expect things to work out. I don't look for problems, and I'm looking for someone who shares my sunny outlook. I know you're out there. When we meet we'll have an 'aha!' moment and we'll both know it.

I also write a paragraph that describes my search for a soul mate who stimulates me mentally, emotionally, spiritually, and physically. I am ready to meet my perfect woman. If that doesn't attract the Babe of my dreams, nothing will.

I put the finishing touches on my profile, and I am very pleased with myself. I have just written the best online dating profile in the long and storied history of online dating. It captures my personality perfectly. If there were awards for online profiles, mine would surely win.

I can see it now. On the live TV show for the Matchie Awards, I am waiting in the audience with all the other nominees. There are lots of men and women nominated in minor categories such as "Best Goofy Photo with a Pet" and "Best Logical Description of Scientific Accomplishment (Engineer Division)." Those of us in the front rows are nominated in the big, prestigious categories. Toward the end of the show, when they announce my name as the winner in the "Best Profile, Man Seeking Woman" category, I smile broadly and dash to the stage wearing a rented tuxedo. I then proceed to thank myself for the wonderful job I did on the profile.

Then, in a moment that will be rerun on cable TV shows for a decade, right along with highlights from *The Jersey Shore* and *Bobbing for Barracudas: Extreme Edition*, I point to a very special person in the audience. "Ladies and Gentlemen, I would like to thank the woman who makes this award especially sweet for me, my wife, who I met online."

The women start to cry, and the men go wild. Afterward, during the many media interviews that I graciously grant, I give a few dating tips and announce my new series of dating seminars. My career as a dating guru is officially launched.

And so my search begins (again) for Babes online. But this time it's different. This time I'm actually not looking for Babes (plural). This time I am ready to find The Babe. This time around I know the drill. I am going to have to look at lots of women's profiles. I will send eight or 10 emails for every response I receive. And now that I know what to expect, I'm okay with those numbers. I am not going to spend any time wondering or worrying about the women who don't respond to my emails. The Zen Dating Master in me is going to assume that they didn't reply because they weren't The One. If they don't respond, they are actually doing me a favor by saving me time—time that I can spend on finding my last and final Babe.

I do a search for women within 20 miles of my zip code, and I start reading profiles. I send out my first batch of emails. "Hi! I enjoyed reading your profile. I, too, love taking walks at sunset..."

Now I wait for responses.

In the meantime, there is a woman in the real world I want to get to know. I have seen her a few times at church. She is tall and beautiful, with long blonde hair and a lanky dancer's body. She bears a striking resemblance to Heather Locklear. The last time I saw her at church, she was chatting with Rupert, a guy I know from my gym. In true Babe Magnet fashion, I walked over to say "hi" to Rupert so he could introduce me to the Babe.

"Chad, this is Lavender."

I smile at her, drinking in the sight of her eyes. "It is a pleasure to meet you." I take her hand and give it a gentle squeeze, holding it for a few lingering moments.

BABE MAGNET RULE #78

Babes dig it when you give them a tender squeezing handshake and not the bone-crushing death grip that guys give to each other when they are showing off their testosterone levels.

"How do you two know each other?" I ask.

"We used to date," says Lavender, without a hint of tension.

"She's my ex-girlfriend," says Rupert.

Well, I stepped right in that pile. But neither Rupert nor Lavender gives any sign of discomfort.

A girl walks up to Lavender. She looks to be about 13 or 14 years old, and she is very tall. So Heather Locklear has a daughter. That's all right, I can deal with it. I introduce myself to the daughter, whose name is Azure. These are not Republican names.

"So, what is your passion?" I ask Lavender.

"Yoga," she responds. "I teach yoga and energy enlightenment."

Oh, God. A woo-woo woman. Well, why not? I have never dated a yoga instructor before. And I have never dated a woman who looks like Heather Locklear, either. By the end of our short conversation, I know where and when Lavender teaches yoga, and I have started to formulate a plan.

Chapter 74: Hello, Yoga Babe

Going to Lavender's yoga class involves some advance planning. I am not a member of the health club where she teaches, which happens to be the most expensive health club in town. In order to get a guest pass to attend the club, I have to visit the club during business hours and talk to a sales representative. Her name is Brianna, and she is friendly, perky, and sexy in a very acceptable, businesslike way. Brianna insists on giving me a complete tour.

I must admit that the facility is impressive. The workout rooms are filled with gleaming, state-of-the-art exercise equipment. There are two exercise classrooms with fully mirrored walls and expensive wooden floors. There is an indoor basketball court, indoor and outdoor hot tubs, and an Olympic-sized swimming pool. There is a staff of buff, attractive personal trainers who, for just $100 a session, will make sure you are not slacking during your workout.

The club is packed. Every treadmill is in use, and every latex-clad Babe walking on every treadmill is wearing earbuds and watching a program on the personal video screen located on each treadmill.

As I tour the facility, I am awed by the number of Babes working out. This place is a Babe Bank, a veritable Federal Reserve Depository of Babes. There are more Babes per square meter than at an open tryout for the next Playboy centerfold.

There is only one problem: the average age of these Babes is 24. I am twice their age—plus a few years. I would love to walk up to one of the Babes and say hello, but I do not want to be called "Gramps."

No, I think I will stick to the original plan. I leave the health club with two guest passes, and I confirm that Lavender is teaching her class on

Thursday at 7 p.m. I also find out that Lavender's last name is Skyes. Her freakin' name is Lavender Skyes. That means her daughter's name is Azure Skyes.

I am definitely headed into woo-woo land.

I have selected my favorite workout clothes, and I have my yoga mat tucked underneath my arm. (Yes, I have my very own yoga mat. If you are going to cruise yoga classes for Babes, it's best to have your own yoga mat. This goes double if you're trying to pick up the yoga instructor.) I arrive a few minutes early for Lavender's class, and I unroll my mat in the middle of the front row. By God, I am going to make sure that Lavender notices that I am here.

She does, of course. She smiles and says hello. The look on her face tells me that she is trying to remember where she's seen me. I decide to re-introduce myself so she won't have to wonder what the hell my name is.

BABE MAGNET RULE #79

Make sure the Babe knows your name. Tell her again if you think she doesn't remember. She will appreciate you for it.

"Hi, Lavender!" I say with a friendly smile on my face. "I haven't seen you since Sunday."

"Oh, hi," she says. Inside her brain she is trying to locate my name. Damn! Is it Chester? No. Chapps? No. What is it?

"Chad," I say. "We met at church."

A wave of relief washes over her face.

"Sure! Hi Chad! I'm glad you came tonight."

"Me, too. I am really looking forward to the class."

We settle in for an hour of intense yoga. I keep up pretty well, especially considering I haven't been to a yoga class since I was a Middle-Aged Babe Magnet In Training. It's clearly an intermediate class, and some of the positions are quite difficult. My Downward Facing Dog is adequate enough, although my butt isn't high enough and my heels aren't low enough. Fortunately, my Mountain Pose (standing still with both feet on the ground) is flawless. But my Forward Fold with palms on the ground—not so much.

What keeps me going is an intense desire to not embarrass myself at the front of the class. It also helps that I get to watch Lavender's toned body do sexually suggestive yoga positions just a few feet away. At the end of class, a few women walk up to chat with Lavender. I roll up my yoga mat with painstaking, time-consuming precision. I time my exit to coincide with Lavender's so I can talk to her as we walk out of class.

I turn up my Babe Charm dial to maximum, and I confidently talk with Lavender about the class, how long she has been practicing yoga, her favorite Indian food restaurant, and the other classes she teaches. As we walk out toward the main entrance of the health club, she asks what astrological sign I am.

"Libra," I reply. "For me, it's always about balance."

"My daughter is a Libra."

Somehow I think being a Libra scores me a few points with Lavender. If so, I'll take them. As we say goodbye she touches me gently (and, I think, affectionately) on the arm.

Have I mentioned what a Major Babe this woman is? She is the most beautiful woman I have ever thought I had a chance of dating. She is a perfect specimen of 45-year-old Babe-aliciousness. Straight blonde hair. A perfect body—5 foot 10 inches tall, long and lean, not an ounce of fat on her, perfect breasts. Perfect teeth. Perfect smile. Perfect skin. Eyes that open right into her soul. She has an Earth Mother presence about her, and she smells gently of flowers and herbs.

Exactly one week later I am back at the health club in the front row of Lavender's class. This time she seems genuinely glad to see me, and we talk at length before and after the class. When I walk her out to her car, I ask if she would like to have lunch with me sometime.

She smiles. "Sure. That would be nice." Lavender writes her phone number on the back of one of my business cards. She hands the card to me and smiles again.

On the drive back home, the wheels of my car never touch the ground.

Chapter 75: Lunch with the Yoga Babe

I call Lavender the next day. Screw the “three day rule” that men use to make women wait for their call. That’s just stupid. Lavender answers her phone and her voice tells me she is happy that I called. We set up a lunch date.

“Do you like Indian food?” she asks.

Honey, I will eat cat food if that’s what it takes to go on a date with you. But it has to be high-quality cat food. None of that cheap generic stuff.

“Sure,” I say. “Indian is great.”

I arrive at Lavender’s favorite Indian restaurant five minutes before our appointed time. The restaurant is nestled in a nondescript strip mall. From the outside, it looks as boring as the sewing store and the collectibles store that it sits between. But inside, the décor is a riot of colors, and it is redolent with the exotic smells of clove and curry. Once you step through the doors, you aren’t in Kansas anymore.

Lavender arrives fashionably late, looking ravishing in an outfit that was trendy in 1968: fur jacket, tight-fitting tan jeans, a small blue top, and a British cap atop her flowing blonde hair. By comparison, I look very conservative in my blue plaid sport shirt, black corduroys, and black leather jacket. If her stunning good looks weren’t enough to catch your attention, her funky clothing would certainly turn your head. I try to give her a hello hug, but she doesn’t hug me back.

Lavender is clearly a regular at this restaurant. The owner and waiters smile and greet her warmly with their delightful Indian accents. They sound like a convention of Dell Computer customer service reps. We are escorted to the best table in the restaurant. Lavender also knows the folks seated beside us. I am enjoying being with Lavender in the midst of all of these people that she knows.

The waiter brings us chai tea and we cover some of the usual date topics—work, kids, siblings, other places we've lived. But I quickly learn that with Lavender, any topic is fair game, even the deepest and most challenging things to discuss on a first lunch date. We talk about the Chinese Zodiac, and I learn that she was born in the Year of the Rat. (Clearly, the Chinese don't know squat about Zodiac signs.) We also talk about astrology, organized religion, and our core spiritual beliefs. I try to make myself as comfortable in Lavender's Woo-Woo Land as I can.

Then we go to the buffet to serve ourselves some food. Lavender is my tour guide to the various Indian dishes on display. Some of the trays hold familiar items—rice, a lentil-based side dish (is it called dahl?), and curry chicken are just a few of the choices. I decide to be brave and help myself to several dishes that I recognize and a few that are new to me.

The food is actually quite tasty. I eat most of what is on my plate as Lavender picks at hers. Our conversation never really stalls, and we have plenty of things to talk about. She seems very interested when I tell her my story of going to a job interview at Bell Helicopters many years ago and deciding I didn't want to work there when I learned they built attack helicopters for the U.S. Army.

I ask her what keeps her busy. She teaches yoga classes and Pilates classes, which I already knew. Apparently, she doesn't have a "real" job with nine-to-five hours, and she sees no reason to get one. There must be a trust fund somewhere, or she has a great alimony package. I also learn that her daughter, Azure, is an 11-year-old fifth-grader, although she looks much older.

Lavender offers to do my astrological chart. She asks my birthdate, plus the time and place of my birth. I give her one of my business cards so she can write the info on the back. I think this means that she's planning to see me again.

As our date is winding down, I deliberately take a good look at Lavender as I try to remember every detail. Her beauty has temporarily blinded me to her woo-wooness, and I am fine with that. Even though she is gorgeous, I will not compliment her looks, because I am sure she's gotten that so many times during the course of her life that she's sick of it. She values deeper, more spiritual things than physical beauty. So I compliment the way she embraces the spiritual aspects of life, and how effortlessly she makes the unseen manifest in her daily experience.

> **BABE MAGNET RULE #80**
> The more beautiful a Babe is, the more often she has been told of her physical beauty by men that she does not know. To stand out from other men, give her a compliment that has nothing to do with her physical beauty.

She beams with a radiant smile. My God, she is stunning. And fun to be with. And, yes, fun to be seen with.

Just as I sign the credit card bill, I notice my throat is feeling restricted. Oh crap, I've eaten something here that I'm allergic to. I have had food allergies before, so I always carry Benadryl with me. Except that I left it in my car. A wave of dizziness passes over me. Crap. Thankfully, I panic just a little, and that kicks in my adrenaline, which clears my head enough for me to walk Lavender to the door.

I give her a hug goodbye. This time she hugs me back like she means it.

"Are you going to be busy this next week?" I ask.

"Yes, we're going to Sedona over the weekend. There's no school on Monday."

"OK. I'll call you when you get back."

I watch Lavender walk to her car—a sporty black Mercedes. I get into my car and swallow a Benadryl. Please, God, don't let me have a major allergic reaction. I have a conference call in 25 minutes, and I have a normal life to lead.

I wonder what I ate that didn't agree with me. The problem is, I ate several new things and I don't even know what ingredients were in them.

If the universe is waving a cosmic Red Food Flag in front of my face right now, I refuse to see it. I'll just take another allergy pill.

The next time we go out to eat, I will to pick a restaurant that serves more familiar food. If I end up seeing Lavender on a regular basis, food just might be the biggest stumbling block.

But have I mentioned how beautiful she is?

Chapter 76: Goodbye, Yoga Babe

My excursion into Woo-Woo Land continues. Lavender Skyes is unlike any woman I have ever tried to date. She floats like a cloud in a world of her own making. She has no predictable schedule from what I can see. She doesn't awaken on a Monday morning and begin a traditional work week. If the whim strikes her, she will pull her daughter out of school for a day or two for an excursion to Sedona or Santa Fe or anywhere else where the cosmic vibes are emanating.

She doesn't answer her cell phone, but occasionally she will return a call. When we speak, our conversations flow unexpectedly like a mountain stream finding its way through a meadow. I find Lavender both intriguing and exasperating.

It has been two weeks since our lunch date, and tonight is our first dinner date. But, as I probably could have predicted, this evening is shaping up to be an unconventional date. Lavender has invited me to her house for dinner, and she has informed me that she wants Azure to spend some time with us.

I arrive promptly at her house in the foothills. From the outside, her suburban tract house is the most conventional thing about her. There's a horseshoe driveway and a few shrubs planted along the walkway to the brick porch. I push the standard-issue doorbell and hear the traditional DING-DONG heard in millions of American homes.

The Brady Bunch façade disappears as soon as Lavender opens the door and greets me with a smile. The smell of incense wafts out the door, and as I walk into the entryway a giant gold Buddha smiles at me. Garlands of flowers surround him, and bamboo stalks create the illusion of an Asian forest. Soft Indian music plays in the background.

Lavender, wearing a slinky long dress that hugs her hips and her breasts, escorts me to the living room. The décor is thoroughly Indian, with tapestries on the walls and a patterned rug on the floor. Large pillows are placed where upholstered chairs would normally be. The only "traditional" piece of furniture is the futon that serves as her couch.

Lavender gives me the grand tour of the house. What was once an ordinary three-bedroom, two-bath tract house has been transformed into a showplace of Asian art and furniture. It is lovely, but totally incongruent for the blonde-haired, blue-eyed American woman who lives here. It's as if Lavender wishes desperately that she had been born of darker-skinned parents in a country on the other side of the globe.

Unlike the rest of her house, her kitchen is quite conventionally American. The center island is surrounded by a microwave, a massive refrigerator, an expensive espresso machine, and an impressive convection oven. The entire room is spotless, and I can't help thinking that Lavender doesn't do a lick of cooking. Sure enough, as she tells me what we're having for dinner she shows me plastic packages of gourmet delights that she has purchased from Whole Foods.

"Do you like wine?" she asks.

"Absolutely."

She hands me a nice bottle of white wine and asks me to open it. Glasses in hand, we walk through her converted back porch to the backyard, which is dominated by an enormous trampoline. The trampoline is surrounded by eight-foot-tall sides of netting so the occupant won't inadvertently bounce across the yard and break his or her neck. Bouncing on the trampoline is Azure.

"Mom! Look at this!" she cries excitedly. Azure then executes a move that involves jumping on the trampoline twice and then bouncing on her bottom. Every child on the planet can do the same maneuver, but Azure seems quite proud of herself. I can see that she possesses no special athletic skill whatsoever.

"That's nice, honey," says Lavender without any enthusiasm.

Lavender and I sit and sip our wine.

"Mom, look at this!" Azure jumps on the trampoline twice, then onto her bottom. In mid-air she tries to get from her bottom back to her feet, but the move proves too complicated for her.

"That's very nice," says Lavender, without looking at her daughter.

Lavender tells me that Azure, the budding Olympic trampolinist, is a wise soul who is quite empathic about people. "I never date anyone Azure doesn't approve of," she says.

What? Did I just hear that correctly? Am I being trotted out here so your daughter can give me an evaluation?

Lavender and I converse on the same bizarre topics that we discussed during our Indian restaurant lunch date. She tells me that she did an astrology chart on me, and the results were very favorable. She also says that we are quite compatible from a Chinese Zodiac perspective. I try to sound happy about this. Maybe if I pass the green tea leaves test and her old-soul empathic daughter likes me, I will get a chance to go out on a date with Lavender—just the two of us. Yee haw!

The three of us eat cold salmon, lentil salad, and some curry rice thing at the picnic table in the backyard. Lavender tries to engage Azure in conversation, but Azure is bored and, quite frankly, she doesn't seem all that bright.

Right about now I am thinking to myself, "This date sucks. I am with the most beautiful woman in this entire zip code, but this is one of the worst dates I have ever had."

And then it gets worse.

"You stay out here, honey, and jump on your trampoline," says Lavender. She walks me into the house and sits me down on the futon. In spite of myself and all of my Babe Magnet training, my heart rate increases at the thought of snuggling with Lavender.

But instead of sitting close beside me, Lavender sits on a pillow on the other side of the room. She then proceeds to tell me all about her ex-husband (Azure's father), and how he has turned into such an unenlightened asshole. He's a crappy father, he doesn't make his alimony payments, and he probably voted Republican in the last election.

"I don't know what has happened to him," she laments. "I get no support from him of any kind."

Oh boy.

Lavender goes on and on. All the while, her annoying little hairy dog is next to me on the couch, sticking her wet nose into my crotch. I gently push the dog away, only to have her return to my penile region with more determination.

To break the mood, which has quickly gone from hopeful to pathetic, I suggest that we go for a walk. Lavender, Azure, and I pile into my car and drive to the park. I take Lavender's hand as we stroll amidst the trees.

I try to direct the conversation to us, the two single adults who are supposed to be on a date. I ask Lavender to describe the best romantic relationship she's ever had. But she can barely get a sentence out without Azure interrupting with, "Mom! Look at this!" or "Mom, watch me do a cartwheel!"

Azure does cartwheels with all of the grace of a three-legged elephant.

"Let's go to your house!" says Lavender suddenly.

Well, why not? It's windy out here, the light is fading, and our conversation is stalled. We pick up ice cream and frozen yogurt and head for my place.

As we park in my driveway, Lavender seems suitably impressed. Inside, I give her a quick tour of my place, and the look on her face tells me that I have passed this portion of the job interview. And that's what this date feels like—an extended job interview. I have to get the Azure stamp of approval, I have to sound supportive when Lavender tells me her sad relationship story, I have to demonstrate that the three of us (me, Lavender, and Azure) can do a reasonable imitation of a family, I have to pass the prosperity test, and finally I have to prove that I am not a slob during the unscheduled home inspection.

The three of us eat ice cream at my dining table. Having passed all of my tests, I should be feeling great right now. Instead, I feel like I have been cheated out of my date with the Yoga Babe. We haven't spent any quality time alone, and even when we were alone we didn't do any serious male-female bonding.

What is the matter with this woman? Doesn't she know how to go out on a date? She's got everything backwards. I'm not ready to even THINK about being a male role model for her daughter. I need to feel a connection to Lavender first.

> **BABE MAGNET RULE #81**
> First, date the Babe. *Then* get to know her kids. If a Babe wants to get her kids involved in your early dates, she is not looking for a lover, she is looking for a father figure for her kids.

Maybe this is how they arrange dates in Woo-Woo Land. Maybe a date is a gathering of everyone in the family, and then all the family members vote on whether the man and the woman should see each other again.

But this approach doesn't make any sense to me. This is our first dinner date, and I don't care what Azure thinks of me. I care what Lavender thinks of me, and what I think of her. I want to talk playfully about what she likes to do for fun and what makes her happy. I want to know how deeply her passion runs, and whether she is ready for a passionate, fun, sexy, brilliant, healthy, optimistic, prosperous, creative, friendly, and modest man in her life.

If I was getting any spark of chemistry from Lavender at all, I might overlook this strange Woo-Woo Land date. But I'm not. And although I am sure that 11-year-old Azure is a fine human being, she isn't special in any way that I can see. She's just an 11-year-old kid, and I don't want to be her daddy.

I admit that Lavender's beauty has blinded me. I admit that her exotic aura has enticed me. But I am so over it. By the time I drop Lavender and Azure off at their house, I already know that I won't be calling Lavender for another date.

Chapter 77: Learning a New Trick

I am underwhelmed by the response to my latest series of online dating emails. Of the 26 emails I sent, I received four responses. When I responded back to these four lovely ladies, I received two follow-up responses. Of these two, I have set up a Meet and Greet date with one woman.

That's a pathetic success rate. If I were a Major League baseball player with one hit in my last 26 at-bats, I would be in the midst of a horrible slump. That's a .038 batting average. Bat boys have higher batting averages than that. Stevie Wonder has a higher batting average than that.

There has to be a better way. What am I doing wrong?

I'm a writer, for God's sake. I wrote a killer profile for myself, and I write fabulous emails to the lovely women online. So what's the problem? Is it my photos? Do I look like a total dweeb?

I search through profiles of more local women. Just before I start sending out emails, I catch a lucky break. My single friend Julia emails me, and we end up having a long electronic chat. She shares with me her recent online experiences. She joined Match.com just two weeks ago, and she has been overwhelmed with responses ever since. "I must be the new Babe on the block," she writes.

In two weeks, she has received more than 300 responses from friendly men. More than 300! Every time she opens her email, it is full of messages from hopeful single men. So how has she dealt with that? "I don't even respond to the long messages," she tells me. "It's too much like work. But if someone sends me a nice, short message, I try to respond with a nice, short reply."

Holy Babe Repellant! I have been going about this electronic communication all wrong. When I send one of my patented, well-crafted, highly detailed, and LONG emails to online Babes, they don't respond to me because IT'S TOO MUCH LIKE WORK. I can't blame them, either, if they are receiving even half as many messages as Julia is.

BABE MAGNET RULE #82

If you discover that you have been doing something that Babes don't like, change it. You can't be a Babe Magnet if you are chasing the Babes away. That's not what a *magnet* is, dude.

So I send out a few emails using a new approach. To SunnyClearBlu I send a one-line email that comments about her love of a particular hiking trail that I also like. I ask DivineKona if she still enjoys playing tennis, and where she likes to play. To Shoegirl626, I comment about her enormous breasts. (Just kidding! Even though I love her enormous breasts, I ask her about her paintings.) I send a total of eight short messages to eight promising Babes.

Maybe this new approach will finally increase my batting average.

By the next morning I have my answer. Admittedly, eight women is a very small sampling. But right now, I am ecstatic at the results. Out of eight emails sent, I have received four responses. The short emails have thus far proven to be far superior to my verbose, self-important emails. Let the correspondence begin!

There is someone knocking at my front door. That must be Love now! At last, a beautiful woman has arrived on my doorstep in search of me. Perhaps she found me online, and using modern detective tools (Google and lots of time on her hands) she has found out where I live. Or maybe she has followed me home from the supermarket, having seen me shopping in the produce section.

No, it is my next-door neighbor Ray. In the many years I have lived next to Ray, I can count on one hand the number of times he has knocked on my door.

He is on a mission. Many months ago, I told him all about how I met Colleen on Match.com. Now he is ready to jump into the online dating pool. "Would you help me write my profile?" he asks. "I'm really boring and I suck at writing."

I agree to help him in exchange for a couple of beers and a burger.

The next evening we drive in his sports car to Barleycorn's. We settle into a booth and a Waitress Babe takes our orders almost before our butts hit the benches. I whip out a pen and a pad and I begin to interview Ray.

"What do you like to do for fun?" I ask brightly, trying to get Ray to relax.

"Nothing. I told you, I'm really boring."

"Ray, I know you play tennis. What else do you do?"

"I work. My ex-wife says I'm a workaholic."

"That's not going to attract a woman," I complain as I sip my beer. I try again. "What kind of movies do you like?"

"I haven't been to a movie in a couple of years," he says, eyeing the breasts on the Waitress Babe as she walks by. "I saw a DVD about new accounting changes in the recent tax bill."

"Jesus, give me something to work with here," I plead.

"I like *Star Wars*."

"Ray, everyone likes *Star Wars*."

How did I get myself into this predicament? I am being set up to fail. From where I sit right now, Ray seems pathetic. And pathetic lives right next door to desperate.

BABE MAGNET RULE #83

Never appear desperate. Women are not attracted to men who are desperate to meet a woman. It's better to NOT CARE whether you attract a woman or not. Because, ironically, not caring (and the confidence that goes with it) is a great way to attract a woman.

Women, especially Babes, can smell desperation. It smells like a cross between a wet dog and stale beer, and it turns a Babe off completely. When she smells that smell, a Babe runs toward the nearest "bad boy" type.

I keep digging, and I get a few tidbits to weave into a profile. Ray doesn't go out for beers, except that he's having a beer with me right now. "I enjoy hanging out at Barleycorn's, which is my favorite local tavern," I write on my notepad. Clearly, I am going to need all of my copywriting and marketing skills if I am to write a profile for Ray that will attract any attention from women. Not only is he boring, but he has no confidence and, apparently, no dating skills. No wonder his ex-wife left him.

Ray doesn't like talking about himself, so I switch to another topic. "What are you looking for, Ray?"

"I want to get laid!" he says with a smile.

"Yeah, well, we can't come right out and say that in your profile. You will chase women away. Can I say that you are looking for your soul mate?"

He looks at me strangely. "Yeah, I guess so—if you think it will help me get laid."

Oh, God. No wonder this man has no love life. He is such a Neanderthal. He is self-centered, yet he has no self confidence. He is not especially attractive, yet he refuses to change his appearance. He is unwilling to consider that he must actually woo a woman, which takes effort and style and class. He is everything that women hate about men.

He reminds me of what I was like a couple of years ago, and I hate him for that.

"All right, Ray. Describe for me the kind of woman you would like to meet. What does she look like?"

He smiles. "I want to meet a woman with really big tits. I've never slept with a woman with really massive, battleship-sized boobs. That would be fun!"

Oh, God. Please give me strength—and patience. I will write an acceptable profile for Ray, even though all he wants right now is to get laid by a woman with breasts the size of the *U.S.S. Missouri*.

As for me, my standards are considerably higher. I am holding out for True Love.

Chapter 78: Red Alert, Captain

Brenda is coming over for dinner in 30 minutes, and I am frantically running around the house picking up stuff and cleaning. I haven't consistently done my housecleaning since the last time I had a woman over to the house, which was many, many weeks ago. There is a lot of cleaning to be done.

I have been seeing Brenda for two months, but this is the first time she has been over to my house. Brenda is yet another Match.com woman. After sending lots of emails that led to many phone calls that resulted in a few Meet and Greets, Brenda was the woman I selected as the best girlfriend candidate. Her online profile was short but interesting, and her photos showed a 54-year-old woman who is very cute. She likes eating at Barleycorn's, and she loves red wine. She enjoys watching the hummingbirds from her kitchen window, and she loves live music.

Once the communication started, Brenda and I were like old friends. We laugh at the same things and enjoy the same foods and movies. We are, by all accounts, very compatible. In fact, when Mueller had a little dinner party last week, I brought Brenda and she was the hit of the party. She is friendly and easy to talk to. Mueller pulled me aside to tell me he really liked her. That's saying quite a bit, because Mueller is very slow to welcome new people into his life.

Now Brenda is on her way to my house. I know this because she sent me a text telling me, "I'm on my way!"

I am cooking Pad Thai for Brenda, and that involves chopping a lot of vegetables. I won't have time to do it in advance. Holy Frozen Dinner! I forgot to take the chicken breasts out of the freezer. They are solid ice. I run them under warm water and leave them to soak. Maybe they will thaw in time.

Brenda arrives right at 6:30 pm. She looks lovely, as always. She really is a very attractive woman. Brenda, who is a real tender-heart when it comes to animals, spends more time greeting Zippy the Poodle than greeting me, and she doesn't give me a hello kiss. But she does hand me a bottle of red wine from Washington State and a take-out box from Jupiter Moon that contains a slice of coconut cream pie and a slice of chocolate cake. I forgot to tell her that I'm not a big fan of coconut.

I open the wine and pour us generous glasses. We're going to drink the entire bottle tonight, whether Brenda knows it or not. I have an agenda. It's time for her to tell me the ENTIRE story about her marriages and divorces. She's done a pretty good job of dodging the issue, but tonight is the night.

I put the Brie in the oven to melt. We sip wine, and I chop veggies. When the Brie is just bubbling, I set it on my bistro table and we munch on the warm cheese and crackers. Brenda tells me all about her recent trip to Washington with her friend Paula. It sounds like they had a great time, but Brenda wanted to visit more wineries than Paula did. That makes sense, since I have already observed that Brenda has definite wino tendencies.

As always, it is very comfortable and enjoyable to be with Brenda. That's what I like best about her. We just click together. Not in a passionate way (there is no passion, no sex of any kind), but in a best friends kind of way.

If I have to say so myself, this Middle-Aged Babe Magnet cooks a mighty fine Pad Thai. We eat my carefully prepared feast, and I continue to ply Brenda with red wine. Then, I finally get her to tell me her entire marriage and divorce story. Before tonight, all she would admit to was being married "more than once." Get this: she has actually been married and divorced FOUR TIMES. And since her last divorce, there was another serious relationship that didn't result in marriage, but ended just four months ago.

Holy Laser Beam to the Gonads. Suddenly, I feel like I am on the set of *Star Trek: The Next Relationship* during an intense battle scene.

"So, how many times have you been married?" I ask.

"Four," she replies.

> FIRST OFFICER: CAPTAIN, WE HAVE RECEIVED AN INCOMING MESSAGE. BUT IT APPEARS TO BE GARBLED.

"I'm sorry, I'm not sure I heard that. Did you say four?"

"Uh-huh."

> FIRST OFFICER: UNIDENTIFIED SHIP APPROACHING.
>
> CAPTAIN: RED ALERT! RED ALERT!

"Four marriages and four divorces, right? How old were you when you first got married?"

"I was 23," she says. "He was 14 years older than me, and he had three kids."

> FIRST OFFICER: CAPTAIN, THEY ARE CHARGING WEAPONS.
>
> CAPTAIN: SHIELDS UP!

"How long did that marriage last?" I ask, trying not to let the turmoil in my chest show on my face.

"Five years."

> FIRST OFFICER: PHOTON TORPEDOES HAVE BEEN FIRED. BRACE FOR IMPACT!

"Then you got married again, and you had a son…"

"Yes," she replies, reaching for the wine glass that I have just refilled for her. "And we were married for two years."

> FIRST OFFICER: THEY HAVE FIRED ANOTHER ROUND OF TORPEDOES.
>
> CAPTAIN: I NEED MAXIMUM POWER TO THE SHIELDS!

She takes a healthy gulp of wine and continues. “After that I married an auto mechanic who was seven years younger than me. He also had a tow-truck business. I learned to drive a tow-truck. That marriage lasted for four or five years...”

“Four or five years, but you’re not sure exactly.”

“Well, I could look it up,” she says. She is starting to slur her words.

> BOOM! (THE SHIP ROCKS.)
>
> FIRST OFFICER: DIRECT HIT. SHIELDS DOWN TO 24%.
>
> CAPTAIN: ENGINEERING, I NEED EVERYTHING YOU'VE GOT FOR THE FORWARD SHIELDS!!!

“And husband number four?”

“Who, the ex-convict?” she exclaims. “He said he never did it. He was framed. The building must have spontaneously combusted.”

> BOOM! THE LIGHTS MOMENTARILY GO OUT.
>
> COMPUTER VOICE: SWITCHING TO AUXILIARY POWER.
>
> FIRST OFFICER: CAPTAIN, WE CAN'T WITHSTAND ANOTHER HIT LIKE THAT WITHOUT THIS SHIP BREAKING APART.
>
> CAPTAIN: EVASIVE MANUEVERS!!!

“How about your last relationship—the guy you didn’t marry?” I ask. “Why did you break up with him?”

“That one got really complicated,” she says, finishing her glass of wine. “He wanted his ex-wife to move in with us into the upstairs bedroom. After several months of *that*, I just had to get out.”

> BOOM! THE LIGHTS GO OUT. THE SHIP SHAKES VIOLENTLY, LIKE THE BACKSIDE OF A GROSSLY OVERWEIGHT MAN WEARING STRETCH PANTS WHO IS RUNNING FOR HIS LIFE FROM RABID HYENAS.
>
> COMPUTER VOICE: HULL BREACH IN 15 SECONDS.

SIRENS WAIL.
CAPTAIN: EVACUATE THE SHIP—NOW!

My face feels like it is melting. But I must press on. I must know *one more thing*.

"Is there anything about any of these relationships that you regret?" I ask.

Brenda is oblivious to the fact that my head is about to explode, and the starship we are traveling in is going to disintegrate at any moment.

"No," she sighs. "I still love every one of my ex-husbands—even the one I didn't marry."

THE SHIP EXPLODES. EVERYONE ONBOARD PERISHES.

I do not share the *Star Trek* adventure that is playing in my head. Brenda doesn't have a clue that I am freaking out. I have figured out that, if I keep seeing Brenda, the *best possible* scenario is for me to become her fifth ex-husband after five years. There is no way in God's big, black outer space that I am signing up for that.

"Do you have any more wine?" she asks.

The poor thing has no idea that this is going to be our last date. But that's no reason to let a perfectly good dessert go to waste.

The chocolate cake was fabulous, by the way.

Chapter 79: Use the Force!

I am freaking out just a little bit. My subscription to Match.com is running out in a couple of weeks (again!), and I still haven't found the new love of my life. Sure, I have gotten to be a much more successful online dater with my efficient use of short, snappy emails. But unfortunately, even though I can successfully contact women, I still haven't found The One. What am I doing wrong?

As I sit in front of my laptop, with the screen filled with profile photos of Babes and Babe Wannabees, I hear a gentle voice in my head.

USE THE FORCE, CHAD!

Great, I've gone from imagining *Star Trek* scenes to replaying *Star Wars* lines. I must really be cracking up. All of the stress of dating is finally getting to me. I keep clicking through the thumbnail images that turned up in my latest search of local women.

USE THE FORCE, CHAD!

I look around, just like Luke Skywalker (played by Mark Hamill) did in Star Wars. Use the Force? What is that supposed to mean?

EXPAND YOUR HORIZONS!

Listen, Obi Wanna Date Kenobi, I need you to be a little more specific here, I think. I go back to the online profiles.

Oh, wait a minute. I get it. I do another online search, but instead of looking for women within 10 miles of my zip code, I expand it to 75 miles. Great Mother of Darth! A whole new supply of women has miraculously materialized.

BABE MAGNET RULE #84

Don't get cocky. Just because you have been dating for a long time doesn't mean you know everything about dating. Even experienced Babe Magnets can learn new things. And that goes double for learning new things about women.

I begin reading profiles of the newly discovered women outside of my geographical comfort zone, and I am delighted by what I find. One woman gets my attention immediately. She calls herself Rareone46, and her subhead reads "Landlocked in a Tropical Body!"

She is 46 years old, divorced, and has three kids—the youngest of which is 17. She is not shy about posting pictures with her profile. There are 15 photos, and she's in eight of them. She is cute, with short blondish hair and a nice smile. There are photos of her smiling at the camera and also shots of her in a bikini while snorkeling, hanging out on a tropical beach, and skiing (but not in a bikini).

She gets bonus points for being brave enough to post a photo of herself wearing a bikini, and even more bonus points for wearing the bikini so well. This woman is a Babe.

Rareone46 starts her profile with a rambling paragraph that doesn't mean a thing. She is just getting warmed up. Then she shares this quote: "Live with intention. Walk to the edge. Practice wellness. Play with abandon ... Laugh. Choose with no regret. Continue to learn. Appreciate your friends. Do what you love. Live as if this is all there is!"

I am totally hooked. If I could get this woman on the phone right now I would ask her to marry me.

But there's more in her profile, and it gets better. She describes herself as "a Tigger, not an Eeyore, always the eternal optimist and out to have fun, fun, fun!" She likes to travel to tropical places. She also likes to visit the mountains. She likes to play poker but she doesn't like to gamble. She hosts festive parties. She plays guitar and writes music.

Somebody pinch me. I am falling in love. I read on.

"I value kindness, love, and affection and am very devoted. I only have my son home now and he is nearly always gone working, at school, or with friends. I say 'good job' to myself, they are flying from the nest... the world is at their feet... and mine now! Care to join me?"

Yes, Rareone46, I will join you right now. Let me just grab my toothbrush. On second thought, I can pick one up wherever it is we are going. A tropical destination, you say?

"My ideal match will also be of Tigger qualities and hopefully will want to live life, not merely exist. Age is attitude in my book. A steady job and a good credit score is practical." (Now she is starting to sound like a fortune cookie. But, hey, she never said she was a professional writer. She's a nurse.) "An inkling for adventure and fun or be able to relax and take in a sunset is a must. Romance and chivalry are not dead. I find a kind gentleman very sexy."

Holy Babe Jackpot. This is the closest thing to the perfect woman for me that I have ever seen on Match.com. I reread her profile, savoring every detail. She is five foot five, slender, and a fan of classic rock. She loves to spend time in her garden, which she says is an extension of her home space.

I cannot believe my luck. I cannot believe that this woman is single. This one is indeed a rare find, and I must send her an email message immediately, if not sooner. But what do I say?

Based upon the inside information I have received from Julia, I am guessing that this woman is new to Match.com, and that she is going to receive about 300,000 emails in the next few days. I have to act quickly, and I have to stand out from the crowd of men who are clamoring for her attention.

I have to write something snappy that she can respond to quickly. It has to be very easy to answer me, otherwise she'll lump me in with all the long-winded guys who want to tell her their life stories or the creepy guys who ask her about the most interesting place she's ever "done it."

I could respond to her Winnie the Pooh reference with something like, "I'm also a Tigger seeking a Tigger." But that's not quite right.

I examine her photos again. I check out the bikini shot several times. Did I say she was going to receive 300,000 emails? Make that half a million. There is a photo of her on a tropical beach. She is wearing the lovely, colorful bikini while crouching next to a sea turtle. OK, that's my hook.

I click on "send an email" and write: "That's a great photo of you and the sea turtle. Where was it taken?"

That's it. Nothing about me. Nothing about her profile and how wonderful she sounds. Nothing about how great she looks in a bikini. No clever little comments that reveal how witty and charming I am.

And now, I wait.

By the grace of God, I don't have to wait long. Before the evening is over I have received a response. She says the photo was taken in Hawaii on the Big Island, and she named the turtle Henry. Henceforth, every sea turtle she sees is named Henry. I get up from my computer and do a little dance of joy. She has taken the bait, and the dialogue has begun.

I write back with a slightly longer email, telling her about my vacation plans for the summer, which include an exotic-sounding trip that Jason and I will take next month to Playa del Carmen, Mexico. (I am really glad that my next vacation isn't to Fresno, because that would not impress her at all.) I ask if she has any fun trips planned.

The next day she responds with a slightly longer message:

"I am staying close to home this summer. I went to Hawaii twice and mostly I have been going to Eden Springs for weekend trips... I have been to Playa del Carmen. If I might suggest, there's a great park called Xcaret nearby. Being a lover of plants, you will enjoy all the vegetation I am sure. Well, feel free to call sometime, Krista." Then she gives me her phone number.

Score! I have moved to the front of Krista's Match.com line. The other 500,000 guys are out of luck.

I call Krista the next day, and we have a very nice conversation. On the phone, she is just as delightful as her online profile would suggest. She has a 17-year-old son, an 18-year-old daughter, and a 21-year-old daughter.

The two girls are off at college during the school year, and Krista is getting psychologically ready for the Empty Nest Syndrome that will begin when her son goes off to college in a year.

I proudly tell her all about my son, Jason, and how he is becoming a fine young man. We seem to have a lot in common. But there is one major problem: distance. More than an hour's worth of freeway driving separates us. I tell Krista that I will probably be driving up to Shelbyville next week, and I would love to meet her then.

"Absolutely," she says. "My schedule is flexible, and I would love to meet you, too."

Two days later I successfully manufacture a reason to visit a client in Shelbyville. I call Krista with the good news. "I am going to be up there for a meeting on Thursday morning," I say. "Can I take you to lunch?"

I expect her to say, "Yes!" She is supposed to be all excited that I have made it a priority to drive up to see her. She is supposed to receive my invitation to lunch with the excitement with which it is offered. Instead, she turns me down.

"Sorry, I am training a new nurse that day, so I can't make it on Thursday."

What? What did she say? Was that a "No"? Have I just been rejected by the finest woman currently on Match.com? Has she just shot me down without providing anything to break my fall? I clutch my heart and pains shoot up my left arm. My head is getting dizzy, I can't breathe, and I feel nauseated.

It is time for Plan B. "If lunch doesn't work for you, how about meeting for coffee and dessert in the afternoon?"

Nope. No can do. She's busy. Busy, busy, busy. Thursday is going to be a very busy day for her. Did she mention that she was going to be busy?

"Are you sure you can't break away at all?" I ask, not willing to believe that I am being totally rejected. Throw me a bone here, little lady. I am driving all the way up to see you, and you won't even do a Meet and Greet?

No. The answer is still no. I am very disappointed, although I try not to make it obvious. But I think she can hear it in my voice. "Do you ever make it down to Springfield?" I ask, hopefully.

"No, sorry," she replies.

Well, hell. I have just been shut down, big-time. Excuse me while I go off behind this bush and lick my wounds. Don't worry about me, though. My head will grow back, eventually, and no one will even notice the scars.

Chapter 80: Shelbyville, Here I Come!

During the next week I lick my wounds from Krista's rejection and console myself by examining the profiles of other women from Shelbyville. There is one other woman who looks quite promising.

She calls herself SkyDreamer99. She is exactly my age, five foot seven with long brown hair and a nice smile. Unfortunately, all of her profile photos show her standing in a garden, and I can't see her face very well. There is more of her garden in each photo than of her. This is a pet peeve of mine, so I'm going to offer this advice...

> **BABE MAGNET RULE #85**
> Get a really good photo taken of yourself for your online profile. Use a "head and shoulders" shot as your primary photo so your prospective dates can see what you look like. It's great to post photos of yourself in your garden or on the beach, too. But your next true love wants to see YOU.

SkyDreamer 99 says she is "definitely the glass-half-full kind of person." She claims to be energetic, and she takes good care of herself. I like this quote from her profile: "I know a little about a lot of things, and a lot about some things, and I'm always looking to learn more."

I send SkyDreamer99 an email saying that her garden looks lovely and I like her positive attitude. By the end of the week we have exchanged several emails and made the jump to talking on the phone. Her name is Michelle, and she sounds lovely but slightly reserved. I promise to call her to let her know when I will be in town so we can meet.

As if by magic—or destiny—my client in Shelbyville needs me to come up for a meeting next week. This will give me a chance to meet a Babe in

Shelbyville. By piggybacking my meeting with a date, I will be doing my part to save the Earth by conserving precious fossil fuels—and I will be making the world a better place by bringing two single people together. Plus, I will be saving lots of travel time—time that I can spend feeding hungry children or working diligently to promote world peace.

Some day in the future I might just win an award for this kind of selfless, global thinking. Just call me the Dali Babe Magnet.

I punch in Krista's cell phone number.

"Hi Krista, this is Chad, from Springfield."

"Oh, HI!!" By the tone of her voice, she sounds very happy to hear from me. I appreciate the fact that she remembers me at all, considering she has probably had millions of online contacts by now.

"I was wondering if I could take you out for dinner."

She says yes and suggests a casual Mexican restaurant for our rendezvous. I hang up the phone and do a little celebration dance in my living room.

Then I call Michelle and arrange a Meet and Greet with her at 5:00 p.m. on the same day. So now I have a Dating Doubleheader scheduled for Shelbyville.

The big day finally arrives. My business meeting ends in the mid-afternoon, and I agree to follow my client, Angelica, to her home for tea and cookies. Angelica is one of those work acquaintances who has become a personal friend, and she knows that I am actively looking for the last love of my life. I tell her that I have two dates scheduled for later today, both of which are the result of Match.com contacts.

"Can you show me how online dating works?" she asks.

Sure, why not? I login on Match.com and give her a quick tour. I show her my profile, and I show her how to do a search. Angelica is a middle-aged woman in search of a middle-aged woman, and she wonders if online dating will work for her.

"I don't see why not," I say.

To prove it, I do a search for her. For the first time in my life I select "Woman Looking for Woman," enter Angelica's zip code, and hit enter. Thirty-two thumbnail photos appear on the screen.

Angelica is utterly fascinated. She is still scrutinizing the profiles of her target women when I leave for Date Number One.

Michelle arrives promptly at 5:00 p.m. I am waiting for her just inside the restaurant, and I watch her walk in. I have been on so many first dates that I can immediately typecast her.

Michelle is a people pleaser. She wants people to like her, and she wants to be adored by a man. At the same time, her divorce has rocked her foundation and she is scared to death. She never, never, ever wants to be hurt again. And yet, she is willing to take that risk because she can't tolerate the alternative. She will not shut down her emotions and learn to live without a man. She will open her heart and hope that the next man she trusts will treat her better than the last.

Her body has the comfortable round curves of middle age. She is pleasantly attractive without being a cover girl. She treads lightly on the ground, unsure of her next step. She stands tentatively inside the restaurant door, not knowing where to look for me. I am sitting on a bench about 20 feet away, and I don't try to ease her discomfort by making my presence known. I watch her look from left to right before she sees me. Even then, she is not sure I am her date until I get up and walk toward her.

She looks visibly relieved when she sees me, because she no longer has to worry about being stood up. But now she is worried that she won't know what to say.

We sit at a booth and I make friendly talk about the restaurant and the weather. It is threatening to rain outside, and the temperature has dropped 20 degrees F. in the past hour. As soon as we have covered the safe topics of conversation, her eyes go blank. She is thinking, "Now what do we talk about?" But she has already planned for this moment. She pulls out a fancy canvas bag, and she proudly invites me to look inside.

I am greeted with a bookstore full of colorful gardening books. There's a book about flower gardening and a magnificent book filled with the finest backyard gardens in Shelbyville. There are nine or 10 wonderful volumes, all carefully chosen with me in mind.

I am touched by Michelle's thoughtfulness. At the same time, I am not sure how to react. What does she want me to do, read a book during our first date while she watches? In my 1.7 million first dates, no one has ever handed me a book to read. Maybe she's thinking that I will borrow some or all of the gardening books and that will give us something to talk about during our next date.

Here's the big thing that Michelle doesn't know yet. There isn't going to be a second date. I am not feeling any spark here at all. None. Nothing. Nada.

The chemistry of attraction is an elusive, mysterious, and hard-to-explain phenomenon, but I feel no chemistry between Michelle and myself. I usually know within two minutes of meeting a woman if there is any chemistry. Even if I don't sense it right away, I surely know it soon—well within the first part of a Meet and Greet.

BABE MAGNET RULE #86

If you don't feel the "chemistry" soon after you meet a woman, there probably won't be any. Unfortunately, there is no way to force the chemistry of attraction—no matter how hard you try.

I have heard that women experience chemistry differently than men do. I think for women, attraction is a more complicated experience. Women have more patience than men in most things, and I suppose that includes waiting to see if they feel an attraction toward someone new. So a man might feel the initial rush of "chemistry" in two minutes, while a woman might not feel that same rush of attraction for a couple of hours.

I am sure Michelle is a lovely person, but I sense that she is not yet ready for a relationship. And I am so ready I can hardly stand it. So I am not going to borrow Michelle's gardening books, because I don't want to have to see her again to return them.

After I flip through the books, I carefully place them back into the canvas bag and slide them across the table to her. She looks mildly disappointed, but doesn't say a word.

To be polite, I stay with Michelle for another 20 minutes. I surreptitiously check my watch periodically. At exactly 6:00 pm I tell her I must be going.

"It was a pleasure meeting you," I say, warmly shaking her hand.

I make no false promises about looking forward to seeing her again.

Chapter 81: Game Two of a Twi-night Doubleheader

It's a full hour until my second date of the evening, so I stroll through the nearby shops. Ironically, I walk into a bookstore—but I decide not to look at any gardening books. Instead, I browse through the Self Help and Personal Relationships titles looking for a book about dating. What I would like to read is a real-life story from a man's perspective about dating after divorce. I would love to read an entertaining account of middle-aged dating that could give me some tips and some insight. I am surprised to learn that there isn't such a book.

Hmmmm. Maybe I'll have to write one.

I slightly misjudge the time necessary to navigate the local rush-hour traffic, so I am five minutes late to the location of the second date of the Twi-night Doubleheader. I am excited, because I am really looking forward to meeting Krista. But I am also just a tad melancholy, because, no matter how it goes tonight, this is my last Match.com first date. My membership has expired and I have chosen not to renew it.

As I drive up, I can already see that Krista is waiting for me outside of the restaurant. Even from a distance she looks just like her online photos, and that's a very good thing because she is cute. She is wearing a short, blue-patterned summer dress that hugs her trim body. As I walk briskly toward her, she looks better and better. My heart starts to beat a little faster in a primal reaction that is completely out of my control.

She greets me with warm smile and a friendly hug. It is a wonderful greeting, and one that I didn't expect from Krista. In the few times I have spoken to her on the phone, my impression of Krista is of a woman who embraces modern life yet appreciates traditional values. I expected to greet her with a chaste hand squeeze, not a full-body hug.

Because I am running late, I am unable to put Babe Magnet Rule #30 into play. So instead I use...

> **BABE MAGNET RULE #30-B**
> If you arrive at the chosen rendezvous spot after your date does, smile and walk in like you own the place. Don't apologize for being late until you have given her a heart-felt compliment.

"It is so great to meet you," I say, smiling broadly. "I have been looking forward to meeting you all day. And I gotta tell you, that dress looks really wonderful on you."

Krista returns my smile, her face lighting up like fireworks.

As we wait for the hostess to seat us, Krista explains why she greeted me so enthusiastically. "I was standing out in front of the restaurant waiting for you, and this little old bald man started walking up to me," she says. "I was saying to myself, 'Please don't let it be him, please don't let it be him.' When he walked past me, I was SO relieved. And then you walked up, and you were exactly how you described yourself."

Krista tells me that she has been on first dates that did not go well because the men completely lied about themselves and their appearances. One man posted 20-year-old photos and then refused to admit it. Another man's online profile said he was six feet tall, but when he showed up he was eye-to-eye with Krista, who is five foot five.

The hostess walks us outside to the patio. But the wind has picked up and it feels like the thunderstorm is fast approaching, so we decide to sit inside. But inside, the air conditioner is cranked up to Full Mama, and it is ridiculously cold. Krista is sitting with her legs clamped tightly together and her arms folded. I think I can even see goosebumps on her arms amidst the freckles. She looks uncomfortably cold.

"Would you like me to get you a jacket?" I ask. "I have a windbreaker in my car." She says yes, and I dash out to get it. She nearly melts with happiness when I put my jacket over her shoulders.

BABE MAGNET RULE #87
Be a gentleman. There are so few gentlemen left in the world these days, and being one is a great way to set yourself apart from all of the jerks that women have been dating.

It isn't until the next morning, when I read her online profile again, that I realize what a big score it was for me to gallantly run out to get my jacket. "Romance and chivalry are not dead," Krista wrote. "I find a kind gentleman very sexy."

Krista orders a bowl of tortilla soup and I order a taco plate, and we settle in to talk. I tell her how attracted I was by her calling herself a Tigger. We both share an infectious optimism, and we are clearly attracted to each other. Krista unconsciously strokes the hair by her neck when I tell her how I started my business. A few moments later while I am talking about the favorite places I have been, she quickly licks her lips as she gives her head a playful tilt. I am feeling the chemistry, too.

We cover all of the normal first-date topics, but then we open up and discuss one of the real taboo subjects: religion.

My singlehood has given me a lot of time to think about God and organized religion. One of the things my ex-wife got in the divorce was our church. We never discussed it in those terms, and I didn't realize right away that it had become *her* church. But some of our best mutual friends also go to the church, and when I tried to sit next to them during the last Sunday service I attended, I felt like an African man at a KKK rally. Sitting in the sanctuary, feeling completely ostracized, got me to thinking about God and what I believe.

I got this wild, heretical idea in my head. What if God doesn't care about what religion we believe? What if it really doesn't matter? What if it makes no difference what religion you practice (or whether you participate in any organized religion at all), as long as you have love in your heart? Isn't love the common denominator of every religion?

Isn't love what it's really all about? And isn't love the reason that all of us single people try so hard to find someone to cherish—someone with whom we can spend the rest of our lives in delicious bliss?

I share some of this wild, heretical thinking with Krista, and instead of looking at me in horror, she nods. She says she has done a lot of thinking about this, too. I tell her about the positive message I hear at the church I now attend. "We believe in Original Blessing. We believe that we were all created in the image and likeness of God…"

Krista smiles in agreement. I am digging this woman big-time.

Then I drop the bombshell. After 1.7 million dates, I know how to cut to the chase. I don't want to waste my time—or hers.

"What are you looking for in a relationship?" I ask her.

The question surprises her, and she sputters for a moment. Then she recovers by saying, "Someone I can trust. Someone I can travel with."

She is intrigued that I have asked her the ultimate dating question—the question that no one asks on a first date. So, she turns the question back to me. "And what are you looking for?"

I smile. For the first time during my singlehood, for the first time during the dating process, I have absolute clarity. "I am looking for the last love of my life," I reply, with a confident smile on my face. "I hope it results in marriage, and I hope to be married for the rest of my life."

Krista looks at me like a deer looks at an approaching 18-wheeler. Then she stands up abruptly and runs screaming out the restaurant.

Just kidding. She actually looks at me with a sparkle in her eyes, as if I have touched something deep inside of her. Perhaps she, too, is looking for the last love of her life.

We talk for an hour and a half. The conversation flows from one topic to the next. I am bonding with this wonderful woman in a way that I have never bonded with anyone on a first date. I do not want this moment to end.

And then I catch her sneaking a peek at her watch. My heart sinks. I thought she was feeling the magic, too—but maybe not.

"Do you have somewhere else you need to be?" I ask.

She smiles sheepishly, knowing she has been busted.

"I was planning to meet my oldest daughter and her friend at a restaurant for salsa dancing," says Krista. Then she pauses for a moment as the wheels in her brain turn. "Would you like to come with me?"

I have an hour's drive to get home. I have to get up early tomorrow for a morning meeting. I have been going nonstop since about 6:00 a.m. this morning. I think Jason made plans for tonight, so Zippy the Poodle is home all alone. I have a million reasons why I can graciously say, "No thank you."

But I don't want to say goodbye to this charming woman.

"Normally, I would respectfully decline," I say. "But you have just made me an offer that I can't refuse. I would love to go salsa dancing with you."

Krista beams. Perhaps she is feeling the magic, too.

Chapter 82: Salsa Dancing for Dummies

I pay the bill for dinner. (Did I already say that a man should always pay for the first date? Oh yeah, it's Babe Magnet Rule #49.) I don't know the streets of Shelbyville very well, so Krista tells me to follow her.

My eyes are riveted on the back of her silver Lexus SUV as she zips through town, and we navigate the twists and turns of the intricate roads.

I have lots of time to think as I drive. One of the things I think about is, "Holy Dancing with the Stars, I took a couple of lessons but I do *not* remember how to salsa dance." But I will deal with this small problem with as much grace and humility as I can muster. The most important thing right now is that my date with Krista is continuing.

We zip up a narrow street past quaint shops and art galleries that have sprouted in centuries-old houses. I follow Krista into a tiny parking lot, where we find the last two spots. We walk up the steps into Del Fuego's restaurant, and I can already hear the band playing.

The place is packed. The five-piece band is playing a sexy salsa song, and a few couples are dancing with hips swaying and arms draped over each other. Krista leads me past the bar to the back of the small room where a group of old folks has just vacated a table for six. The Date Gods are definitely smiling down on us. It is as if the universe is saying, "I want you kids to have a WONDERFUL time together tonight. You need a chance to get to know each other."

"This is great!" says Krista. "My daughter and her friend are on their way, and they are bringing my nephew and his friend from England."

Great Mother of the Queen! Am I going to meet everyone in this woman's family during our first date?

Krista offers to buy me a glass of cabernet, and in the spirit of 21st century dating I graciously accept. Krista and I try to pick up our conversation where it left off, but it is difficult to hear over the music. The good news is that Krista and I have to lean in close to hear each other, and sometimes I have to touch her arm or speak right into her ear. We are getting more physically intimate simply because we have to in order to communicate.

Krista's daughter appears, along with her best friend. They are both 21 years old and both named Amy—so I only have to remember one name. I also meet Brrruurighhh and Stmmmpppss, both from England. I don't catch either of their names, but I enjoy talking to them because I love hearing their accents.

Amy and Amy are on a mission to dance, so they cajole the two Brits onto the dance floor, and they shame Krista and me into joining them.

As a man, I love dancing because it presents such a great way to connect with a woman. But as I lead Krista to the dance floor, holding her hand for the first time, I chastise myself for not taking more salsa lessons. I know how to do the West Coast swing and the four-count swing. But I don't have a drop of Latin blood in me, and once, when a woman tried to teach me how to swivel my hips to a salsa song, I felt like a hopelessly Caucasian doofus.

I try to explain this to Krista as we stand on the edge of the dance floor, so Amy #1 gives me a quick lesson. I almost get the basic steps down and I am working on my hip swivel when we change partners. Now I have my arms around Krista.

The dance becomes secondary to the intoxication of the physical contact. I hold Krista while I smile and gaze into her eyes. Even in the dim light on the dance floor, her green eyes shine with excitement. I lean in close to her, and her hair is alive with the soft fragrance of flowers. When the band plays a slow ballad, I wrap my arms around Krista's waist and feel the delightful female curves of her body pressed gently against mine. The sensation of her breasts on my lower ribs is almost more than I can bear.

During an upbeat song, I lead Krista through as many four-count swing moves as I can remember. It ain't salsa, but the guitar player smiles when he sees we are having so much fun.

The band takes a break and we head back to our table.

"You're a great dancer," says Krista. Ah, a positive attitude and a few good moves have left her with an inflated opinion of my dancing skills, and I am pleased.

Krista's son, Jeff, stops by with his girlfriend. They are both only 18, so they can't legally stay in the bar. Krista hands Jeff money and he disappears after saying hello and goodbye to everyone.

We stay for nearly two hours, dancing and listening to the band. Krista and I talk when the 20-somethings go off to dance. Considering I did not expect to be at a salsa bar in Shelbyville with Krista after a full day of work and two Meet and Greets, I feel energized. Krista's kids, nephews, and friends are helping me feel very welcome, and Krista is giving me a jolt of excitement that I haven't felt since I have been single.

By the time we venture outside toward our cars, I have a new spring in my tired legs and a new Babe on my brain. Krista agrees to give her nephew a ride home, so our goodbye is brief. It is the only part of the date that disappoints me. I wanted to give Krista a kiss. I wanted to hold her in my arms and tell her how much fun I had with her tonight. I wanted to hug her again and feel her body pressed to mine.

But with a quick wave she is in her car and gone. I am left alone in the dark parking lot with visions of this new Wonder Babe dancing in my head.

I will call her tomorrow and thank her for a fabulous evening. I will thank her for the best first date of my life.

During the next hour while I am driving home, my smile never fades.

Chapter 83: I've Just Seen a Face

The world of popular music is filled with songs about meeting a new person and thinking of her until the word *infatuation* comes into play. I love James Blunt's song, *You're Beautiful,* because every man has had the experience of seeing someone for the first time and just being completely knocked out by her.

> My life is brilliant.
> My love is pure.
> I saw an angel.
> Of that I'm sure.
> She smiled at me on the subway.
> She was with another man.
> But I won't lose no sleep on that,
> 'Cause I've got a plan.
>
> You're beautiful. You're beautiful.
> You're beautiful, it's true.
> I saw your face in a crowded place,
> And I don't know what to do,
> 'Cause I'll never be with you.

But that song is about unattainable, unrequited love for a stranger. The song that keeps playing in my head right now is *I've Just Seen a Face* by the Beatles.

> I've just seen a face
> I can't forget the time or place

Where we just met, she's just the girl for me
And I want all the world to see we've met
Mmm, mmm, mmm, mmm mmm mmm

Had it been another day
I might have looked the other way
And I'd have never been aware
But as it is I'll dream of her tonight
La, di, di, da di di

Falling, yes I am falling
And she keeps calling me back again

(©Copyright Northern Songs)

I call Krista the afternoon after our first date and try not to gush. Gushing is not a manly man thing to do. Men don't emote. We play it cool. We stay aloof and we don't say much—until we just can't hold it in any longer.

From my own personal experience, however, I know that women appreciate hearing about how men feel—especially when it's good news. And women hate it when they have to wonder whether or not the man that they just met has feelings for them.

BABE MAGNET RULE #88
If you go out with a woman and you had a great time, call her the next day and tell her. Thank her for a wonderful evening. Tell her that she is wonderful. And tell her that you would really like to see her again.

So that's just what I do. "I would really like to see you again," I tell Krista.

I can feel her smile coming through the cell phone. "That would be nice," she says.

The soonest we can work a date into our busy, two-city schedules is the following weekend. Now I have an entire week to spend in lovely anticipation of seeing Krista again. I find myself thinking of her often. When I drive past a Mexican eatery, I think about sitting across from her in a cold restaurant and watching her eyes sparkle. I hear Carlos Santana playing a salsa-beat song on the radio, and I smile at myself for not having taken more salsa dancing lessons.

I let two entire days go by before I can stand it no longer and call Krista again.

"Hi, I was just thinking about you," I say, in my best friendly but non-gushing voice. Again, the sound of her smile comes through. I like the sound of Krista's smile.

I know better than this. I know better than to get excited about a woman I have just met. I know that you shouldn't make wedding plans after one date. I know this from the experience and wisdom that 1.7 million dates gives a person.

I replay the scenes from our first date in my head. The hug when she greets me. My gallant dash to the parking lot to get her my jacket. The instant attraction. The flowing conversation that deftly weaved between safe topics and meaningful ones. The change of venue to the salsa club. Holding Krista close while we danced. The drive home, when I was already missing her.

I tell myself not to get too excited. But I don't listen.

The week finally passes. I have deliberately filled my days with work and my nights with busyness. Now it is early on Saturday afternoon on a picture-postcard, blue-skies day, and I am driving my BMW at 75 miles per hour toward Krista's house.

You might think that a Middle-Aged Babe Magnet such as myself would be smiling smugly to himself as his fine German automobile speeds toward the rendezvous with his date. You might think that the aforementioned Middle-Aged Babe Magnet would be cool and calm, because of his vast dating experience. After all, this is just a second date.

But the truth, is I am excited. I have been looking forward to seeing Krista for an entire week, and as I drive down the Interstate I feel the blood pumping through my body in delicious anticipation.

Halfway between my house and Krista's house, in a spot that can literally be described as The Middle of Nowhere, I hear strange noises from the back of my car. It sounds like the world's largest truck, traveling at 160 miles per hour, has snuck up behind me. I quickly check my rear-view mirror and see no truck. But the noise continues.

I take my foot off the gas and slow down. Now the loud humming sound behind me is joined by a flap-flap-flap noise. Son of Goodyear, my right rear tire has just committed suicide!

I pull off on the side of the road to assess the situation. My tire is dead dead dead. Cars and trucks are whizzing past at incredible speeds, blowing hot gusts of wind at me as they pass. I am dressed in elegant casual clothes for my date with Krista, and the last thing I want is to be stranded at the side of a gritty, noisy Interstate highway.

This is not what I envisioned for today. For a moment, I lament my situation and I curse the Dating Gods. Why, oh why, must this be my fate? Today was supposed to be a truly great day in my life. Why, of all times, why did I have to get a flat tire NOW?

Wait a minute. This doesn't have to ruin my day. WWTD (What Would Tigger Do) if faced with this situation? I can decide right here and right now that a crummy flat tire IS NOT going to ruin my day. I can choose to handle this setback as the minor inconvenience that it is.

I pop open the trunk and look for the spare tire. It's underneath the trunk cover. But I have never changed a tire on this car, and I can't find the jack. That's okay. That's what I have a AAA membership for. I whip out my trusty smartphone and dial the number for roadside assistance.

The customer service rep is clearly out of state, because when I describe where I am, she acts like I am speaking Russian. But she finally finds my location on her map, and she says a truck will be out to fix my flat in 45 minutes. Great.

Wait a minute—45 minutes isn't so great. If I have to sit by the side of the road for 45 minutes before the truck even gets here, then by the time the tire gets changed and I am back on the road, I will be more than an hour late for my date with Krista.

I do not want to make a Babe of Krista's caliber wait that long.

All right, I am going to race them. I'll bet that I can change my tire before AAA even gets here.

I go back and start looking for the tools and the jack. A-ha! The tools are hidden in a compartment underneath the trunk lid. I never would have found them if I wasn't desperate.

How long has it been since I changed a tire at the side of the road? Probably 20 years—but I still remember the tricks. I loosen the lug nuts while the wheel is still on the ground. Then I set up the jack and start turning. Magically, the car rises from the ground. This is working. I am not going to let a flat tire come between me and my Babe.

In 20 minutes I have wrestled the old tire off and the new tire on. My hands are black with tire grime, but the job is done. I have beaten AAA at its own game.

I call Krista to tell her the news. "I got a flat tire on the Interstate, but I have already changed it," I announce proudly. "So I'm running 30 minutes late, and I'm going to need to wash my hands when I get to your house."

She is kind and gracious. "Don't worry about being late," she says. "Just drive safe."

I want to see her now more than ever.

Chapter 84: Listen to the Music

Back on the road, I have 30 more minutes to think as I drive ever closer to Krista's house. It occurs to me for the first time that if Krista were using the conventional wisdom, she would not have asked me to pick her up at her house.

Conventional wisdom tells women NOT to invite a man to her house until she knows him well enough to trust him. Dating websites, such as www.datingwithoutdrama.com, are filled with cautious advice for women about setting up dates with men that they meet online. Meet in a public place. Make sure your friends and family know about your date and how long it is expected to last. Have someone call your cell phone after your date. And DON'T invite your date to your home right away.

After one date and several phone calls, Krista trusts me enough to let me pick her up at her house for our second date. I take that as a huge compliment. It means that she already thinks I am someone special. Well, my dear, the feeling is very mutual.

Krista's house is in a rural community northeast of Shelbyville. Technically, it's not out in the country, but it feels that way to me. My house in Springfield is in a densely packed suburban neighborhood where the lots are 1/5th of an acre. But as I drive through the winding roads of Krista's master-planned community, the houses are luxuriously spread out on two-acre lots. I turn onto Krista's dirt road and then her gravel driveway, and it feels like I am in a different world.

Krista greets me with a warm hug. I slip into her bathroom to wash up and change into the spare shirt that I conveniently had in my car. She gives me a tour of her lovely, sprawling one-story home. No wonder she lives way out here. This is a little slice of heaven, with views that stretch across wide open land under a sky that never ends.

Krista offers me a glass of ice water, and we sit on the porch for a while and just talk. The day is glorious, and the views from her back patio are stunning. I tell Krista the obligatory story of my flat tire, emphasizing my decision to not let it spoil this wonderful day. "So much of life is an attitude, a choice," I say. "I decided not to let a minor inconvenience cast a dark shadow on our day together."

She smiles. My day begins right here, with her.

I am smitten with this woman, and it feels marvelous. We talk about the busy week just past, and we talk about things that make us happy.

"I love travelling to tropical places," says Krista.

My mind jumps forward to the two of us, sunning ourselves on a tropical beach. I know it is too soon to have thoughts like this, but, again, I cannot help myself.

I drive us into Shelbyville for the Summer Arts Festival. The streets of downtown are blocked off, and the entire old part of town has been transformed into an open air marketplace featuring art and artisans. Colorful flags fly from the streetlights, and music fills the air.

The artists' booths are filled with impressive paintings, jewelry, exotic handmade clothing, sculpture, and creative arts of all shapes and types. Krista and I are not in the mood for buying, but we delight in looking at the artwork and comparing our tastes. I am drawn to the scenic photographs. She loves the colorful shawls and shoes.

We stroll over to the plaza to listen to a band playing a Latin-tinged modern rock. We join the bodies in front of the stage swaying to the music. I look over at Krista, who is enjoying the music in that glorious, unselfconscious way that only women can. Men just can't relax and let the music move their bodies in the same way. Men hear the music, but women *feel* it. Krista catches me watching her, and she smiles.

As we wander through the crowded streets, I buy some funnel cakes from a street stand. There is no place to sit and eat, so I walk us over to the shady steps leading to a small shopping area. We munch, we talk, and we watch the steady parade of people walking by.

I am feeling the beginnings of romantic passion for Krista, and I want to make my feelings known. I want her to know that I do not want to be "just friends." I do not want to go out with her on a few dates and then get blindsided by her confession that she doesn't feel "that kind" of attraction for me.

So it's time to send a message. Ready or not, I am going in for our first kiss. I lean in slowly, and our lips touch for the first time. I can tell she is surprised; she didn't see this coming. That's okay. Our first kiss is friendly, not passionate. But I have made my intentions known in a powerful, physical way. And I will always know that our first kiss happened right here on these steps, for all of Shelbyville to see.

We spend hours walking around the festival, and then I take Krista to my favorite local restaurant. Pablo's Kitchen is a small, funky place on a side street that is frequented by locals and savvy tourists. The food is lovingly hand-prepared from scratch, and if you didn't know any better, you might swear you were in the heart of old Mexico. The restaurant is tiny, and there is almost always a line of patrons waiting outside the door. The only way Krista and I can get a seat is if we share a table, so we consult with each other and both feel adventurous enough to sit with strangers.

We are seated with two single women, Miranda and Jenni. They are both friendly and attractive middle-aged ladies. Both of them have perfectly coiffed dark hair and perfectly manicured nails. I bet they are both single.

Krista and the two ladies instantly become old friends. The four of us share a bit about our backgrounds, and Krista and I confess that we are on our second date. Jenni can't believe it. "You seem so comfortable with each other, like an old married couple," she tells us, "except you still have that spark between you."

When Krista excuses herself to use the restroom, Jenni tells me, "She is beautiful, inside and out." I agree totally.

It's still light outside when we walk out onto the street. I am having a wonderful time, and I don't want this date with Krista to end.

"What do you want to do now?" I ask.

Krista pauses, as if she isn't sure. "Well, a friend of mine who lives outside of town has built a house on 10 acres of land. Every year she hosts a private music festival. We could go out there and listen to the live music."

I know that as the man, I am supposed to plan the dates. It is clearly stated in...

BABE MAGNET RULE #89

Women love a man with a plan. This is especially true for dates early in a relationship. Be the man, take the lead, plan the dates. Taking charge and planning wonderful dates will make your Babe feel special.

I have planned the date thus far. But this lovely woman has a creative streak and a spontaneity that I love. I have already scored sufficient dating points by demonstrating that I am a man with a plan. Perhaps a little unplanned diversion with the lovely Krista is just what this Middle-Aged Babe Magnet needs.

BABE MAGNET RULE #90

Don't be afraid to be spontaneous—especially if it will make your Babe happy.

"A music festival sounds wonderful," I say. "Let's go for it."

We drive to the hills and travel back into time.

Krista's friend Roxanne is an old hippie. If she didn't attend the original Woodstock music festival, she should have. Her property is a loosely organized compound of ramshackle "homesteader" buildings that look like they are just waiting for a strong wind to topple over. Now her long dirt driveway is littered on both sides with old parked cars bearing bumper stickers reading "Free Tibet" and "Do Not Meddle in the Affairs of Dragons, for You Are Crunchy and Good with Ketchup." As soon as we open the car doors to the gathering dark, the sound of a rock band greets us.

We are transported to a mini-Woodstock festival, with hippies roaming around dancing to the music. It is a flashback to a college party scene in the late '60s or early '70s. We make a monetary donation and approach the outdoor stage. Clearly, no one with construction skills participated in the creation of the bandstand. But it doesn't matter. The music is great, and a throng of people are dancing and singing along. The world is a cool and righteous place.

We dance. We sing. We consume an alcoholic beverage or two. And Krista and I grow closer. During a break between bands, I tell Krista that I have tickets to an upcoming concert, and ask her if she wants to go.

"Who's playing?"

"I don't want to tell you yet. Do you want to go out with me again?"

"Yes."

"It's James Taylor."

"Yes!" She gives me a hug and a kiss. This time she kisses me with passion.

It is long after dark when we drive back to Krista's house. We end up back on her porch, talking. And then we are kissing. We are standing up, wrapped in a full-body embrace—and we are making out like a couple of teenagers. The kissing is VERY passionate, and I don't want it to end. The feel of our mouths and tongues together is so sensuous and so wonderful that I cannot imagine anything better in the world right now.

We kiss until our lips get sore. Alas, it is time for me to leave.

There is music playing in my head as I make the long drive back home. Once again, our date was filled with music. Everything about Krista is musical.

Chapter 85: A Bigger World

I have done such a good job of shrinking my geographic world. I live in a suburban house that is only 1.5 miles from my office. My favorite supermarket lies halfway between the two. My bank is inside the supermarket. Nearby are a bookstore, a Whole Foods Market, a bagel shop, a Wal-Mart, a coffee shop, an auto repair shop, and almost everything else I ever need.

My whole world is conveniently located in a 1.5 mile radius. This is the world that I deliberately created for myself.

In my final five years in California, I drove 46 miles to get to work. Then I drove the same 46 miles back home at night. It was a minimum of one hour each way. On busy traffic days, my commute took an hour and 15 minutes. On Friday evenings I was on the road for at least an hour and a half.

When I moved out of the big city 20 years ago, to the far frontiers of Springfield, I vowed to never tolerate a long-distance commute ever again. I started working out of my house, where my commute was the 10 paces from my bedroom door to my home office door. Five years ago, I moved into an office building that was a whopping mile and a half from my home, and that commute felt like a LONG way to go to work.

Now Krista comes along, and with her comes the dilemma of geography. Now the person I find myself thinking about throughout the day is 70 miles away.

Curse you, Match.com, for making it so easy to connect with women who are outside of my geographic comfort zone! And yet, when I think about Krista, my heart is aflutter with butterflies, and I wouldn't have it any other way.

Before our first date, Krista told me that she never comes down to Springfield. That was not true. She has a daughter in college down here, and she comes down to visit a couple of times a month. Krista didn't want me to know this in the beginning, because she wanted me to want to see her enough to make the drive to Shelbyville.

I can understand the logic in that. In the old-fashioned arena of dating—and let's face it, much of what comprises the world of dating is based on old-fashioned behaviors and even older genetic differences between the sexes—a woman is the prize who must be earned. The man must prove himself worthy of the prize, and one way to do that is to travel across vast distances to see her. I am indeed fortunate to live in the age of BMWs and not the age of covered wagons.

When I call Krista to ask her out on another date, she tells me that she's going to be down in Springfield on Wednesday.

"Really?" I say. "Would you like to go to the baseball game with me on Wednesday night?"

"I would love to," she says, and I can hear her lovely smile across the cell phone airwaves.

I call Mueller to see if he's planning to use his season tickets for Wednesday.

"No, would you like to go?"

"Absolutely. I have a new Babe I want to take to the game."

He wants to hear all about her. I tell him the "guy" basics without going into too many details. She lives in Shelbyville. She's a nurse. She has three grown kids. She is a Babe. I like her body, and I like her mind.

If Mueller and I were women, this conversation might have lasted two hours. But I'm off the phone in two minutes. I did not tell him that Krista makes my heart go pitter-patter. I did not tell him about her hazel-green eyes or her infectious laugh. I did not tell him about how much I have been thinking about her in the past three weeks.

I don't want to jinx this by saying too much too soon.

Krista arrives at my house for our date, and I give her the walk-through tour. Compared to her spacious home, my house seems small and modest. But I have some interesting furniture and décor, and she especially likes the Asian pieces that I bought at an auction last year. My giant jade horse catches her eye.

"No one needs a 200-pound jade horse," I admit. "But I got caught up in the auction fever, and I decided to go for it."

"I love it," she says.

"Everyone should buy something frivolous that they really want at least once in their lives," I said. "Mine just happened to be a jade horse."

Zippy the Poodle is happy to meet Krista. He sniffs her thoroughly, delighting in the smells of her dog, Trucker. We don't have much time for hanging out, though, so I drive us to the stadium so we can be there for the first pitch.

I love driving my car with Krista in the passenger seat. I love our relaxed, free-flowing conversations. So far, I love everything about this woman. I love her smile. I love the chemistry between us. I love the way she stimulates my mind.

I know that at some point I am going to discover something about her that really bugs me. But right now, I can't imagine what that might be.

We settle into Mueller's seats for the game, and Krista is suitably impressed. We are in the fourth row, right behind the visiting team's dugout. We're so close that we can yell at the players, and they turn around to see who is yelling at them.

We're also in prime foul ball territory, and I explain how I once saved a woman sitting in the row behind us from certain plastic surgery by grabbing a foul ball that was inches away from her face.

Krista has a worried expression on *her* face.

"Don't worry, I will protect you," I say, chivalrously.

She smiles. I know that Krista loves it when I behave like a gentleman. It makes her feel like a lady—like a cherished, desirable lady. So I am going to keep behaving like a gentleman, because this gentleman *loves* to make this woman happy.

BABE MAGNET RULE #91

When you find something that makes your Babe happy, keep doing it.

I was raised with baseball. I played Little League baseball, and my father took my brother and me to see the Detroit Tigers play. Although football has surpassed baseball as America's favorite sport, I still love the game. I understand the rules and the strategy, and I'd like to think I know the game well enough to be a pretty good manager.

As the game unfolds before us, I try to explain it all to Krista without sounding like a pompous know-it-all. (Women hate pompous know-it-alls, and they hate it when a man talks down to them.) I tell her about the foul tip rule on the third strike. I explain the logic of bunting a base runner forward. I answer her questions when the umpire calls a balk. It's fun to educate her about the game, and she seems to appreciate my patient answers to her questions.

We also talk about our jobs and our lives. One of the things I like about attending a baseball game is that its slow pace gives you plenty of time to talk.

"Sometimes Mueller and I will go to a game and spend the whole time talking—mostly about women and relationships," I explain. "We have to remind ourselves every once in a while to watch the game so we won't get whacked by a foul ball."

That's how it is with Krista, too. We talk the whole time. There just happens to be a baseball game going on in the background. Walking back to the car after the game is over, I take Krista's hand in mine. It feels very comfortable and natural to be holding her hand as we walk through the parking lot.

We drive back to my house and I invite her inside. Jason's truck is parked in the driveway, so I tell Krista that I would like to introduce her to my son.

Jason smiles and shakes her hand warmly. Bless his heart. All of the parental nagging about good manners did generate results. He is gracious, and so is Krista. There is no tension in the room at all. Krista relates easily to Jason, and tells him about her kids.

Krista has a long drive home, so I walk her out to her car. There in the street, in the middle of a hot summer night, we passionately make out.

I'm talking passion, real melt-your-clothes-off passion. You can see the heat waves radiate from our bodies.

If Jason weren't home, I would take Krista back inside right now and ravish her body. I want this woman more than I have wanted anything in a long, long time. But somehow I contain myself, and Krista gets into her car for the long drive home. We kiss one more time through her open window.

"I would really like to see you again," I tell Krista.

"I would like that, too."

I will tell her this again and again, because it's true. Every time I see her I want to see her again.

Chapter 86: Cue the Hallelujah Chorus

I am stuck in the longest business meeting in the history of business meetings. There are four of us sitting around a conference table. We are examining a 100-page printout of an Excel file that contains the names, attributes and descriptions of landscape plants. The two plant geeks are arguing about whether *Miscanthus sinensis* will grow in the southern part of the state without any supplemental water.

I look at my watch. Again. I have looked at my watch every three minutes for the past four hours. If these two plant geeks don't shut up soon, my head is going to explode.

I am getting paid handsomely for attending this meeting. This is a big project that the State Engineer has contracted me to coordinate. We are creating the official list of low-water plants for the entire state, and I need these plant geeks to give us the accurate information that will make this database work.

But Holy Composted Cow Manure, this feels like torture right now.

The plant geeks can't keep from telling each other stories about each plant species.

"Did you see the size of the *Agave utahensis* next to the post office on 4th Street?"

"I know, can you believe it?"

"I didn't know they got that big."

"Rob Finklemansteinerberg, you know, he used to work down at All States Horticulture, discovered a variety that gets big enough to ..."

They go on and on and on.

The good thing about this meeting is that it's in Shelbyville. And the *really* good thing about this meeting is that after it's over, I am going to see Krista. The plan for our date was for me to take her to lunch, but that's not going to happen now. I call her to apologize and tell her to eat without me.

Back to the droning of the plant geeks.

Finally, I am able to leave the meeting and drive to Krista's house. I grab a sandwich on the way to keep from starving to death.

It's the middle of the afternoon by the time my car tires crunch along Krista's gravel driveway. I am worn out from The World's Longest and Most Boring Business Meeting, but I am excited to see Krista.

She is wearing an orange summer dress that is tight-fitting at the top but loose and long at the bottom. Her sun-bleached hair dances on the tops of her shoulders. "I am glad you made it," she says with a smile. She greets me with a hug and a kiss.

"I am glad to see you, too. I was beginning to wonder if I would ever get here."

She serves me iced tea and invites me to sit on the couch. We chat for a while, and then we get onto the topic of music. Way back before I met Krista (a month and a half ago), I learned from her Match.com profile that she wrote songs. I ask her to sing me one of her original compositions.

At first she declines, with feigned modesty. But it doesn't take too much coaxing for her to agree to sing me a song. She retrieves her guitar from the other room, and I am surprised that it is a crummy little guitar that she has had since high school. I don't consider myself a talented musician, and I am certainly not an expert on guitars, but I have learned enough about instruments from my guitar teacher to know that Krista's guitar is a glorified toy.

The instrument isn't much, but she plays it with skill and confidence. Her finger picking is superb. I wish I could play guitar that well. But it's her voice that knocks me out. Her voice is powerful and melodic; her tone and pitch are perfect. This woman has the vocal chops to pass the Simon Cowell test. She has an *American Idol* voice.

I am completely blown away. Krista could be a professional singer. This woman has skills. I try not to gush when I tell her how much I love her singing. She beams.

Krista wants to go for an afternoon hike, and normally I would think that this is a fine idea. But here we are all alone in this big, comfortable house, and her son isn't expected to be back for many hours. I want to make love to this woman, and I want to make love to her now. It's time for me to put my Babe Magnet seduction skills to the test.

I park myself on the couch next to Krista so that our thighs are touching. Then I gently stroke her hair and give her a kiss. Her mouth softens, and we are sharing the most passionate kiss I have ever experienced in my entire life.

The damn bursts, and all of the feelings and all of the passions that have been building up since we first started exchanging emails wash away our inhibitions and hesitations. We are in the moment, and we are on the cusp of a new love.

Krista abandons her plans for an afternoon hike. We go with my plan instead.

But before Krista will make love with me, she lets me know that the only way our relationship will move forward is if we are monogamous. She is looking for a commitment. No woman has ever told me that, and I love this woman's virtue.

Absolutely, Krista. You are the only Babe that this Babe Magnet wants.

We don't just make love, we *invent* lovemaking. It is as if our souls are bonding, and they are using our physical bodies because that is what's available to them.

Our bodies fit together perfectly. Our minds meld. Our energy combines and co-mingles, and the music inside each of us is the perfect harmonic note for the other.

Time slows to a crawl so we can savor every delicious moment. It's so wonderful to feel each other, skin to skin. Our bodies join together in a divine union. It is nothing short of heavenly as our hearts open to each other.

The Hallelujah Chorus, sung by an angelic version of the Mormon Tabernacle Choir, reverberates in my ears.

I am not going to describe the details of our lovemaking. I have no desire to share this sacred moment with the world. But let me just say, in all humility, that it was the most amazing and most impressive performance of my life. I was the Michael Jordan of lovemaking. I was the Babe Ruth of lovemaking. I was the Albert Einstein of lovemaking (without the bushy mustache and the crazy hair).

Winston Churchill once said, "Everyone has his day, and some days last longer than others." Well, this was my day, and I lasted and lasted and lasted.

We lay, totally spent, in total rapture. Even though I have just experienced the best loving of my life, already the voice of my little Male Ego is starting to talk to me. It says, "Oh my God, what if she thinks that will happen every time you make love?" I don't want her to expect me to be Superman forever.

Gently, like a politician trying to lower expectations, I tell Krista, "It may not always be that good."

Krista smiles. "You're right. Next time it could be BETTER."

After we walk down from Passion Peak, Krista makes dinner for us. Then we take Trucker for a walk through the neighborhood as the sun is going down. I take a photo of Krista, so I can remember this afternoon for the rest of my life. She looks right into the camera and smiles. On her face are peace, tranquility, and contentment.

Life is so wonderful I can hardly stand it. No, let me rephrase that. Life is wonderful—and I am loving every minute of it.

Chapter 87: The End of the Road

I thought 70 miles was a long-distance relationship. How about 1,500 miles? That's the distance between Krista and me right now, and it is *killing* me.

Jason and I flew to the Yucatan Peninsula in Mexico for our already-planned annual father-and-son vacation. We chose Mexico because Jason wanted to speak Spanish, and we chose the Mayan Riviera side of the country because we didn't want to get kidnapped by a drug cartel and end up on *Headline News.*

The weather here is tropical—hot and steamy. The locals are friendly because they want our money. The resort where we are staying is picturesque and perfect. It was created to appeal to wealthy tourists, and no expense has been spared. The hotel's lobby spills out into an entertainment area and bar, which features an open-air view of the vast landscaped grounds, the resort swimming pools, and the beach.

I bought the all-inclusive package, so everything we eat and drink is paid for. Jason, who eats like an NFL linebacker, is in Food Heaven. He can eat whenever he wants to at any of the seven restaurants on the property. I have discovered the delightful seduction of the tropically prepared Mojito, and I have lost track of how many of them I have consumed.

But there is a downside to hanging out as a father-and-son team in paradise. Virtually everyone else here is a couple. There are the young newlyweds and the dating couples. They lounge by the pools and order free drinks every time the friendly waitresses come by. There are the middle-aged couples who are rediscovering the sparks in their relationships. They don't lounge in the sun as much as the younger folks, but they hang out in the shady outdoor bars, laughing and talking. There are even older, gray-haired couples who nap on the beach in private cabanas.

And then there is Jason and me. I am missing Krista, *mi nueva novia*. And Jason is missing Brittany, his college sweetheart.

Even though Jason and I are having our best vacation together ever, I vow to never again come to a tropical resort without a Babe. I would love to be experiencing this paradise with Krista.

I know that Jason feels the same way about being "stag" in a land of romantic couples. "Dad, if you want to send me and Brittany here as a college graduation present, that would be great."

Because I am in a foreign country—and in a resort area with spotty cell phone coverage—I only get to talk to Krista twice during the week I am gone.

"I miss you!" and "I wish you were here" can only go so far in describing how deeply I miss Krista and how much I want to see her again. Two months ago I didn't even know her. Now I can't get through a day without thinking about her 100 times. And seeing all these couples laughing and holding each other tenderly as they bask in the sunshine makes it all the worse.

While we are in the *Riviera Maya*, Jason and I venture into the jungle to climb a Mayan pyramid, take a ferry to Cozumel and go snorkeling, and turn our white gringo bodies a lovely shade of sunburn. Jason even experiences Mexican culture when he loses his official visitor's declaration form and must pay every peso in his wallet to a bribe-happy airport bureaucrat just to escape the country.

As soon as we land in Houston, Jason is on the phone with Brittany and I am on the phone with Krista. We have had our fill of father-and-son time, and it's time to connect with our sweeties.

Two days later I am driving up the Interstate to visit the wonderful Krista at her wonderful home. I am starting to appreciate the 70 miles that separate us. During the travel time, I have a chance to think and reflect. On this fine early evening, as the sun grows heavy in the western sky, I have time to reflect on one of Mueller's favorite aphorisms about dating—which he originally got from me.

"Dating is a numbers game," he says. "You just have to go out with a lot of women until you find your soul mate."

I have played the dating game as if that were true. I did the male equivalent of what women call "kissing a lot of frogs." But now I'm not so sure I approached dating from the right perspective. I think I had it backwards.

Dating may be a numbers game, but the only number that matters is ONE. Because the goal is to find the one person with whom you really want to spend your life.

That thought leads me, naturally, to Krista. Throughout my 1.7 million dates, I have not fallen for any woman the way I have fallen for Krista. The way I feel about her defies any logical description. She is comfortably prosperous, but she is not the richest woman I have dated. She is very attractive, but she is not the most beautiful woman I have dated. She has a fun personality, but she is not the most vivacious woman I have dated. And given the distance that separates my house from her house, she is not the most conveniently located woman I have dated.

But none of that matters to me now. Krista is the woman I want. She has set a new standard—of virtue, chemistry, attraction, integrity, and desirability.

When Krista greets me at her door with a passionate hug and a kiss that shows how much she has missed me, I feel as though I have arrived home. My heart feels very much at home with her.

The passion that envelopes us cannot be contained. Krista had planned to cook us a fabulous dinner, and her dining table is set with her finest silverware and china. Crystal wine glasses are waiting to be filled. We ignore the Martha Stewart accoutrements as we leave a trail of clothing that leads to the bedroom.

I had worried about setting the bar too high with my first superhuman sexual performance. I shouldn't have. There is magic happening here. Magic happens every time Krista and I are together.

Is there anything as delicious as a new romance? Is there anything as wonderful as newfound passion? Is there anything as satisfying as reaching the final destination after years of travel?

Krista lies in my arms. Our romance is still so new that neither of us wants to jinx it. Neither of us wants to say the wrong thing or do something stupid to ruin the mood. A new romance is like a wild bird, which can easily be spooked into flying away.

She cannot bring herself to say the "L" word. Instead, she looks deeply into my eyes and says, "I adore you."

I cannot say the L word either. I do not want to scare this little bird away.

"I adore you, too." But I already know that I love her.

When I began my journey into Middle-Aged Babe Magnethood, I truly believed that I would find love. I believed that my perfect match, my perfect lover, was out there somewhere, waiting for me to let her into my life.

Maybe I did things the hard way. Maybe I spent too much time working on my Middle-Aged Babe Magnet persona. Maybe the whole Middle-Aged Babe Magnet thing was just a crutch to help me feel better about myself while I (slowly) got myself ready to receive the woman of my dreams.

I am ready now.

I know that my relationship with Krista is just beginning, and I know that love brings no guarantees. But right now I am absolutely sure that Krista is THE ONE for me. I am falling madly, deeply, and passionately in love with her. And when I gaze into her eyes, I see her love gazing back at me.

So I end this story with one final Babe Magnet Rule. This, ladies and gentlemen, is the most important one of all:

BABE MAGNET RULE #92
A Babe Magnet knows when to stop chasing Babes and commit himself completely to the woman of his dreams.

The End

Check out the Middle-Aged Babe Magnet blog at

http://middleagedbabemagnet.blogspot.com

To subscribe to Chad Stone's free eNewsletter, send an email to:

babemagnetchad@aol.com

www.ingramcontent.com/pod-product-compliance
Lightning Source LLC
Chambersburg PA
CBHW071404090426
42737CB00011B/1342

* 9 7 8 0 9 8 5 0 4 7 9 1 7 *